ONEplus Therapy

and

Common Emotional Problems

ONEplus Therapy
and
Common Emotional
Problems

Windy Dryden

Onlinevents Publications

First edition published by Onlinevents Publications

Copyright (c) 2024 Windy Dryden and Onlinevents Publications

Windy Dryden
136 Montagu Mansions, London W1U 6LQ

Onlinevents Publications
38 Bates Street, Sheffield, S10 1NQ
www.onlinevents.co.uk
help@onlinevents.co.uk

ISBN: 978-1-914938-33-7

Contents

Preface

In this book, I will discuss my approach to single-session therapy (SST), which I call ONEplus Therapy, and show how it can be applied to common emotional problems for which clients seek therapeutic help. These problems are:

- Anxiety
- Depression
- Guilt
- Unhealthy regret
- Shame
- Unhealthy anger
- Hurt
- Unhealthy jealousy
- Unhealthy envy

My purpose in writing this book is to demonstrate how it is possible to work in a focused way using what I refer to as the ONEplus Therapy mindset. This mindset allows the therapist to use a combination of practical strategies that stem from the mindset and the approaches that the therapist favours to help the client with one of these common emotional problems. I see ONEplus Therapy as a blend of what the client brings to the process and what the therapist brings to the process. The client brings to the ONEplus Therapy process their knowledge of themself, how they have tried to address the nominated emotional problem before, their strengths, and the external resources upon which they can draw as they address their nominated emotional problem. The therapist brings to the ONEplus Therapy process their professional knowledge about the common emotional problems listed above, their skills in quickly developing a good working alliance between themself and their client and in addressing emotional problems in a focused way and helping the client to effect change in their nominated emotional problem.

In my experience, many clients are open to the possibility of addressing their emotional problems quickly, often in a single session, and do not want to enter a lengthy therapeutic process. For these clients ONEplus Therapy is ideal, and it is a shame that professional training courses in counselling and psychotherapy have neglected the needs of this group.

Of course, some clients want to access ongoing therapy and should ideally be provided with what they think will help them. Many therapists are available to help them to do so. No attempt should be made to foist ONEplus Therapy on this group of clients. Indeed, no attempt should be made to force therapists to practise ONEplus Therapy (or SST) when uninterested. However, this book is not written for this group. It is written for therapists interested enough and sufficiently open-minded to learn how to help clients benefit from a very brief focused form of therapy designed to help them take away something meaningful from the session that they are willing to implement in their everyday life (the 'ONE' in ONEplus Therapy), knowing that more help is available should they require it (the 'plus' in ONEplus Therapy).

Windy Dryden
London, Eastbourne
February 2024

Part I

ONEplus Therapy

PREAMBLE

In the first part of this book, I will begin, in Chapter 1, by discussing ONEplus Therapy, explaining what it is and what it is not. Then, in Chapter 2, I will detail and discuss the ONEplus Therapy mindset, which facilitates the practice of this mode of therapy delivery. Following on from this, in Chapters 3 and 4, I will outline my own way of implementing ONEplus Therapy, showing in Chapter 3 how this practice is shaped by principles of good practice stemming directly from the ONEplus Therapy mindset and in Chapter 4 how my work is informed by ideas from Rational Emotive Behaviour Therapy (REBT) and by other sources.

1

What Is ONEplus Therapy?

The world of counselling and psychotherapy does not need another brand of therapy to add to all the other brands currently available. I hear you ask what is wrong with the perfectly good term, 'single-session therapy'. I changed the name of my single-session therapy practice precisely because I considered the term 'single-session therapy' neither perfect nor good. Let me explain why.

Difficulties with the Term 'Single-Session Therapy'

It matters what things are called, and therefore clarity is essential when considering what name to give to a way of working therapeutically with people. If you went to a restaurant and ordered, let's say, fried liver, chips and peas, you would expect to be served fried liver, chips and peas. If you were served grilled liver instead of fried liver, you would complain, and the same would be true if you were served mashed potatoes instead of chips and cauliflower instead of peas.

So, what would you think if you heard the term 'single-session therapy' for the first time as a therapist or a client? You would be forgiven if you thought that single-session therapy was a therapy that lasted for one session. After all, doesn't it meet the 'fried liver, chips and peas' test?[1]

---

[1] An alternative to the 'fried liver, chips and peas' test is the 'Ronseal' test (Dryden, 2024). In 1994, a British company called 'Ronseal' which manufactures wood stain, paint and preservatives, developed a slogan to explain and demystify its products. It was 'Ronseal. It does exactly what it says on the

Jeff Young (2018: 46), who is a leading exponent of single-session therapy (SST), admits that the term 'single-session therapy' is inaccurate but deals with this situation in the following way:

> In short, while SST is a misnomer, it is a great name for challenging the traditional thinking about the therapeutic change process and for challenging traditional ways of providing services.

In other words, Young considers that the sacrifice of clarity concerning terminology is worth the advantages gained in the challenge posed to traditional therapeutic thinking posed by the term 'single-session therapy'. While I understand Young's position here, I disagree with it. I think it is possible to be accurate in what one calls one's work *and* pose a challenge to traditionalism.

In my experience as a trainer in this field, I have found that no matter how many times I have asserted that 'single-session therapy' does NOT inevitably mean that the person only has one session and that in SST, we do not aim to restrict people from accessing a range of therapeutic services, the offending term does lead people to make such assertions.

Difficulties with the Term 'One-At-A-Time Therapy'

Michael Hoyt (2011), a colleague of Moshe Talmon at the Kaiser Permanente clinic in North California in the mid to late 1980s, penned the term 'One-At-A-Time Therapy' (OAATT) as an alternative to single-session therapy. This term conveys that therapy takes place one session at a time and sometimes only occurs one time. It has been interpreted as meaning that while a client can have multiple therapy sessions, these can only be

---

tin'. This caught the public imagination to the extent that the phrase is used internationally and is now a commonly used slogan. The Ronseal approach to the question, 'What is SST?', then, is: 'Single-session therapy is a therapy that lasts for one session.'

accessed one session at a time. Thus, a person cannot access a block of therapy sessions or ongoing therapy. The term 'One-At-A-Time Therapy' has been utilised in UK university and college counselling services. This is the only way students can access counselling in several of these agencies. Also, in some of these agencies, while students may have several counselling sessions, these can only be booked one session at a time two weeks after the first (and if relevant) subsequent sessions.

As seen above, the term 'One-At-A-Time Therapy' lacks clarity. While people do not think that OAATT precludes further help being offered, this help is restricted to one session at a time. Specific modes of therapy delivery (e.g. blocks of therapy sessions or ongoing therapy) are not available to clients who wish to access further help after the first session.

ONEplus Therapy

I use the term ONEplus Therapy to describe my SST work because, as I have said, I am not happy with the terms 'single-session therapy' and 'One-At-A-Time Therapy' for the above reasons. But why 'ONEplus Therapy'? I wanted to find a term that (i) emphasised that a significant purpose of this mode of therapy delivery is to work with the client to help them achieve their stated wants from their first visit while (ii) making it clear that more help is available and (iii) I wanted these two ideas to be explicit in the title.

Let me now explain the spelling and the spacing of the term, which for me, need to be precise. Thus, it is 'ONEplus Therapy' and not 'ONE plus therapy', 'oneplus therapy', or 'one plus therapy'.

1. I decided to capitalise the word 'ONE' to make clear that the raison d'être of the work is to work with the client to help them on their first visit.

2. The word 'plus' indicates that more help is available to the person at the end of the session, but it does not specify the form that such further help should take. Thus, with the term 'plus', there are no restrictions placed on the further help offered as occurs with OAATT, where further help can only be accessed one session at a time. With 'ONEplus Therapy', the person who wishes further help is invited to choose from the range of therapeutic services the independent practitioner or agency offers and is informed of the waiting time for accessing these services. Furthermore, the client can access that further help at the end of the session[2] or after an agreed period designed so that the person can implement what they learned from the session and decide at the end of the agreed period whether they need further help.

3. To emphasise the integration of the 'let's help you in one' and 'further help is available on request' ideas, there is no space between 'ONE' and 'plus' in ONEplus Therapy.

Definition of ONEplus Therapy

Let me conclude this chapter with the following definition of ONEplus Therapy (Dryden, 2023a).

> *ONEplus Therapy is an intentional form of therapy delivery where the therapist and client contract to meet for a session of therapy and work together to help the client to achieve their stated wants from that session on the understanding that further help is available to the client on request.*

---

[2] Most people in the SST community consider that it is best to give clients an opportunity to implement their learning from the session before they can access further help. These people argue against offering clients further help at the end of the first session, unless there is a very good to do so.

2

The ONEplus Therapy Mindset

The key feature in helping a client in ONEplus Therapy is the mindset that the therapist brings to the work. Cannistrà (2022: 1) states that a mindset is 'the therapist's series of beliefs which influence the actions and decisions taken in the course of their work.' In this chapter, I will discuss the main elements of the ONEplus Therapy mindset, which the therapist is advised to bring to this work.

In doing so, I will be mindful of the focus of this book which is to show how ONEplus Therapy can be used with the common emotional problems for which clients seek therapeutic help. I will also be mindful that most of my readers will likely be steeped in the conventional therapy mindset.

One Session or More? Be Open to Both Possibilities

At the end of the previous chapter, I defined ONEplus Therapy as a way of working therapeutically where the therapist and client agree to meet with the intention of helping the client achieve their stated wants by the end of the session while acknowledging that further help is available if needed. The ONEplus therapist brings this mindset to the work and is open to both possibilities.

There is a risk that when a therapist begins to practise ONEplus Therapy and thinks they have to help a client in one session, then if the client indicates that they want further help, they, the therapist, have failed. Alternatively, if a therapist begins the work under the influence of the conventional therapy mindset, they will think they have failed if the client does not want to return for a second session. Being open to both possibilities – helping the client in one session and providing the client with further help when requested – without thinking that either scenario represents therapeutic failure is a crucial feature of the ONEplus Therapy mindset.

In working with common emotional problems (CEPs), it is important to recognise that the therapist can sometimes help the client in one session, and at other times clients request more help.

When the client's solution to their nominated CEP[3] is based on a reframing of their problem, a more realistic inference about the adversity they are facing, a validation of their response or the implementation of new behaviour, this often *can* be achieved in a single session.

Suppose the solution is based on developing a new attitude and behaviour underpinned by this new attitude. In this scenario, while this solution *may* be achieved in one session – when the client thinks that they can implement an action plan developed with their therapist without further help – it is also the case that the client requires more than one session to achieve this. Additionally, suppose the client is unsure whether they need more help. If this is the case, what some call a 'purposeful pause' is introduced to enable the client to determine what happens when they independently implement the solution. At the end of this hiatus, the client decides whether or not to access further help.

The therapist (and client) will only know which way forward the client will choose when the end of the session is reached. The important thing is that the therapist considers each outcome equally satisfactory and conveys this at the end of the session while outlining the client's options.

Help at the Point of Need

If ONEplus Therapy were a plant, it would flourish in therapeutic soil known as 'help at the point of need'. When a person decides to seek therapeutic help, then, at that point, they are often the

---

[3] In this book, I refer to the problem with which the client wants help as their 'nominated' problem.

most open to change. If that is the case, the client needs to be seen as quickly as possible at the point of their need rather than at the point of the therapist's or agency's availability. If they are seen at the point of their need, this facilitates them to get the most from the first session, and many such clients will be helped in one session. In my view, the therapeutic potency of ONEplus Therapy begins to ebb away if the person has not been seen within a week of making an appointment. Consequently, if a practitioner or agency is going to introduce ONEplus Therapy into the suite of therapy services they offer, this means, as stated above, seeing clients at the point of their need.

Helping clients at the point of need is the defining feature of what I call 'open-access, enter now'[4] services. These services offer therapy to those who have a problem for which they are seeking help and know they can get that help soon after they enter the building which houses the service.[5] These services are open to all who wish to access them.

It Is Possible to Conduct a Session without Prior Knowledge of the Person

In ONEplus Therapy, I agree with my colleagues who work in 'open-access, enter now' services that it is possible to help someone without knowing much about them. I have learned this experientially, having done over 700 demonstrations of single-session therapy[6] over many years (Dryden, 2021).

When I work with someone in ONEplus Therapy on their nominated CEP, I ask them at the outset, 'What do you think I

---

[4] 'Open-access, enter now' services were previously known as 'walk-in' services. However, latterly, the view is taken that the term 'walk-in' is not welcoming to people who cannot walk.

[5] Open-access, enter now services are increasingly being offered online as well as face-to-face.

[6] I am intentionally using the term 'single-session therapy' here and do so in its 'Ronseal' sense since these demonstrations are literally single sessions of therapy with no prospect of additional help, at least from me. This is made clear to volunteers at the outset.

need to know about you and the problem for which you are seeking help that, if I didn't know, from your perspective, I would not be able to help you?' This puts the onus on the client to inform me of information they deem vital for me to know. This is in sharp contrast to the conventional therapy mindset when the therapist or agency representative carries out an assessment session designed to find out information about the person, and their problems to enable the therapist or agency to offer the client what the practitioner or agency thinks will benefit the client. While there is nothing wrong with this practice and the conventional therapy mindset on which it is based, it is not appropriate when practising ONEplus Therapy.

What I need to know about the client initially in ONEplus Therapy is their nominated emotional problem and what they want to achieve by the end of the session concerning this problem.

As I will discuss at the beginning of Chapter 3, it is my practice to send a client a pre-session questionnaire before their session with me, While the primary purpose of the form is to encourage the client to prepare for the session so that they can get the most from it, I do ask them to send the form back to me before we meet so that I can also prepare myself for the session. My preparation is based on my wish to understand what was in the client's mind when they completed the questionnaire so that I can orient myself to their problem and what they want to achieve from the session. However, as it sometimes happens that the client changes their mind between completing and returning the questionnaire and attending the session, I will check their current position on the problem they wish to discuss and their session goal. For this reason, some ONEplus, SST and OAATT practitioners prefer not to look at the client's pre-session questionnaire before the session, and others do not ask for the form to be returned to them.

View the Session as a Whole, Complete in Itself

There are several differences between a therapist bringing the ONEplus Therapy mindset to the session and a therapist bringing the conventional therapy mindset to the session. I will mention two in the present context.

First, the therapist who brings the ONEplus Therapy mindset to the session is confident that they may be able to help the client in one session but is open to the possibility that the client may need more help. By contrast, the therapist who brings the conventional therapy mindset to the session is doubtful that they can help the client in one session and is confident that the person will need more help.

Second, the therapist who brings the ONEplus Therapy mindset to the session sees the session as a whole with a beginning, middle and end. It may lead to another session, but equally, it may not. Given this view, this therapist paces the session well and does not try to cram too much into the session. By contrast, the therapist who brings the conventional therapy mindset has one of two views. Some such therapists see the session as a prelude to further sessions. As such, they will tend to carry out an assessment which prepares for therapy to begin later in the process. Others tend to think that if they are to see a person once. Then they will want to give that person as much as possible. As I will discuss in the section below entitled 'Less Is More', this will result in the client being overwhelmed.

Potentially Anyone Can Be Helped in a Single Session

Another learning from 'open-access, enter now' services is that the therapist needs to believe that anybody can be helped in a single session. This does not mean that everyone will be helped in a single session. Thus, the committed ONEplus therapist will go into the session with an open-minded, 'can help' attitude, while the therapist undecided about ONEplus Therapy but working in this way will go into the session with a doubtful, 'probably can't help' attitude.

Indeed, the latter therapist will tend to have doubts about being able to help anyone who raises a problem of any complexity or alludes to having other problems when discussing their nominated emotional problem. They will consider offering the client further sessions as soon as they reveal either of the two scenarios.

The idea that anyone can be helped in a single session means that the therapist or agency does not have to assess the client for their suitability for ONEplus Therapy. Indeed, such activity is contraindicated for two reasons. First, the time devoted to conducting a suitability assessment is better spent doing therapy with the person. Second, no reliable criteria indicate who will benefit from ONEplus Therapy and who will not.

Focus on the Person and Their Problem, Not the Disorder

Therapists who are used to thinking about a client's disorder will tend to be pessimistic about practising ONEplus Therapy.[7] Whenever I run a training workshop on ONEplus Therapy, one of the most frequently asked questions that I get asked is, 'Can you use ONEplus Therapy with "x" disorder' (Dryden, 2022a)? My response is, 'What is the person's name, and what do they want to achieve from the session?' Thus, if ten people with borderline personality disorder seek help from a ONEplus therapist, they will tend to want to achieve different things. Their diagnostic status is no impediment to being helped. However, if anyone has a disorder or wants to achieve something from ONEplus Therapy that I cannot help them achieve, then I will say so. This is part of being transparent as a ONEplus therapist, which I will now discuss.

---

[7] ONEplus therapists who practise solution-focused therapy will want to skip over this section.

Be Transparent

As mentioned above, the therapist needs to be transparent about several salient issues about ONEplus Therapy. Thus, the therapist needs to be clear about the following:

- What ONEplus Therapy is and what it isn't.
- The therapist or agency's confidentiality policy and cancellation policy, if relevant.
- What they can and can't do as a ONEplus therapist.
- What further help options are available to the client if requested at the end of the session,[8] and what are the waiting times to access these, if known.
- Their reservations about the client's goal, mainly if this goal serves to maintain rather than solve the client's problem.
- The rationale for making interventions before asking for the client's permission to proceed.

A number of the above points must be made explicit before the client can be expected to give their informed consent to proceed with ONEplus Therapy. I don't think therapists with a conventional therapy mindset would disagree with the principle of transparency. However, they may feel uncomfortable about the content of some of the points listed if they are asked to practise ONEplus Therapy as part of their job.[9]

---

[8] See footnote 2 on p. 14.

[9] In the same way that clients who don't want ONEplus Therapy should not be compelled to have it (see the next section), therapists who do not want to practice ONEplus Therapy should not be compelled to do so. When they refuse to do practice ONEplus Therapy in an organisation that has just introduced this mode of therapy delivery, this becomes a human resources issue and not a therapeutic issue.

In ONEplus Therapy, the Client Is in Charge

One of the central principles of ONEplus Therapy is that the client is in charge of much of the process. Thus, clients are in charge of the following in ONEplus Therapy:

- Deciding whether to access ONEplus Therapy or not.
- Choosing which of their common emotional problems they want to nominate.
- Selecting their session goal.
- Deciding on the therapeutic focus for the session.
- Selecting the solution to their nominated emotional problem.
- Determining the nature of their action plan.
- Deciding what their therapeutic takeaways are from the session.
- Deciding whether to seek further help after the session (with a suitable break) and, if so, choosing what type of help they think would be most helpful.

By saying that the client is in charge in ONEplus Therapy, I am not proposing that the therapist has no say in these matters. Far from it. Thus, if the client's proposed solution to their problem is likely to maintain their problem rather than solve it, the therapist should explain why. However, the client is ultimately in charge of whether or not to accept the client's reasoning, although in my experience, most accept it, not because the therapist is making the point but because they can see that it makes sense.

Conventional therapists also say that the client is in charge, but this is not true in certain critical respects. Thus, when a therapist or agency decides what form of therapy the client should have after an assessment, this is not putting the client in charge. When the client is given a block of sessions[10] when they want less, this is also not putting the client in charge.

---

[10] For reasons that are not made clear, a block of sessions often comprises six therapy sessions.

The Power of Now

The ONEplus therapist argues that the only time they know they will be seeing the client is in the here and now when they are seeing the client. Given this, the ONEplus therapist asks themself, 'What do I want to offer the client given that I may never see them again?' The response is invariably: to provide them with the help that meets their stated wants from the session. Thus, before and during the session, the therapist does not assume that the client will return for more help or that they will not return either because they have received the help they wanted or because they haven't found the process helpful.

This contrasts with the conventional therapy mindset, where the therapist structures the therapy process so that the first contact is an assessment and serves as a prelude to the help to be provided in future sessions. Thus, in conventional therapy, the therapist assumes that the client will return for a second session after the assessment session and that they will keep returning until the end of treatment has occurred, usually, but not always, as determined by the therapist or agency. Indeed, in conventional therapy, clients who decide not to complete the entire treatment because they have gotten the help they were seeking tend to be regarded as 'dropouts' from that treatment.

Less is More

I mentioned in the section above entitled 'View the Session as a Whole, Complete in Itself' that the therapist who practises ONEplus Therapy from a conventional therapy mindset tends to think that since they may only see a client once, they have to give that client as much help as possible. This leads them to cram in the help they typically give over several sessions. The result is that the client gets overwhelmed and takes away very little from the session. Such a therapist also tends to send the client a lot of information after the session in the form of attachments and links to further material and organisations that may be helpful to them. Again, this only results in client overload and confusion.

The ONEplus therapist needs to appreciate that less is more in this mode of therapy. Helping the client focus on one problem for which they are seeking help, and assisting them in finding a solution to this problem which they can implement after the session has finished, is what the ONEplus therapist should aim for.

I say to my ONEplus clients that we will meet for *up to* fifty minutes because if we finish before then, I do not want to use any remaining time on a new issue, given that doing so will detract from the work I have done on the client's nominated emotional problem.

Small May Be Beautiful

Related to the 'less is more' principle, 'small is beautiful' refers to the idea that if a client can be helped in ONEplus Therapy to take a small step forward in the session towards solving their nominated emotional problem and assisted to build on that step after the session, then this is regarded as a good outcome in ONEplus Therapy

Take Nothing for Granted

In ONEplus Therapy, keeping an open mind and taking nothing for granted is important. It may seem that a client has the resources to solve their nominated emotional problem, but they may not be able to do so. Conversely, a client may be bereft of resources but still be able to help themself. This is why the answer to the question of who can and cannot be helped in ONEplus Therapy is to let them have ONEplus Therapy and see if it helps them.

3

My Practice of ONEplus Therapy with Common Emotional Problems (CEPs): Contributions from SST/OAATT

In this chapter and the following one, I will discuss how I use ONEplus Therapy to work with clients seeking help for common emotional problems. In this chapter, I will outline principles of my practice generally accepted by most ONEplus/SST/OAATT practitioners. In the following chapter, I will discuss how I ally this practice with ideas informed by Rational Emotive Behaviour Therapy (REBT) – see Dryden (2019) – and other therapeutic approaches.

Encouraging the Client to Prepare for the Session

When a client contacts me and, after some discussion, decides they want to access my ONEplus Therapy service, I send them a pre-session questionnaire to complete and return before we meet for the session. The primary purpose of the questionnaire is for the client to prepare for the session so that they can get the most from it. Having said that, it is not mandatory, and I would not refuse to see a client for ONEplus Therapy who did not want to complete it. Also, while it is helpful for me to see the questionnaire before I see the client, this is unnecessary. I have a wealth of experience doing live demonstrations of ONEplus Therapy while knowing nothing about the volunteer client before the session (Dryden, 2021).

As already pointed out, it sometimes happens that the client changes their mind about which common emotional problem to discuss after completing and returning the questionnaire. Therefore, I find it helpful to check with them at the outset that the problem they mentioned they wanted help with on the form is still current.

If the person has taken the time to complete the form, it is my practice to thank them for doing so and to ask them for permission to refer to this during the session. If they have a copy of the form to hand, I encourage them to refer to it if they wish.

A ONEplus Therapy Session with CEPs Requires a Structure

The first (and perhaps only) session in ONEplus Therapy to help the client with their nominated emotional problem requires structure. The following is such a structure that features in my practice of ONEplus Therapy.

1. Starting therapy from moment one.
2. Agreeing on the purpose of the session.
3. Establishing the working alliance quickly.
4. Establishing that the client is looking for help with emotional problem-solving.
5. Identifying and working towards the client's end-of-session goal.
6. Co-creating a therapeutic focus with the client and maintaining it.
7. Understanding the client's nominated emotional problem in context.
8. Focusing on what the client has done before concerning the problem.
9. Focusing on the client's internal strengths and external resources.
10. Being solution focused.
11. Promoting in-session rehearsal of the selected solution, if feasible.
12. Helping the client develop an action plan.

13. Inviting the client to summarise the session.
14. Focusing on the client's takeaway(s).
15. Encouraging generalisation whenever possible.
16. Reviewing with the client their options for further help.
17. Ending the session well so that the client leaves the session with their morale restored.

Please be advised that I am not advocating that the above points be used as a step-by-step guide to the practice of ONEplus Therapy, and I am certainly not proposing a manualised approach to this mode of therapy delivery. These areas are covered in most ONEplus Therapy sessions but not necessarily in the order presented here. Thus, I am not putting forward a treatment protocol. Indeed, in some cases, the therapist and client will not deal with one or more of these areas.

Starting Therapy from the First Moment

In most cases, when a person seeks therapy from a practitioner offering conventional therapy practised from a conventional therapy mindset, they will be engaged in one or more processes that are not designed to be therapy, which, in this case, I mean helping the client to solve their nominated emotional problem. Thus, they may be assessed to see which therapy is most suitable for them and how long this therapy is likely to last, a case history may be taken from them, or the therapist may engage them in developing a case formulation designed to explore connections between their problems, how past events may have contributed to their problems and how they may unwittingly maintain these problems. These practices may be therapeutic but are not seen as constituting therapy by those undertaking them. They are pre-therapy processes.

Alternatively, these practices are absent in some therapeutic approaches (e.g. person-centred therapy). Instead, the client is encouraged to begin the therapeutic approach in any way they choose with minimal structuring by the therapist. This free-form exploration may take place over several sessions.

In contrast, in ONEplus Therapy, I do not engage the client in any of these pre-therapy practices or encourage the client to talk in an unstructured way. Instead, focused therapy is begun from moment one. Since I do not know if I will see the client again, I decide to use the time we do have together focused on helping the client with what they have come for, dealing effectively with their nominated emotional problem. Of course, the client will be offered more help if required, but I do not know the client's response to this offer. It is quite likely that the client will choose not to return. In many cases, this is because they have been equipped with a solution that they can implement to solve their nominated emotional problem after the session has finished.

Clarifying at the Outset the Purpose of the Session

One of my preferred ways of beginning a ONEplus Therapy session is as follows:

> *Windy*: From your perspective, what is the purpose of
> our conversation today?

The client's response indicates if they understand the purpose of ONEplus Therapy, which, in the present context, is to help the client identify the means to deal effectively with their nominated emotional problem. Their response also indicates if they have ideas about the purpose of the session that is at variance with its objective. If so, I will clarify what I can offer to help the client with their nominated emotional problem.

Establishing the Working Alliance Quickly

When I give a training workshop or short presentation on ONEplus Therapy (or single-session therapy), perhaps the most frequently asked question is, 'How can you develop a good therapeutic relationship with a client in one session when this usually takes several sessions?' (Dryden, 2022a). My answer is as follows.

Using my elaboration of Bordin's (1979) working alliance concept (Dryden, 2011), which is comprised of four domains: bonds, goals, views and tasks, I begin by ensuring that the client and I have shared *views* about the form of help they are accessing and that I am offering. I then elicit their session *goal* and work with the client to achieve this goal. In doing so, I offer them the core conditions of empathy, unconditional acceptance and transparency and collaborate with them throughout the session, all of which are important elements of the therapeutic *bond*. Finally, I work with them to find a solution to their nominated emotional problem, which represents our shared *tasks*.

Research has shown that when a client has developed a good working alliance with their therapist, they are more likely to benefit from a single therapy session than when the therapeutic dyad does not develop a good alliance (Simon, Imel, Ludman & Steinfeld, 2012).

Clarifying that the Client Is Looking for Help to Solve Their Emotional Problem

In this book, I am concentrating on how ONEplus Therapy can help a client with their emotional problem with which they have become stuck. If the client states that they are looking towards me to help them (a) gain a greater understanding of their problem, (b) express their feelings about their problem, or (c) feel understood or validated by the therapist, then I need to find out how they think that these forms of help will help them solve their emotional problem. This is not to say that these forms of help are not helpful. They are when they facilitate later emotional problem-solving. However, on their own, they will usually not help the client to achieve what they seek – specific help to solve their emotional problem.

When a client nominates these other forms of help and does not see their role in facilitating emotional problem-solving, I assist them in making this connection. If they are steadfast in wanting one of these other forms of help, and that alone, then I will help them see the implications. In such a case, I may be unable to help them solve their emotional problem.

Identifying and Working Towards the Client's End-of-Session Goal

ONEplus Therapy is goal-directed, and the client puts forward that goal. It is important to distinguish between two sets of client goals. The first is known as the session goal, which relates to what the client wants to achieve by the end of the session. The second is known as the problem-related goal, which, as the term makes clear, is the goal related to resolving the problem. The following figure shows the relationship between the two sets of goals.

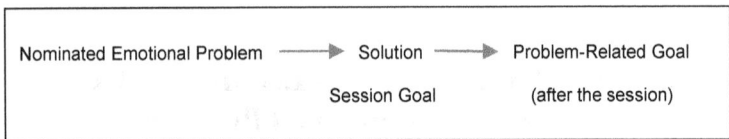

Nominated Emotional Problem	⟶	Solution	⟶	Problem-Related Goal
		Session Goal		(after the session)

As this figure shows, the session goal is often equivalent to the solution to the client's problem. Thus, when a client says that they want to learn how to deal with their anxiety by the end of the session, in terms of the figure, their nominated emotional problem is anxiety and 'dealing with' anxiety is equivalent to the solution. After the session, the person's problem-related goal is pursued by implementing the solution aided by the action plan to be developed later.

Co-Creating a Therapeutic Focus with the Client and Maintaining It

Once I know the client's nominated emotional problem and session goal, I can create a focus that contains these two elements. From there, the work proceeds, and I am responsible for maintaining the focus. This may mean interrupting the client if the latter goes off track. The best way to do this is to give the client a rationale for interrupting them and then ask for their permission to do so. In my experience, this helps to keep the session focused on helping the client achieve their session goal.

Understanding the Client's Problem in Context

To help the client develop a solid solution to their nominated emotional problem,[11] I need to help myself and my client understand the latter's emotional problem in context. This would include the adversity that is centrally featured in the client's problem, the thinking and behaviour associated with the issue, the situations in which the problem occurs and how the client unwittingly maintains their problem through failed attempts to deal with it.

Focusing on What the Client Has Done Before Concerning the Problem

As can be imagined, time is at a premium in single-session therapy (Dryden, 2016a). In the present context, this means that I do not want to waste time discussing potential solutions to their nominated emotional problem that the client has already tried and found wanting. Consequently, it is helpful for me to review with the client what they have done to address their problem. In doing so, my goal is to encourage the client to make future use of

---

[11] Single-session therapists who favour solution-focused therapy would probably omit this step.

elements of attempted solutions that were helpful and to discard solution attempts that proved unsuccessful. My aim here is to help the client build on valuable things that they have done in the past rather than start from scratch.

Focusing on the Client's Internal Strengths and External Resources

This concept of 'building on', which I discussed at the end of the previous section, is an important feature of SST. Perhaps this is most evident when I come to help the client to identify both their internal strengths and the external resources that are available to them and that they can make use of during the emotional problem-solving process.

Internal Strengths

There are several ways in which I can approach the issue of helping the client to identify their internal strengths.

- *I ask the client directly for their strengths.* I can pose this question on the pre-session questionnaire form or during the session. If they do not nominate strengths, I can ask one or both of the following questions.
- *What would a good friend say your strengths are?*
- *What would you say about your strengths if you were asked about them at an interview for a job you really want?*
- *I infer the presence of strengths from what the client says during the session and put these to the client for their view.* For example, I may say, 'From what you have said, I think you have shown remarkable resilience in putting up with such a difficult situation for a long time. What's your view?'

Tough-Minded and Tender-Minded Strengths

In my view, strengths may be tough-minded (e.g. resilience, grit, self-discipline) or tender-minded (e.g. compassion, kindness, empathy). If a client provides one type, then it is helpful for me to enquire about the presence of the other. Indeed, the term 'internal strengths' may pull for the tough-minded type. The alternative term 'internal resources' might be used in this case.

External Resources

I often use the phrase, 'Only you can do it, but you don't have to do it alone', as a way of introducing the client to the idea that they have access to resources outside of themself that may be useful as they embark on the process of emotional problem-solving. Three types of external resources are helpful for my client and me to consider in this respect.

Who's On Your 'Team'?

A successful tennis player such as Rafa Nadal will have a group of people who travel with him while he plays in tournaments on tour. Collectively this group is known as 'Team Nadal'. Each person on the team has a particular role, and if Nadal wants help with something, he will go to the person whose job is to provide it. I have used the concept of 'team' to good effect because it suggests that the client has several people on their 'team' who have the person's 'back' and can support the person. It also suggests that different people on their 'team' can support them differently as they strive to solve their emotional problem, and they can go to the person who can offer them the type of help they need at any point.

Organisations

There may be several organisations that could provide help to the client as they strive to deal effectively with their nominated emotional problem. This help may be through advice, information or support groups.

Self-Help Resources

There is a wealth of self-help material available in book form or on the web that could support the client as they tackle their nominated emotional problem. If I am going to suggest self-help material to the client, then this should be as relevant to the work the two of us have done in the session as possible. I will only suggest one self-help resource to my client. To suggest several such resources is to run the risk of confusing or overwhelming the client.

Being Solution Focused

Earlier in this chapter, I made the point that a solution is something that the client uses to address their problem in a way that helps them to achieve their problem-related goal. In effect, a solution renders the client's problem a non-problem.

Common solutions involve reframing, attitude change, inference-based change, behavioural change, situational change or a combination of these factors. To help the client find an effective solution to their nominated emotional problem, I need a good understanding of each of the nine common emotional problems for which clients seek help. As I mentioned in the preface, these common emotional problems (CEPs) are anxiety, depression, guilt, unhealthy regret, shame, unhealthy anger, hurt, unhealthy jealousy and unhealthy envy.

In addition to drawing on my professional knowledge about these CEPs and how they can be best addressed, I help the client construct a solution by drawing on some of the following factors:

- *Their internal strengths, as discussed above.*
- *The resources in their environment that may be of use to them.*
- *Role models.* A good role model is someone whom the client can look up to and who struggles to implement a solution but comes through in the end.

- *Guiding principles.* In this context, a guiding principle is a principle that guides the client to achieve their goal.
- *The client's prior helpful and unhelpful attempts to solve the problem.*
- *Exceptions: When the CEP does not occur.*
- *Instances of the client's goal occurring.*
- *The client's experiences of solving the problem in a different area.* I will then help them to transfer these experiences to the solution of their nominated CEP.
- *The opposite of the client's problem-maintenance factors.*
- *The client's view of what will solve the problem.*

In co-constructing the solution with the client, the therapist needs to bear in mind two points:

- Complex problems do not always require complex solutions.
- Different methods can be used with different clients.

Promoting In-Session Rehearsal of the Selected Solution, if Feasible

Once the client has chosen a solution, I will help them rehearse it in the session. The purpose of this rehearsal is to allow the client to try out the solution to see if they can commit to implementing it after the session. The rehearsal may lead to an immediate commitment to the solution, the tweaking or the rejection of the solution in favour of another.

Using imagery, roleplay, and chairwork are common ways I encourage my client to rehearse the solution.

Helping the Client to Develop an Action Plan

While there are occasions where I can help the client solve their problem in one visit, most of the time, results are achieved by the client later outside the session. As such, I need to help the client develop an action plan to implement the solution after the session with me.

A Good Action Is Based on Solid Foundations

These are:

- The client is prepared to take responsibility for implementing the plan.
- What the client has agreed to do needs to be clear. Therefore, the more specific the solution delineated in the action plan, the better.
- The client can integrate the action plan into their everyday life.
- The action plan contains an inbuilt reminder to encourage the client to remember the purpose of implementing the plan.

A Good Action Plan Has Several Components

These components are as follows:

- *What* the client has agreed to do (i.e. the aspects of the solution).
- *Why* the client has agreed to do it.
- *When* the client has agreed to implement the solution.
- *Where* the solution is to be implemented.
- *Who* is the solution to be implemented with.
- *How often* is the solution to be implemented.

Identifying and Dealing with Potential Obstacles to Action Plan Implementation

It would be nice to think the client would implement the action plan without difficulty, but this is unrealistic. Therefore, I have found it essential to help the client identify, in advance, potential obstacles to them implementing the solution as specified in the action. Once we have identified these potential obstacles, I help the client formulate a way of dealing with them effectively should they occur.

Ending the Session on a Good Note

As William Shakespeare noted in the title of one of his comedies, *All's Well That Ends Well*, it is good when things come to a satisfactory conclusion. This is undoubtedly the case at the end of the first (and perhaps) only session of ONEplus Therapy that my client may have with me. Thus, I strive to end the session on a good note. This involves several features,

Inviting the Client to Summarise the Session

A good indication that the ONEplus Therapy session is coming to a close is when I have helped my client to develop an action plan as described above. The first thing I do when moving into the end phase of the session is to invite the client to summarise the session in their own words. Therapists are generally trained to summarise on behalf of clients as a way of bringing matters together. However, given the emphasis on client empowerment in ONEplus Therapy, I prefer to ask the client to summarise the session. After all, the client will be more influenced by how they see what we discussed and what they will take away from the session than by how I see these things.

In my experience, a good client summary includes what we discussed, the solution to their nominated CEP that we developed, how the client will implement this solution and what they have learned from our conversation that they will take away with them. Thus, I listen for these issues in the summary and may add to it if I consider that the client has omitted something. When I do this, however, I invite the client to add my point to their summary only if it makes sense to them to do so.

Focusing on the Client's Takeaway(s)

A client takeaway in ONEplus Therapy is what the client says they will take away from the session. It usually includes the solution and one or two other points that have meaning for the client to remember and, if relevant, implement after the session has ended. If the client has not included the solution they developed with me during the session, I enquire about this. The client may say that they included this in their summary, or, occasionally, they may indicate that they have doubts, reservations, or objections (DROs) to the solution. If so, I discuss their doubts and see where this leads us. If they still have DROs related to the solution at the end, this may signal the need for more help. However, as in all other cases, the client will decide about this. I don't see it as my job to do so in ONEplus Therapy.

Encouraging Generalisation Whenever Possible

A major way that I can increase the potency of ONEplus Therapy is by asking the client if they can see ways in which they can generalise their selected solution and/or takeaways to other areas of their life. If so, I will briefly ask them how they envision this. It is important for me remember, however, that there will be little time for me to elaborate on this issue with the client.

Reviewing with the Client Their Options for Further Help

After, the issue of generalisation has been dealt with, it is usually time for me to address the issue of further help with the client. In doing so, I will outline the options as I see them while ensuring that I present them in an even-handed way and stressing that whichever option the client chooses is OK.

- Option 1: The client has achieved what they have come for and does not want further help.
- Option 2: The client would like to reflect on what they have learned from the session, digest their learning, implement their selected solution, let time pass before deciding if they need further help.
- Option 3: The client requests further help at the end of the session. This may be another single session, an agreed number of sessions or ongoing therapy. If the client requests a form of help that I don't offer, I will suggest how they may access such help. As I pointed out in the footnote on p. 14, many SST therapists would not include this option because they would want to encourage the client to get the most out of the first session. The client can only do this if they implement the solution several times and determine whether or not they want more help once they have done so. The exception to this would be if the client would suffer as a result of not being offered more help at the end of the session.

Ending the Session Well so that the Client Leaves the Session with Their Morale Restored

Before I bring the session to a close, I give the client a final opportunity to tell me anything that they haven't told me about the issue at hand that they want to tell or to ask me anything that they need to ask me so that we can finish on a good note, hopefully with their morale restored.

*

In the next chapter, I discuss what I bring to my practice of ONEplus Therapy from sources other than the general single-session therapy practice literature that I have discussed in this chapter.

4

My Practice of ONEplus Therapy with Common Emotional Problems (CEPs): Rational Emotive Behaviour Therapy and Other Contributions

In this chapter, I discuss ideas that inform my practice of ONEplus Therapy that don't necessarily stem from the SST literature. It is the integration of these ideas with more standard ways of implementing ONEplus Therapy/SST practice that I discussed in the previous chapter that makes my ONEplus Therapy work unique. In presenting these ideas I, do so to describe how they inform *my* practice of ONEplus Therapy. I am not suggesting that they should inform *your* practice of ONEplus Therapy, and I am certainly not presenting them as ideas that should inform *the* practice of ONEplus Therapy with common emotional problems.

This chapter is divided into two parts. In the first part, I discuss ideas that come from Rational Emotive Behaviour Therapy that inform my practice of ONEplus Therapy (Dryden, 2019). In the second part, I discuss ideas that don't have a particular source but are ones that I have found useful to implement in my ONEplus Therapy practice.

Contributions to My ONEplus Therapy Practice from Rational Emotive Behaviour Therapy (REBT)

Each practitioner of ONEplus Therapy has their own therapeutic approach and they bring their own ideas deriving from these approaches to help clients with their common emotional problems (CEPs) using this mode of therapy. I myself have my own approach to therapy and I will now make clear the ways in which I have applied concepts from Rational Emotive Behaviour Therapy that help me encourage clients both to face and deal with their CEPs in ONEplus Therapy (Dryden, 2019).

What Is REBT?

Albert Ellis developed Rational Emotive Behaviour Therapy as an approach to cognitive behaviour therapy in the mid-to-late 1950s (Ellis, 1957). In summary, it holds that people disturb themselves about adversities mainly because they retain a set of extreme and rigid attitudes towards such adversities. They, therefore, need to develop an alternative set of flexible and non-extreme attitudes towards the adversities in order to deal healthily with them.

Although REBT is an attitude-based approach to therapy, Albert Ellis, REBT's founder, rather than referring to 'attitudes', called them 'beliefs' and distinguished between rational and irrational beliefs as mediating between adversities and psychologically healthy responses in the former case and between adversities and psychologically disturbed responses in the latter case (see e.g. Ellis, 1994). I regard the term 'belief' as having several different meanings, and I have come to realise that it tends to lead to confusion (see Dryden, 2013). What Ellis said about the roots of psychological disturbance and health is represented more accurately by the term 'attitude' rather than the term 'belief'. An attitude is thus 'an enduring pattern of evaluative responses towards a person, object, or issue' (Colman, 2015).

Moreover, instead of using the terms 'rational' and 'irrational', which Ellis favoured (see e.g. 1994), which many consider pejorative, I have adopted the more descriptive and non-pejorative terms 'flexible and non-extreme' and 'rigid and extreme' to refer to attitudes leading to healthy responses to adversities and to attitudes leading to disturbed responses to adversities respectively (Dryden, 2016b).

Helping Clients Distinguish between Healthy and Unhealthy Negative Emotions

In using ONEplus Therapy to help clients with their CEPs, I have adopted the REBT distinction between healthy negative emotions (HNEs) and unhealthy negative emotions (UNEs). When, as we shall see, a client chooses a CEP to discuss in ONEplus Therapy, an adversity is generally at the core of the problem. In ONEplus Therapy and other forms of therapy delivery, common adversities discussed by clients include criticism, rejection, threat and failure. As an adversity is, by definition, negative, then the client will experience a negative emotion about it, even if they are dealing constructively with it. This emotion, however, although it is negative in feeling tone, will, in effect, be healthy. What is more, according to REBT theory, this HNE will be associated with behaviour whose nature is mainly constructive, and thinking this will mainly be non-ruminative, realistic and balanced.

In contrast, when a person deals unconstructively with the same adversity that occurs when they consider they have a common emotional problem, they will also feel negatively, but this emotion, although again negative in feeling tone, will, in effect, be unhealthy. Thus, a UNE will be associated with behaviour that is mainly unconstructive and thinking that will mainly be ruminative and highly negatively distorted in nature.

In discussing a person's goal in relation to their nominated CEP, they often say that they want to feel OK or neutral about the adversity at the heart of their problem. I will explain in response why this is unrealistic. This is because feeling OK or neutral about a problem would indicate that it didn't matter to them that the adversity occurred, whereas, in reality, it does matter to them that the adversity occurred. They would have preferred it if it had not occurred. If the therapist accepts the client's goal as being to feel OK, this would mean encouraging the client to deceive themself, and this, in my view, is not a good therapeutic strategy.

I will then help the client to acknowledge that when they face the adversity underlying their nominated CEP, they can choose between experiencing an HNE or a UNE about the adversity. Common adversities and the UNEs and HNEs associated with them are listed in Table 1 (see p. 45).

Getting to the Heart of the Matter

In ONEplus Therapy, I find it productive to spend time working with the client to get to the core of their problem. In supervising therapists who are learning to become ONEplus Therapy practitioners, I have found that they struggle with getting to the core of the client's CEP. The therapist has to give themself permission to take their time to acquire as much personalised information about the client's nominated problem as they require so that they can help the client in a way that allows them to respond constructively to the adversity that features in their nominated CEP.

In order to get to the core of the matter, I need to do two things. I have to help both myself and my client to be clear about (1) their UNE and (2) what disturbed them most. Table 1 shows the framework I keep in mind when working with clients to get to the core of the matter of their nominated problem. When I am finding it difficult to help both of us to ascertain what they were most disturbed about, I find it useful to use a method which I term 'Windy's Magic Question'.

Table 1   Common adversities and the UNEs and HNEs

ADVERSITY	NEGATIVE EMOTION	
	UNHEALTHY	HEALTHY
- Threat	Anxiety	Concern
- Loss - Failure - Undeserved plight (experienced by self or others	Depression	Sadness
- Breaking your moral code - Failing to abide by your moral code - Hurting someone	Guilt	Remorse
- Doing something you wished you had not done - Not doing something you wished you had done	Unhealthy Regret	Healthy Regret
- Falling very short of your ideal in a social context - Others judging you negatively	Shame	Disappoint-ment
- The other is less invested in your relationship than you - Someone betrays you or lets you down and you think you do not deserve such treatment	Hurt	Sorrow
- You or another transgresses a personal rule - Another disrespects you - Frustration	Unhealthy Anger	Healthy Anger
- Someone poses a threat to a valued relationship - You experience uncertainty related to this threat	Unhealthy Jealousy	Healthy Jealousy
- Others have what you value and lack	Unhealthy Envy	Healthy Envy

Using Windy's Magic Question

In using my 'magic question' technique to identify what the client is most disturbed about in the situation where their chosen problem occurred, I undertake the following steps:

Step 1.   I ask the client to specify an example of their problem and describe succinctly the situation in which this problem occurred.

> In this example, I am working with Jean who has a problem with anxiety. She specified feeling anxious while waiting for a team meeting to begin at work.

Step 2. I focus on the situation in which my client disturbed themself (i.e. where they experienced their UNE).

> Jean focused on the following situation in which she felt anxious: 'I'm anxious while waiting for the team meeting to begin.'

Step 3.   I ask my client to imagine first that the situation cannot be altered. Then, I ask them to identify the one factor that would significantly reduce or even get rid of their UNE in the situation.

> Jean identified the following factor which would have reduced her feelings of anxiety: 'Not being criticised by the team leader.'

Step 4. The opposite is probably what the client was most disturbed.

> What Jean was most disturbed about: Being criticised by the team leader.

In using my Magic Question technique, I do not allow my client to change the actual situation in Step 1. If they were to do so, it would not help either of us to identify the adversity at the core of their problem.

Helping Clients Identify the Extreme/Rigid Attitudes Underpinning Their Problem and the Non-Extreme/ Flexible Attitudes that Could Solve This Problem

When my client and I have agreed on what is the main adversity at the heart of their nominated CEP, I ask them to express to me their understanding about why they have a disturbed emotional response to this adversity. They often reply that it is the adversity itself that causes them to have the response. I then ask them if they want to know my 'take' on this. (This question is a little disingenuous because I don't expect my client to say 'no', but by saying 'yes' they give me permission to proceed, which in turn leads them to listen to me with more attention.)

Table 2 summarises the difference between my view and theirs.

Table 2   The client's view of their problem vs REBT's view of their problem

Client's View of Problem	REBT's View of Problem
Adversity	Adversity
↓	↓
	Rigid/Extreme Attitude
	↓
↓	↓
Problematic Response	Problematic Response

Using Windy's Review Assessment Procedure (WRAP)

When the client has told me that they wish to know more about my 'take' on their problem and what might account for it, I use what I call Windy's Review Assessment Procedure (WRAP) to assess the attitude underpinning their chosen problem. I will use the example of Jean (see above) to demonstrate this. In the following, I talk directly to Jean.

1. At this point, we know that your emotion is anxiety and that your adversity is 'Being criticised by the team leader'.

2. We also know your preference, which is, 'I would prefer it if my team leader does not criticise me.'

    [I know this because my work is guided by REBT (Dryden, 2022b), which states that whenever a client has an emotional problem, it is based on their having a preference either for something to happen or for something not to happen (as in Jean's case).]

3. What we don't yet know is which of two attitudes your feelings of anxiety are based on – a flexible or rigid attitude.[12] So are your feelings of anxiety based on Attitude #1 ('I would prefer it if my team leader does not criticise me and therefore he absolutely must not do so') or Attitude #2 ('I would prefer if my team leader does not criticise me, but he does not have to do what I want')?

    [If Jean does not see that her feelings of anxiety are based on Attitude #1, I would discuss this with her until she understands this 'rigid attitude–unhealthy negative emotion (UNE)' connection.]

4. Now answer the following question: 'If you had a strong conviction in Attitude #2, how would you feel about the prospect of your team leader criticising you?'

---

[12] The WRAP technique can also be used to identify non-extreme attitudes and their extreme attitude alternatives (see Dryden, 2022b).

[If Jean does not say 'concern' or some suitable synonym, I would discuss this with her until she understands this 'flexible attitude–healthy negative emotion (HNE)' connection.]

5. You now see clearly that your healthy feelings of concern are based on your flexible attitude ('I would prefer it if my team leader does not criticise me, but he does not have to do what I want') and that your feelings of anxiety are based on your rigid attitude ('I would prefer it if my team leader does not criticise me and therefore he absolutely must not do so').

6. Does it make sense for you to set concern as your emotional goal in this situation and see that developing conviction in your flexible attitude ('I would prefer it if my team leader does not criticise me, but he does not have to do what I want') is the best way of achieving this goal?

[If Jean has any doubts, reservations or objections to doing so, I will discuss them with her. This last point is crucial from a ONEplus Therapy point of view. Setting 'concern' as Jean's problem-related goal is what I am asking her to do and seeing that developing conviction in her flexible attitude is the solution that will help her to achieve this goal after the session has ended.]

Encouraging Clients to Develop a Flexible Attitude

I mentioned in the brief description of REBT (see 'What is REBT?' above), that this approach maintains that disturbed responses to adversities are based on extreme and rigid attitudes while healthy responses to these adversities are based on non-extreme and flexible attitudes. One of the aspects of REBT informing the way I practise ONEplus Therapy with clients with CEPs is helping them develop non-extreme and flexible attitudes towards the adversities at the heart of their problems. My work with Jean, discussed in the previous section, was informed by this idea. I will focus in this section on helping clients develop, where relevant, flexible attitudes towards adversity, and in the next three sections I will discuss, again where relevant, how I help them develop non-extreme attitudes to adversity.

What's the Difference between a Flexible Attitude and a Rigid Attitude?

By a flexible attitude, I am referring to a situation where in some vital sphere of their life a person maintains an attitude that they don't have to be spared from getting what they don't want or don't have to get what they do want. By a rigid attitude, I am referring to a situation where in the same crucial sphere of their life someone holds an attitude that they must not get what they don't want or must get what they do want. The idea that is common to both attitudes is of what matters to them, what is important to them, or what they prefer. In my work with Jean (see above) I gave an example of this and have summarised this position in Figure 1 (see p. 51).

When the client can distinguish between these attitudes, I ask them which one they want to proceed with. Invariably they select the flexible attitude, so we discuss how they can do this (see below on 'Helping Clients Examine Their Attitudes' and 'Helping Clients Strengthen Their Conviction in Their Non-Extreme and Flexible Attitudes').

Desire / What is Important / What Matters

> *I would prefer it if my team leader does not criticise me....*

| *... and therefore, he must not do so* | *... but that does not mean that he must do what I want* |

Rigid Attitude   **Flexible Attitude**

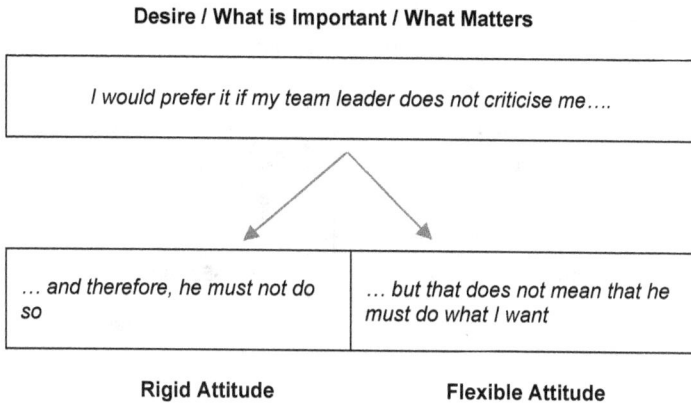

Figure 1   Difference between a rigid and flexible attitude

Encouraging the Client to Develop a Non-Extreme Attitude

REBT posits, as already mentioned, that psychologically healthy responses to adversities, in contrast, are based on a set of non-extreme and flexible attitudes. Psychologically disturbed responses to these same adversities are based on a set of extreme and rigid attitudes. REBT theory also argues that when clients maintain flexible attitudes, these often lead them to maintain one or more alternative non-extreme attitudes. Conversely, when they maintain rigid attitudes, these often lead them to maintain one or more extreme attitudes. Table 3 shows this position (see p. 52).

Just as I would help clients develop flexible attitudes where relevant, I would help them develop one or more non-extreme attitudes, again where relevant.

Table 3   Rigid attitudes lead to extreme attitudes and flexible attitudes lead to non-extreme attitudes

Rigid Attitudes	Flexible Attitudes
↓	↓
Extreme Attitudes	**Non-Extreme Attitudes**
• Attitudes of Unbearability	• Attitudes of Bearability
• Awfulising Attitudes	• Non-Awfulising Attitudes
• Devaluation Attitudes towards Self/Others/Life	• Unconditional Acceptance Attitudes towards Self/Others/Life

Helping the Client Develop an Attitude of Bearability

At the core of a client's nominated emotional problem there is sometimes an attitude of unbearability. An attitude of bearability is my term for the healthy alternative to this attitude. I outline the components of each attitude in Table 4 (see p. 53).

When clients see the relevance of developing an attitude of bearability, I help them put this into their own words to form the basis of the solution to their chosen problem.

Table 4   Differences between attitudes of unbearability and bearability

Struggle Component

It would be a struggle for me to bear being criticised by my team leader....	
Attitude of Unbearability	**Attitude of Bearability**
... and I couldn't bear it	*... but I could bear it* *It would be worth bearing* *I am worth bearing it for* *I would be willing to bear it* *I am going to bear it* *Taking action in ways that are consistent with the attitude of bearability*

Helping Clients Develop a Non-Awfulising Attitude

If the client mentions that they 'awfulise' their experience and think that this component is at the heart of their chosen problem, my strategy is, rather than helping them to take the badness out of badness, helping them to take the horror out of badness. This is known as a non-awfulising attitude, which is the healthy alternative to an awfulising attitude. I outline the components of each attitude in Table 5 (see p. 54).

When clients see the relevance of developing a non-awfulising attitude, I help them express this in their own words to allow them to understand for themselves the solution to their chosen problem.

Table 5   Difference between attitudes of awfulising and non-awfulising

Evaluation of Badness Component

It would be bad if I am criticised by my team leader....	
Awfulising Attitude	**Non-Awfulising Attitude**
...and therefore, it would be the end of the world	.... but it would not be not the end of the world

Helping Clients to Develop an Attitude of Unconditional Self-Acceptance

In situations where clients have problems of low self-esteem, I cannot obviously help them solve these problems in a single session. However, as a ONEplus therapist what I am able to do is to offer clients a framework to deal with their self-esteem issue from that point onwards. I suggest, in this respect, that the client might consider using the framework shown in Table 6 (see p. 55) to develop an attitude of unconditional self-acceptance rather than of self-devaluation.

Table 6   Difference between attitudes of self-devaluation and unconditional self-acceptance

Negative Evaluation of a Part of Self

It would be bad if I were criticised by my team leader....	
Self-Devaluation Attitude	**Attitude of Unconditional Self-Acceptance**
... and if this happens, it would prove that I am worthless	*... but this would not prove that I am worthless. It would prove that I am a unique, complex, unrateable, fallible human being capable of doing a myriad of different things, some good, some bad and some neutral.*

When clients see the relevance of developing an attitude of unconditional self-acceptance, I help them, as before, to express this in their own words so that it allows them to understand for themselves the solution to their chosen problem. In addition, I use Figure 2 (see p. 57; see also 'Utilise the Visual Medium as Well as the Verbal Medium', p. 62) to demonstrate the same point but doing so visually. This figure depicts the 'Big I – little i' technique, which illustrates that our 'self' (or 'Big I') is made up of many different elements or 'little i's' and that no single one of these elements can define the self.

Helping Clients to Develop an Attitude of Unconditional Other-Acceptance

If clients have an anger problem related to another person or group of people, it is likely that an attitude of other-devaluation and a rigid attitude underlie this anger. Helping them to address their anger problem, in my view, involves them developing a flexible attitude towards the other person's behaviour (see

'Encouraging Clients to Develop a Flexible Attitude', p. 49) and an attitude of unconditional other-acceptance (see Table 7, p. 56).

Table 7   Difference between attitudes of other-devaluation and unconditional other-acceptance

Negative Evaluation of a Part of Self

It would be bad if my team leader criticised me	
Other-Devaluation Attitude	Attitude of Unconditional Other-Acceptance
... and this would prove that he is worthless	*... but this would not prove that he is worthless. It would prove that he is a unique, complex unrateable, fallible human being capable of acting well, poorly and neutrally.*

Helping Clients to Accept Reality

I was feeling good after writing 16,000 words of a previous book (Dryden, 2023a) not only because I was enjoying writing it but because I was ahead of schedule. However, when I was about to start work on the draft, I couldn't find a way to open the file as it had been corrupted. I, therefore, bought an online tool that was supposed to recover the text of what I had written, but all it actually did was reformat the USB drive so that I lost the file altogether. What's more, I had forgotten to back up my work!

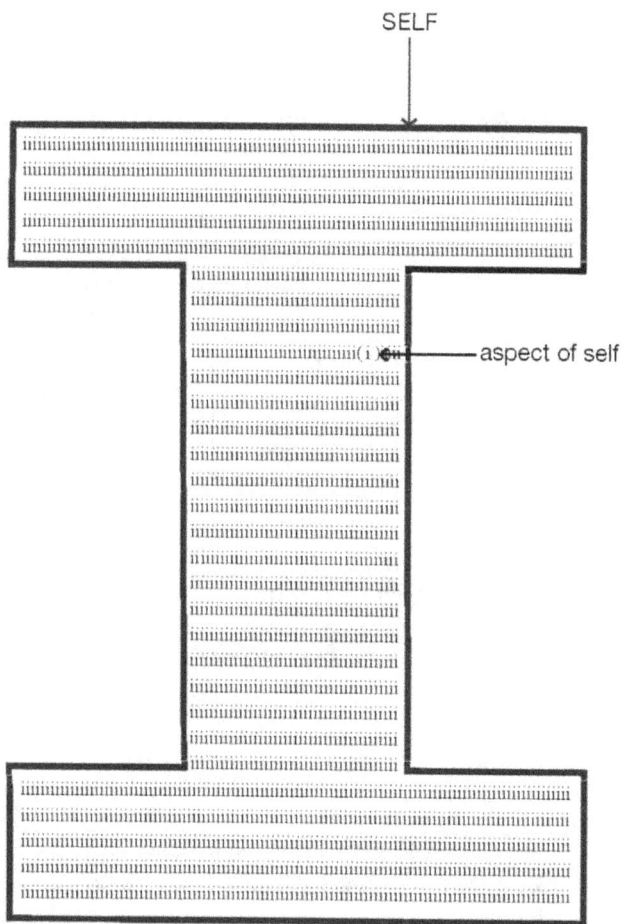

Figure 2 The 'Big I – little i' technique

How did I respond to this? After a struggle, I accepted reality. This, in effect, meant the following:

- I acknowledged that I had lost my file and had not backed up my work.
- I accepted that I really did not like the fact that this had happened.
- I recognised that all the conditions were there, unfortunately, for this to take place and that things did not have to be different. They had to be just the way they were. Why was this? Because that's what had happened. Reality has to be reality!
- I decided to email myself the work from that point onwards and also that I would back up my work to two different files. This would ensure that, even in the event that my file was corrupted again, I would have copies of my work.

When it is appropriate, I mention the above incident, and my strategy for dealing with it, to clients if they want me to say more about how I view the acceptance of reality.

Helping Clients Examine Their Attitudes

In ONEplus Therapy, in which time is at a premium, I look for an efficient method of helping clients to stand back and examine the two sets of attitudes underpinning their disturbed responses to the adversity underpinning their problem (extreme/rigid attitudes[13]) and their healthy responses to the same adversity (non-extreme/flexible attitudes[14]). In this section, I will discuss two ways of doing this: (1) using the choice-based examination method and (2) using persuasive arguments.

---

[13] These extreme attitudes are: attitudes of unbearability, awfulising attitudes and devaluation attitudes (see Tables 4–7).
[14] These non-extreme attitudes are: attitudes of bearability, non-awfulising attitudes and unconditional acceptance attitudes (see Tables 4–7).

The Choice-Based Examination Method

I adopt the choice-based method with clients' rigid attitudes and their flexible alternatives and/or the most relevant extreme attitudes and their non-extreme alternatives. In using this method, I ask clients to focus on both attitudes and choose which of them is true and which is false, which is logical and which is illogical, and which is healthy and which is unhealthy, as well as giving reasons for their choice.

Using the Choice-Based Examination Method with Rigid and Flexible Attitudes

In employing this method with my client's rigid and flexible attitudes, I encourage them to focus on both of these attitudes and I ask them the following questions.

- Which of these two attitudes is true or consistent with reality and which is false or inconsistent with reality and why is that the case?
- Which of these two attitudes is logical or sensible and which is illogical or nonsensical and why is that the case?
- Which of these two attitudes is largely helpful to you and which is largely unhelpful to you and why is that the case?
- Which of these attitudes do you want to choose to develop going forward and why is that the case?

Using Persuasive Arguments

I consider the 'Choice-Based Examination Method' as the most structured way of helping clients examine both their extreme and non-extreme attitudes and their rigid and flexible attitudes at the same time. It is also important, though, for me to help clients develop their own methods of examining these attitudes, focusing on using arguments that are persuasive to them. The following are some examples of applying this more creative approach to examining attitudes.

TEACH YOUR CHILDREN

With this method, I take an attitude pair (for instance, a rigid and flexible attitude) and ask clients to decide which of these attitudes they would like to teach a child or a group of children about whom they care and/or for whom they have responsibility. In teaching the child(ren), I take care to ask the client to explain the reasons for their choice in a way that the child(ren) can understand.

WHICH ATTITUDE WOULD YOU LIKE TO HAVE BEEN TAUGHT?

In this method, I take the pair of attitudes and ask clients which of these two attitudes they would have liked to have been taught growing up and why that is the case. I also ask them to make clear why they would not have liked to have been taught the other attitude.

USE DIAGRAMS

Some clients prefer, or are more receptive to, points being made visually rather than verbally. If this should be the case, draw a diagram to help your client to accept the non-extreme/flexible attitude rather than the extreme/rigid attitude. Figure 2 shows an example of this[15] which depicts the 'Big I – little i' technique. As described earlier, this technique demonstrates that the 'self' (or 'Big I') comprises many different aspects or 'little i's. It also shows that the self cannot be defined by its aspects.

Helping Clients Strengthen Their Conviction in Their Non-Extreme and Flexible Attitudes

Once clients have indicated that they wish to strengthen their non-extreme and/or relevant flexible attitude from this point

---

[15] See the 'Helping Clients to Develop an Attitude of Unconditional Self-Acceptance' (p. 54). See also 'Utilise the Visual Medium as Well as the Verbal Medium' (p. 62).

onwards, I do two things which are in accordance with traditional ways of practising ONEplus Therapy/SST/OAATT.[16] First, I suggest how clients can rehearse the attitude in the session. I do so because the non-extreme/flexible attitude represents, in ONEplus Therapy terms, the solution to the client's problem. When they have committed themself to this solution, I then work with them to develop an action plan by which they can implement this attitude in relevant contexts using behaviours which will be the support and foundation of the conviction in the attitude they have developed.

Other Contributions to My ONEplus Therapy Practice

In this part of the chapter, I will discuss eight ideas that inform my practice of ONEplus Therapy which I have learned are important in helping clients to get the most of their first (and perhaps) only session of therapy with me. These ideas do not stem from any particular school of thought.

Making an Emotional Impact

In my view, ONEplus Therapy is most effective when the client engages both their 'head' and their 'heart' so that they can take away one or two principles from the session that are personally meaningful to them and which, when implemented, can help them make meaningful changes in their life. As such, I strive to make an emotional impact in my work with my ONEplus Therapy clients without pushing to do so. This involves a delicate balance between making the session a non-emotional cognitive experience for the client where they engage their 'head', but not their 'heart' and a situation where they are flooded with affect and cannot process what they experience. In making the session

---

[16] See 'Promoting In-Session Rehearsal of the Selected Solution, if Feasible' (p. 35) and 'Helping the Client to Develop an Action Plan' (p. 36).

emotionally impactful for the client I make use of one or more of the following concepts.

Finding and Using Something that Really Resonates with Your Client While Helping Them

When I carry out a ONEplus Therapy session, I am always looking for something that may resonate with my client. My view is that the ONEplus therapeutic process is enhanced when the client resonates with something that we are discussing and is. My search for resonance occurs in three areas.

USING LANGUAGE THAT IS MEANINGFUL TO THE CLIENT
When a client is experiencing affect in the ONEplus Therapy session, they use language that is personally meaningful to them. In order to hold the resonance in the session, I will use (but not overuse) the same words as they use and will resist the temptation of using synonyms that may have the same objective meaning as the words used by the client but lack their subjective meaning.

USING RELEVANT IMAGERY
Sometimes a client may use an image to describe their experience, and this often seems to have emotional resonance for them. I will use this image not only to express my understanding of the client's experience but in modified form which may contribute to the client's solution to their nominated CEP.

UTILISE THE VISUAL MEDIUM AS WELL AS THE VERBAL MEDIUM
It is said that a picture is worth a thousand words and I have certainly found at times that a client will resonate more to something shown to them through the visual medium as opposed told to them through the verbal medium alone. Thus, when the client is discussing a relationship about which they have doubts respect to the behaviour of the other, I may wave a red flag to indicate understanding of their position and as a

stimulus to change (e.g. 'What would you have to do so that I stop waving my red flag?').

USING STORIES, PARABLES AND METAPHORS

I have found telling the client a suitable story, parable or metaphor is useful because it tends to be memorable. However, I do check whether the client has understood the point of the story, etc. because otherwise the power of the intervention will be lost. I refer the reader to Dryden (2024) for examples of these stories, parables and metaphors.

USING HUMOUR

Albert Ellis (e.g. 1977) used to argue that since emotional disturbance can be seen as taking things *too* seriously, the therapeutic value of humour can be to encourage the client to see an adversity, for example, in a different, less serious frame. To do this well, the therapist and client need to share a similar sense of humour and the client should experiences the therapist's humour as a caring challenge, rather than a personal attack (see Lemma, 2000).

USING SELF-DISCLOSURE

I have found that the judicious use of self-disclosure can help the client resonate with a possible solution to their CEP. First, it is important that I ask the client if they are interested in my experience before I tell them about it. When they give me their permission, I tell them that I struggled with the same or similar issue with which the client is currently struggling, but that I dealt with the issue by implementing a solution that the client may also find helpful.

Refer to Your Client's Core Values to Promote Change

I agree with my Acceptance and Commitment Therapy colleagues who argue that the client's core values provide powerful motivation for emotional problem solving (Flaxman,

Blackledge & Bond, 2011). Given that, I have found it useful spending time discovering the client's values. I use them in different ways, but in general they are useful to help a client see that short-term discomfort is worth bearing when doing so helps them client pursue value-driven goals. It is also important to help the person keep their values in mind as these are often forgotten when discomfort is experienced in the moment and the client experiences a strong urge to eliminate this discomfort. Here, as suggested above, a story, parable or metaphor is useful as is an image to help the keep refer to these values in times of struggle. Having them rehearse this process in imagery is particularly helpful with some clients.

Utilising the 'User Manual' Approach

If you were to purchase an electrical gadget, for example, it will probably come with a user manual, the purpose of which is to tell you the gadget works and how you can get the best out of it. I use the 'user manual' concept in ONEplus Therapy in two ways. First, I encourage the client to discover how they typically function so that they can accept themself and get the most from themself based on the knowledge. Second, I encourage the client to discover how another person typically functions so that they can accept the person and act towards that person according to how they are and how the client demands them to be.

Helping the Client to Respond to Their Initial Reactions

Often, clients come to ONEplus Therapy with what I call 'elimination' goals. For example, they say things like I want 'not to feel anxious' when asked what they want to get from the session. As described above in the section on REBT entitled, 'Helping Clients Distinguish between Healthy and Unhealthy Negative Emotions' (see pp. 43–44), I help the client who voices such a goal to understand the following:

- It is not possible to eliminate anxiety (or other disturbed emotions) from the human emotional repertoire.
- For every unhealthy negative emotion such as anxiety there in a healthy negative emotion alternative. For example, concern rather than anxiety when facing a threat.
- It is realistic and constructive to experience a healthy negative emotion in the face of an adversity. It is neither realistic nor constructive to feel calm or 'OK' in this circumstance.
- I can help the client begin this process of change in the session, but, in general, I can't help them complete it. As such, finding, rehearsing and planning to implement a solution based on the above points is do-able by the end of the session.
- During the process of change the client will initially default to experiencing their unhealthy negative emotion (e.g. anxiety).

I have found it particularly helpful to make this latter point because some clients become discouraged when they begin to experience their unhealthy negative emotion. For these clients, I explain that it is very common for this to happen and when it dos that have a choice between becoming discouraged and giving up the process of change or using the occurrence of their initial response as a cue to implement whatever solution that came up with in the session. Magnus Magnusson who used to present the TV programme, *Mastermind*, had a phrase he used when the buzzer sounded to end the round of questioning after he had started a question. It was 'I've started, so I'll finish.' I use what I call the anti-Magnus Magnusson principle with clients on this point. This is, 'I've started but I don't have to finish.' This reminds the client that beginning to be anxious is not the problem: failing to respond constructively to this anxiety using their selected solution is.

Using the Book Analogy

A similar issue occurs when clients fail to see their problem in a wider context where 'process' is the important theme. Neglecting the process nature of a problem and its solution often lies at the heart of a client's issue and certainly neglecting this process will not help the person sustain the implementation of their selected solution.

To emphasise the process nature of the problem-solution process, I use what I call the 'book analogy'. Thus, in Chapter 1, a client experiences a problem. If they give up at that point they are, in effect, closing the book and making the book a one-chapter book. However, let's suppose that Chapter 1 occurs and the client responds to the problem with the solution that we have developed in the ONEplus Therapy session. This becomes Chapter 2. Furthermore, let's suppose that in the midst of implementing the solution they experience an obstacle and stop implementing the solution. This becomes Chapter 3. Then, in Chapter 4 they stand back and deal with the obstacle and resume implementing the solution. I will outline these two scenarios and ask the client which book they would like to follow: the one-chapter book or the four-chapter book. In using this technique, I suggest as many book chapters as are needed, but it is important that the book ends on a productive note, mirroring the idea the client will solve their common emotional problem in the end.

Helping the Client to Understand the Problem before Suggesting 'Tips and Techniques'

Quite a few clients come to ONEplus Therapy hoping to get 'tips and techniques' to deal with their nominated CEP. The way that I view this request is that they are asking for a solution to their problem. However, if the client uses the term 'tips and techniques', then I will also use this term rather than the term 'solution'.

In my experience, the selection of tips and techniques to help the client deal effectively with nominated CEP is best founded on an understanding of their problem and I will put this point to my client before proceeding. If they are doubtful about this way of proceeding, I ask them whether it is better for them if we find a tailor-made, bespoke set of tips and techniques or a set that is 'off-the-peg' as might be offered to anyone. This helps them to get the point that a solution is best selected once the problem has been properly understood.

Helping the Client to Develop Confidence by Doing Things Unconfidently

One of the session goals that clients often want to set in ONEplus Therapy is for them to feel confident about doing something that they currently do not feel confident about. This is actually a problem-related goal as we will see, but the realisation of how to achieve this can be achieved by the end of the session.

When the client states such a goal, I engage them in a conversation concerning how confidence tends to develop. I can best do this by asking them if they have ever had the experience of not being confident about doing something and later feeling confident about doing that very same thing. As virtually everybody has had that experience, the client invariably replies in the affirmative. I then ask them to give me an example of how they brought about this shift. What they say is as follows:

- They began by feeling unconfident about doing something that they wanted to do.
- With help, they began the task even though they felt unconfident.
- They persisted with the task because it was worth it for them to do so and learned from their mistakes.
- In doing this, they gradually became increasingly confident at doing the task until they reached their desired level of confidence.

After they have outlined the process similar to that outlined above, I can show they that they have already had the experience of achieving their stated goal before and, thus, they can see that all they need to do is to transfer the experience to their nominated problem. However, while this realisation can be achieved in the session, the experience of becoming more confident at their desired activity can only be done after the session, and to this end, I help them to develop an action plan so that they can implement their solution and achieve their problem-related goal.

The above is a good example of how to utilise the client's past experience in constructing a present goal and is far more telling than if I outlined the process of developing confidence didactically or even Socratically, without reference to the client's past experience.

I utilise the same process as that outlined above when the client sets as their goal becoming competent at a task or becoming comfortable at doing something (see below).

Helping the Client to View Discomfort as a Friend and Not as an Enemy

We tend to live in what I call the 'age of comfort' where being comfortable in the moment is prized and often prioritised over the therapeutic value of doing things uncomfortably. If the client has become used to getting rid of presently experienced discomfort, they come to view discomfort as the enemy.

If you think of it, the achievement of personal change is often accompanied by discomfort, and this needs to be understood by the client and it is my task as a ONEplus therapist to help them appreciate this. I do this by again helping them to search for a past experience of personal change that was accompanied by discomfort and where they became comfortable with the change again after repeated practice. In doing this, I help them to see that 'If it ain't strange, it ain't change', for personal change involves the process of bearing a state of unfamiliarity until one becomes familiar with the desired behaviour.

In doing this, I help the client see that when dealing with their nominated CEP, discomfort is their friend and not their enemy – to be experienced rather than eliminated.

Helping the Client Distinguish between Enthusiasm-Based Motivation, Fear-Based Motivation and Reason-Based Motivation

Quite often in ONEplus Therapy, the issue of motivation is raised by clients, and the most common way that they discuss this topic is them not having the motivation to do something that they want to do and/or that is in their interests to do. In talking about this issue with a client, I have found it useful to make the distinction between 'enthusiasm-based motivation', 'fear-based motivation' and 'reason-based' motivation. In doing so, I make the following points to clarify which type of motivation they lack and which type of motivation they would ideally like to have prior to doing a task.

- *'Enthusiasm-based motivation'* represents a feeling of enthusiasm for doing what the person thinks they need before starting it.
- *'Fear-based motivation'* represents the fear that the person feels they need to experience before they do the task. The fear concerns the possibility that the person may not meet a deadline and it is this fear that is motivating the person.
- *'Reason-based motivation'* represents the good reasons the person has to do the task.

In my experience, when motivation is involved in a client's CEP, it is usually because they have relied on 'enthusiasm-based motivation' or 'fear-based motivation' to drive them forward and both, in different ways, contribute to the client's problem rather than to its solution. On the other hand, 'reason-based motivation' does have the potential to contribute to a good solution to the client's issue if they are willing to forgo the other type of motivation that they have previously relied upon.

In the next part of the book, I will discuss how I apply ONEplus Therapy to the nine common emotional problems for which clients seek help. These are: anxiety, depression, guilt, unhealthy regret, shame, unhealthy anger, hurt, unhealthy jealousy and unhealthy envy.

Part II

Applying ONEplus Therapy to Common Emotional Problems

PREAMBLE

In this second part of this book, I will outline how I apply ONEplus Therapy when helping people with nine common emotional problems (CEPs). These are: anxiety, depression, guilt, unhealthy regret, shame, unhealthy anger, hurt, unhealthy jealousy and unhealthy envy. In doing so, in each chapter, I will outline the ideas that I bring to the practice of ONEplus Therapy with a specific CEP. I will then present a transcript of my actual work with someone who is seeking help with the CEP in question. I will comment on my work on the transcript as the session unfolds. At the end of each transcript, the volunteer offers their reflections, on their experience of the session and what they made of it going forward.

5

Helping People with Problems with Anxiety

Anxiety is perhaps the most common emotional problem for which clients seek therapy, in general, and ONEplus Therapy, in particular. It features in the new name for the National Health Service's provision for the treatment of psychological problems in the United Kingdom – the NHS Talking Therapies service for anxiety and depression.

Helping the Client to Understand and Deal with Anxiety

In this section of the chapter, I will discuss what I have to offer clients seeking help with anxiety. Remember that in ONEplus Therapy, I will only offer a client my perspective when they are clearly struggling to understand or deal with their nominated emotional problem. When this occurs, I will ask my client if they are interested in my 'take' on their nominated emotional problem and how they can deal with it. If they are interested, I will share it. If they are not, I won't.

While, as mentioned above, anxiety is probably the most common emotional problem for which clients seek ONEplus Therapy, many of these clients know very little about anxiety that will help them deal with their anxiety problems. Consequently, let me outline several ideas and concepts that I have found useful to introduce into my conversation with clients that can help them understand and deal with anxiety.

The Two Main Components of Anxiety

Anxiety[17] has two major components. First, it is based on a set of rigid/extreme attitudes that the person holds towards something that they deem to be threatening. Second, it is based on the person's inference that they won't be able to deal with the threat. It follows that I may need to help a client with the first, second or both components.

Non-Anxious Concern is the Healthy Alternative to Anxiety

I mentioned in Chapter 4 that I am informed by the distinction made in REBT between unhealthy negative emotions and healthy negative emotions. As shown above, anxiety is clearly an unhealthy negative emotion and is experienced as such by clients in general. If I ever ask a client why they regard anxiety as a problematic emotion, I am met with a quizzical look which says, 'Isn't it obvious!'

The healthy alternative to anxiety is not the absence of anxiety or a less intense form of anxiety. It is what I call non-anxious concern, which, like anxiety, has two major components. First, it is based on a set of flexible/non-extreme attitudes that the person holds towards the same threat as in anxiety. Second, it is based on the person's appraisal that they will be able to deal with the threat.

The Behavioural and Thinking Concomitants of Anxiety and Non-Anxious Concern

In Table 8 (see pp. 75–8), I present the main features of anxiety and non-anxious concern. You will see from this table that both anxiety and non-anxious concern are about threat. In anxiety, as mentioned above, the person processes this threat with rigid/extreme attitudes, while in non-anxious concern, they process the threat with flexible/non-extreme attitudes. You will

---

[17] In this section, I will be discussing anxiety, which is psychological in nature. Sometimes, anxiety is related more to medical issues.

also see from this table that the behavioural and thinking concomitants of anxiety and non-anxious concern are very different, and it is these concomitants that help me and my client to see clearly if they are experiencing anxiety or non-anxious concern. If the former, the behavioural and concomitants of non-anxious concern help the client see what they need to do and think as they implement a co-created attitude-based solution to their anxiety problem.

Table 8   Anxiety vs non-anxious concern

Adversity	• You are facing a <u>threat</u> to your personal domain	
Basic Attitude	RIGID/EXTREME	FLEXIBLE/NON-EXTREME
Emotion	Anxiety	Concern
Behavioural Concomitants	• You avoid the threat	• You face up to the threat without using any safety-seeking measures
	• You withdraw physically from the threat	• You stay in the situation and take constructive action to deal with the threat
	• You ward off the threat (e.g. by rituals or superstitious behaviour)	• You do not employ any attempts to ward off the threat. You see the value of facing it and dealing with it directly
	• You try to neutralise the threat (e.g. by being nice to people of whom you are afraid)	• You employ no neutralising methods preferring to deal with the threat directly if it happens
	• You distract yourself from the threat by engaging in other activity	• You face the threat if it occurs without distracting yourself from it
	• You keep checking on the current status of the threat hoping to find that it has disappeared or become benign	• You develop a plan to deal with the threat if it happens and get on with the business of living without checking on the status of the threat

Table 8 (continued)

Behavioural Concomitants *(continued)*	• You seek reassurance from others that the threat is benign	• You make your own mind up if the threat is benign. If it is, you go about your business. If it is not benign then you deal with it
	• You over-prepare in order to minimise the threat happening or so that you are prepared to meet it (NB it is the over-preparation that is the problem here)	• You prepare to meet the threat but do not over-prepare
	• You seek support from others to help you face up to the threat and rely on them to protect you from it by handling it for you	• You seek support from others to help you face up to the threat and then take constructive action by yourself rather than rely on them to handle it for you or to be there to rescue you
	• You tranquillise your feelings so that you don't think about the threat	• You think about the threat and remind yourself how you can deal with it and that you have the resources to do so. You do this without tranquillising your feelings
	• You overcompensate for feeling vulnerable by seeking out an even greater threat to prove to yourself that you can cope	• You deal with the threat as it is and accept your feelings of vulnerability as you do so. You do not overcompensate for feeling vulnerable by seeking a deal with a greater threat

Table 8 (continued)

Thinking Concomitants	Threat-exaggerated thinking	
	• You overestimate the probability of the threat occurring	• You are realistic about the probability of the threat occurring
	• You create an even more negative threat in your mind	• You view the threat realistically
	• You ruminate about the threat	• You think about what to do concerning dealing with threat constructively rather than ruminate about the threat
	• You underestimate your ability to cope with the threat	• You realistically appraise your ability to cope with the threat
	• You magnify the negative consequences of the threat and minimise its positive consequences	• You are balanced in your thinking about the negative and positive consequences of the threat
	• You have more task-irrelevant thoughts than in concern	You have more task-relevant thoughts than in anxiety
	Safety-seeking thinking • You withdraw mentally from the threat	
	• You try to persuade yourself that the threat is not imminent and that you are 'imagining' it	
	• You think in ways designed to reassure yourself that the threat is benign or if not, that its consequences will be insignificant	

Table 8 (continued)

Thinking Concomitants (continued)	• You distract yourself from the threat, e.g. by focusing on mental scenes of safety and well-being	
	• You over-prepare mentally in order to minimise the threat happening or so that you are prepared to meet it (NB once again it is the over-preparation that is the problem here)	
	• You picture yourself dealing with the threat in a masterful way	
	• You overcompensate for your feeling of vulnerability by picturing yourself dealing effectively with an even bigger threat.	

Disturbed Emotional Responses to Anxiety

Quite often, people make themselves disturbed about their anxiety (e.g. ashamed, depressed, guilty etc.)[18] If this is the case with my client, I need to discuss with them whether we should focus in the session on their original anxiety or their meta-emotional disturbance. My client and I may or may not have time to address both in the first (and perhaps only) session of ONEplus Therapy. However, if we have time, then I will definitely try to cover both issues with the client as long as they feel able to take away something meaning with respect to both problems.

Perhaps the most common form of meta-disturbance with respect to anxiety is anxiety about anxiety. When this happens, and the client wants to focus on this 'secondary' disturbance, I help them to discover what it is about their 'primary' anxiety that they consider to be most threatening. I then help them to appraise this threat more realistically and help them to see that they can deal with the threat.

---

[18] When a person disturbs themself about their original disturbance, this is known as meta-emotional disturbance

In general, when helping my client to deal with their meta-disturbance about anxiety, I strive to help them in three ways. First, I help them understand that the feeling of anxiety is painful but usually not dangerous. Second, I help them to see that they can bear feeling anxious even though they think that they cannot bear it. Third, I encourage them to view anxiety as a sign that they are a fallible human being who is holding a rigid and extreme attitude towards threat. It is not evidence that they are a weak person.

Common Attempts to Deal with Anxiety Often Serve to Maintain It

Since anxiety is a painful emotion which affects several parts of the person's body and physiological functioning, it is natural (but not constructive) for the person to try to get away from these feelings as quickly as possible rather than stay in the situation and deal constructively with the threat.

However, attempts to eliminate anxiety only serve to maintain or increase it. Realistic, mindful acceptance of anxiety is the healthy alternative to elimination. This involves the client acknowledging that they feel anxiety and that it is unpleasant. They then decide to let the anxious feelings remain so that they can deal with them and the threat that they are about in an effective way.

Similarly, when a client attempts to avoid or withdraw from threat, they, again unwittingly, only serve to maintain their anxiety. Instead, as noted above, they need to face the threat and deal with it effectively.

Another way in which the person maintains their anxiety problem is to stay in the closet with respect to the threat that they find anxiety-provoking. Trying to hide from others and from oneself that one is anxious only serves to make one's anxiety problem worse in the long run, and when this happens, I encourage my client to look at the factors that lead them to stay in the closet and the factors they would need to be present for them to come out of the closet. I then work with them to achieve the latter.

Helping the Client to Deal Healthily with the Issue of Loss of Control

One of the most common threats people experience when anxious is loss of control. I have found it useful to help clients who experience such anxiety to consider the following:

- It is important that the client is clear about what they are in control of (largely themself) and what you are not in control of (largely others and events involving others).
- If the client holds a rigid and extreme attitude towards loss of self-control this will lead them to think that they will lose complete control of themself if they begin to lose such control.
- If the client holds a flexible and non-extreme attitude towards loss of self-control this will lead them to focus on how to respond when they begin to lose such control. They will tend not to think they will lose complete control of themselves.

Helping the Client to Deal Healthily with Uncertainty

Another common threat that people experience when they are anxious is uncertainty. I have found it useful to help clients who experience such anxiety to consider the following:

- Uncertainty in the face of threat does not on its own lead to anxiety.
- If the client holds a rigid and extreme attitude towards such uncertainty this will lead to anxiety. This attitude will lead them to think that if they do not know they are safe, then they are in danger.
- If the client holds a flexible and non-extreme attitude towards such uncertainty this will lead to non-anxious

concern. This attitude will lead them to think that they are probably safe even if they do not know for certain that they are.

- Thus, it is quite probable that the client is safe even when they are facing uncertainty. Uncertainty is not a sign of danger. It is a sign that they are in a state of not knowing. This may be an unpleasant state, but that is all that it is.
- The client should only seek reassurance if they are able to be reassured in the longer term (i.e. they are reassurable). Continually seeking reassurance when they are not reassurable, will maintain their anxiety problem.

Transcript of My Work with a Person with a Problem with Anxiety

Therapist – Volunteer: Windy – Jen
Venue: PESI UK on 12/05/23
Time: 21 minutes 39 secs

Windy: So, Jen, what's your understanding of the purpose of our conversation this afternoon?

[*This is my typical way of beginning a ONEplus Therapy session. It helps me to understand very quickly if the volunteer and I are on the same page concerning why we are meeting.*]

Jen: I am hoping that I could get some help with a specific problem I have about a fear that I have.

Windy: You're not sure if you have that or you are sure?

Jen: I'm very sure I have it.

Windy: So, would you be prepared to share what that problem is?

Jen: I would be delighted. I ... have a fear about having my blood pressure taken.

Windy: Right, OK. If you knew that it was going to be normal, would you still fear it?

              [At the outset, I am beginning to assess Jen's problem. In doing this, I am trying to find out what she is most anxious about. So, I use what I call the subtraction method. Would Jen be anxious having her blood pressure taken if she knew it would be normal? However, I have not asked her what she wants to achieve by the end of the session which is an error.]

Jen: No.

Windy: So, you're not scared of your blood pressure being taken. You're scared of what the results would show you.

Jen: Kind of. What happens is, when I go to the doctor and they take it, it goes really high, and the doctor reacts. So ... that's contributed to it.

Windy: So how does the doctor react?

Jen: She says, 'Oh, I think we need to take it again and again and again,' and ... *[pause]* looks a bit anxious.

Windy: OK. Do you take it on your own at home, in the comfort of your own home?

Jen: Yes, I've done that before and ... that's the problem I'm having at the moment. My doctor has said, 'I need you to do it twice in the morning and twice in the evening for a week,' otherwise she's not going to give me my repeat prescription for HRT. So, I'm having difficulty even doing that, even doing it myself. I have a machine.

[Again, I wished that I had asked Jen to make her goal explicit. It is implicit in what she is saying throughout the session that she wants to take her blood pressure, but in her mind, anxiety prevents her. It doesn't, as we will see.]

Windy: Have you ever had one of these things that monitors your blood pressure all the time and it randomly goes up or down?

[A much better question at this point would have been to ask Jen what she has previously done to solve the problem and what the results of these self-helping attempts were.]

Jen: I haven't.

Windy: How would you feel about that?

Jen: ... *[Pause]* I think part of me would probably think it was really helpful and another part would probably be a bit triggered by it.

Windy: Triggered in what sense?

Jen: ... *[Pause]* Well, I'm not sure if I would know if it was taking my blood pressure. I guess I would.

Windy: Yeah. I mean, I've had one of these things myself. All of a sudden it goes. You don't know when it's going to happen but it just does.

Jen: Yeah. So, there would probably be an element of, when I was aware of that, it would activate my threat system, as it were.

Windy: So, what is threatening for you then about having your blood pressure taken, since you mentioned threat?

Jen: That there's something wrong with me.

Windy: Like what? Anything in particular?

Jen: Yeah. I only have one kidney that functions, and I was told that … if my blood pressure went up, it would be an indication that there was a problem, and I might need to have my kidney removed. So, I guess there's an underlying fear.

Windy: So, you've got one kidney, is that what you're saying?

Jen: Well, one kidney that functions and one kidney that doesn't function.

Windy: And they would be taking away the one kidney that doesn't function?

Jen: Hmm-mmm, yeah.

Windy: And what impact would that have on your life?

Jen: … I don't know.

Windy: You don't know?

Jen: No. I probably would be OK with one kidney.

Windy: I think you probably would, from what I know. I'm not a doctor so don't hold me to it, but I hear that people can and do function well on one kidney.

Jen: Yeah.

Windy: Let's suppose you followed it through like this. You could say, 'I'm the kind of person that would tend to get anxious when they have their blood pressure taken. So, I'm just going to have to factor that in.' By the way, do you explain that to the doctor ahead of time?

     [*Like many people, when Jen gets anxious, she avoids or withdraws from the threat (taking her blood pressure in case she finds out there is something wrong with her) and thus does not think things through. I call this 'ostrich thinking'. My approach is to invite her to think things through.*]

Jen: Yeah. I mean, I've had quite a few health problems in my life, so I think I've focused a lot of that trauma into having my blood pressure taken. So, she knows, but … she's being quite strict at the moment with me, and I have to go in and do it in the room.

Windy: If you followed it through in terms of what we've been talking about: 'I'm the kind of person who tends to get anxious about having her blood pressure taken. So, I may have to experiment with different ways of doing it – either doing it myself or taking this thing and see what happens. If I do have high blood pressure and the worst comes to the worst and

I'm going to have to have one kidney out, I can live on one kidney.' Do you get to the end of the story or do you stop it somewhere early?

[*Here, I am using my 'book analogy' (see Chapter 4) to see if this might form the basis of a solution*]

Jen: … [*Long pause*] I don't think I've really gone to the end of that story. I think where I go to is, if my blood pressure goes up very high … something could happen to me.

Windy: Right, and, if that happens, would you like that to be known and dealt with or would you like not to know that?

Jen: I'd definitely like it to be known and dealt with.

Windy: So, if we factor that into the story, into the narrative, it would be, 'I'm the kind of person who gets anxious about having their blood pressure taken, but I'm going to have it taken anyway because it's in my interest to do that. I'll let the doctors know. They might react, they might not. They might give it to me at home. I'll take it. That might work, that might not. I'll even wear this 24-hour thing. But, if it happens that my blood pressure does go high, I'd like to know about it so something can be done. And, if the worst comes to the worst and I have to lose a kidney, I can function well on one kidney.' Now, if you really went through the whole of that narrative before you had your blood pressure taken almost, what difference do you think that would make to you?

Jen: … [*Pause*] It sounds logically … really an obvious thing, that, if I do have a problem with my blood pressure, I need to have it dealt with.... [*Pause*] And it feels do-able at the moment.... [*Pause*] I'm just wondering how I can get over that reaction that I get, which normally involves avoidance.

Windy: I understand that, in terms of if you don't avoid that reaction. Let's be clear here, what's the reaction that you've been avoiding?

Jen: Well, first of all taking my blood pressure here, and secondly going to the doctor.

Windy: So, if you don't avoid that and you say, 'Look, I have a tendency to avoid that. I'll build that in, because naturally I'd want to avoid anything that's threatening, so I'm going to build in the idea that, yeah, part of me wants to avoid it, but I'm not going to. I'm going to face up to it. And I am going to get anxious about this.' So, in a way, trying not to get anxious would have what effect on you?

Jen: It would probably make me more anxious.

Windy: That's right. 'I've got to be calm when I have my blood pressure taken.' It's interesting. It reminds me of this guy who, in the 1930s, wrote a book. I'm not quite sure what he's called, but he was a famous relaxation expert. Do you know what the book was called? *You Must Relax.*[19]

[*Here, I am taking the tack of helping Jen to construct a process-based narrative where she accepts that she is anxious rather than try to eliminate anxiety.*]

---

[19] Written by Edmund Jacobson (1934). See References.

Jen: Yeah.

Windy: Can I share something of my own experience?

Jen: Please. Thank you.

Windy: It's not in the area of blood pressure. It's in the area of Alsatian dogs. I was bitten by an Alsatian dog. So, I'm saying that my natural tendency is to avoid Alsatian dogs as a result of that experience. But I'm not going to. I'm going to allow for the fact I'm going to be anxious and I'm going to approach them. So, I did that. Do you know what happened eventually? I was savaged! No, I wasn't. I got over my anxiety. Now, if you regularly did that with your blood pressure and just say, 'I'm going to be anxious. I'm doing it anyway but I'm going to be anxious.' Eventually, what do you think would happen?

                [*This is an example of therapist self-disclosure that I discussed in Chapter 4.*]

Jen: I think I will get used to it in an exposure therapy approach.

Windy: That's right, if you allow yourself to be anxious. I think, as you say, you've factored all this in with other illnesses. How do you think that's got entangled in your mind?

Jen: I think it's since my dad had a stroke and he thinks it's because his blood pressure went up when he was having a medical procedure, which is quite possibly magical thinking.

Windy: Well, I don't know, but is he medically trained?

Jen: He isn't.

Windy: So that's his version, isn't it? And how's that affected you, do you think?

Jen: I guess it's focused. There's more anxiety around … blood pressure and having this white-coat hypertension, which I now have on my medical records, and he does as well.

Windy: So, if the doctor wore blue it would make a difference?

[*I am not sure my attempt here at humour was noticed by Jen.*]

Jen: Yeah.

Windy: If you're scared that there's something wrong, you'll find something wrong. But, if we work it through, because I think that you don't work it through. I think you stop it at Chapter 1: Jen gets anxious because she thinks that there might be something wrong with her. That's it. End of story. And I'm saying there's a Chapter 2 and a Chapter 3 and a Chapter 4, and you're not reading the whole book and you're not reading the book repeatedly. And I'm just curious about what would happen if you really read the book and worked it through, saying, 'If there's something wrong with me, I'd rather have it known and dealt with than not and, if I do have to lose a kidney, that wouldn't be great.' We're not having a 'I'm losing my kidney' party for Jen type of thing. It would be bad, but you could live a life.

[*Here, I am bringing all the elements that we discussed in the form of a process-based narrative that includes anxiety as an early part of the process rather than excludes and incorporates a worst-case scenario that she can live with.*]

Jen: Yeah, and I think what happens with me is I ran a therapy service in a hospice for 12 years, and so my experience of people with high blood pressure and losing kidneys was always end of life. So, I go immediately to the end of the book.

Windy: Yeah. Because they had problems with both kidneys, didn't they?

Jen: Yeah, many things.

Windy: Yeah, exactly. I think you could factor that in, in a self-compassionate kind of way: 'Of course, I can understand that about me. I'm going to be anxious about that. I've got the history about that – my dad, this story. Yes, I'm going to be anxious, but I still can get to the end of the story. And, as I go, I can still take my blood pressure and see what happens.' How often are you taking your blood pressure, Jen?

[*Here, I am incorporating these historical elements into the narrative and suggesting that Jen could adopt a self-compassionate stance about these elements.*]

Jen: Well ... I haven't done it for some time, but I think I will probably do it after this session.

Windy: Well, what would happen, do you think, if you did it every day?

Jen: That's what my doctor wants, every day for a week.

Windy: Well, yeah, but your doctor's not doing what I'm doing. He wants to just say, 'Take it every day,' not, 'I'm gonna give you help to do that,' but, 'Take it every day.' But what do you think would happen if you were to go through that particular process? Let's hear you go through that process now. Why don't you mention it out loud?

[I am inviting Jen to rehearse the solution as discussed in Chapter 3.]

Jen: I think what will happen is the first few times I'll probably feel more anxious, and it'll probably be higher. And then probably the second day it will be a bit more settled. I think, if I see a more settled reading, it will be easier to do it the next time and the next time and the next time.

Windy: Yep. And, if it's not having a settled reading, it's a high reading, what are you going to do?

Jen: I'm going to fill in my piece of paper that my doctor's given me and go to the doctor.

Windy: That's right. And there's either going to be something that needs to be done or nothing that needs to be done.

Jen: Yeah.

Windy: But, if you really add in the bits that we're talking about: 'I understand all too well what I'm anxious about. I haven't had a great health history. I've been around people with kidney issues, I've been around my dad and blood pressure. Of course I'm going to be anxious. But that doesn't mean I can't not take it. I'm going to be accepting of me for being anxious and I'm going to take it and I'm going to learn to take it and we'll see what happens.' As far as I can see at the moment, the worst that's going to happen to you is that you'll live a productive life on one kidney. Is that right?

Jen: I think that's right. The irony is my supervisor has only got one kidney and he's a doctor, so he keeps telling me I'll be fine.

Windy: This is not a kidney problem or a blood pressure problem. This is an attitude problem, isn't it?

[*This is an important point.*]

Jen: … [*Pause*] Yeah.

Windy: You're going into the first scenario with the blood pressure, what's your view on that? When you're anxious, what's your view on that?

Jen: Thinking it's going to be bad.

Windy: Right. How bad?

Jen: Well, very bad. The worse I think it's going to be the higher it goes, which is my experience.

Windy: Exactly. So, I think what you're doing is what we call catastrophising. Again, it's understandable, for God's sake, with the factors that you're talking about.

Jen: … Yeah.

Windy: But, if you don't catastrophise the catastrophising –
'Oh my God, I'm catastrophising! Oh my God.' So,
I think it's about you rehearsing a narrative that
allows you to see the whole picture plus being a bit
more systematic about taking your blood pressure,
because I think part of the reason is that you,
understandably, want to not take your blood
pressure.

*[Here, I suggest to Jen that it is meta-
catastrophising that is the problem here, not the
catastrophising on its own]*

Jen: Yeah.

Windy: So, what do you think will happen if you regularly
reviewed that narrative from beginning to end and
regularly took your blood pressure?

Jen: I think the anxiety would subside and I think my
tendency to catastrophise would reduce.

Windy: And are you willing to see if that's going to happen?

Jen: Yep.

Windy: Do you have any doubts about doing that?

Jen: Well, I don't think it's going to be easy, but I think
the more....

*[I was too quick to cut Jen off here and respond to
her point about it not being easy. I wished I had
allowed her to make her point.]*

Windy: Jen, you never told me you wanted the easy solution
to this problem. Why didn't you tell me about that?

So how are you going to view the fact that it's not going to be easy?

[*Here, I bring in humour again*]

Jen: With acceptance and compassion.

Windy: Yeah, and just say, 'Yeah, it's not going to be easy.'

Jen: Yeah.

Windy: But is it worth doing?

[*In retrospect, I could have made more of the constructive reasons for having her blood pressure taken and taking it herself and encouraged her to keep these reasons in mind at salient points in her life.*]

Jen: Definitely worth doing. I can't avoid it anymore.

Windy: I disagree with you. You can avoid it. Of course, you can avoid it. But it sounds like that you don't want to avoid it any longer.

[*Here, I show Jen that she has choices even when she thinks she doesn't*]

Jen: I don't. I mean, I want to get more prescriptions.

Windy: You volunteered for this for a reason, haven't you?

Jen: I did, definitely.

Windy: What was the reason?

Jen: Because my doctor texted me this morning to tell me to make an appointment ASAP.

Windy: What, with Dryden? 'See Dryden immediately!' So, have you got what you've come for today?

              [*Humour again*]

Jen: I have, yeah.

Windy: People like my props. I could get another prop out here. If you asked me to use this, I would've done it for you. You've got your high blood pressure, now you don't. You've got your fear, now you don't.

              [*Here, I am using one of my props – a magic wand*]

Jen: Thank you.

Windy: Thank you. And let's get the comments of the folks.

              [*This session was a live demonstration held at a large online workshop, and at the end of the session, I typically invite the audience to make comments and ask myself and my client questions about what they observed*]

My Comments

There are some things I like about this session, but a lot of things I don't like. I have included the transcript here for several reasons. Primarily, it shows how a very brief intervention can be used in health psychology, where psychological interventions can help people deal effectively with their health concerns. In this flawed ONEplus Therapy session, I helped Jen in just over 20 minutes to construct a solution which she could use to help her to take her own blood pressure regularly. Two weeks after this session, I sent Jen the transcript of our conversation, and she wrote back in response, 'I have now managed to take my blood pressure for a week, and I feel very relieved.' We will see later if she maintained this gain after a period of about two months when she provides her reflections on the session and what she took from it (see below).

Now, why do I say that there are a lot of things I don't like about my work in this session? I say this because I did not show how I could have used more general ONEplus Therapy skills, such as: asking explicitly for Jen's session goal, discovering her previous attempts to solve her problem, eliciting and using her strengths, asking her to summarise the session, encouraging her to mention her takeaways and inviting her at the end to tell or ask me anything that she would have wanted to tell or ask me when she reflected on the session afterwards. For context, this was a live demonstration of SST at a large online workshop, and I remember feeling pressed for time as I was behind on my schedule for the day.

What I liked about the session was that I helped Jen construct a solution which incorporated the following features: It put her experience in the form of a process-based narrative from the beginning, where she was anxious about having her blood pressure taken to the end where she saw that she could deal with life, should she need to, with one kidney. I helped her to incorporate her anxiety-based reactions into the narrative that she would more naturally have wished to exclude and invited her to remind herself of her contextual experiences (i.e. with her father and her work as a therapist in a hospice) with self-compassion. I could have spent more time helping Jen to be more active in co-creating this solution, but as I said above, I was pushed for time.

You may note that I drew more from Acceptance and Commitment Therapy (ACT) and narrative therapy than I did from REBT in my conversation with Jen, which shows that ONEplus Therapy is pluralistic in practice, where the therapist draws from therapeutic sources that best provides a solution to the client's problem.

Jen's Reflections on the Session: 03/09/23

When I signed up for the PESI Masterclass in Single-session Therapy with Windy Dryden, I had no idea that I was about to share my phobia for having my blood pressure taken in front of 700 people.

I enjoyed Windy's style and provocative humour. I thought it was an opportunity to face my fear.

Recently diagnosed with ADHD, I'd had some high BP readings in the surgery. My GP wondered about 'white coat hypertension' but wasn't keen for me to take ADHD medication.

I felt nervous, particularly as I am a coach and therapist and there were colleagues and clients present. However, I was working on avoidance, and I decided that it was a good opportunity for exposure therapy.

Windy helped me feel reasonably relaxed and started to ask me about this fear.

What struck me was his direct yet compassionate questioning, when he inquired if I would be worried if I knew my BP would be low. I said no, as there would be nothing to fear.

I realised that it was the vulnerability and fear of the unknown which triggered me. He asked me if I had high blood pressure, would I want to avoid knowing about it, or would it be better to have it checked and appropriately treated. I said of course I would want to know and be treated for it, as well as establishing lifestyle changes which would improve my health.

He gently remarked that he didn't think I had a phobia, I just didn't have the right attitude.

That interrupted my pattern of health anxiety which was an old story for me. That reframe made absolute sense. I was catastrophising about serious illness and death. No wonder I felt bad! The idea that I might choose to ignore a health risk and resist professional help and therefore keep myself stuck in a paralysing state of fear just felt silly. Instead of my usual self-criticism and shame, I was able to smile at myself with compassion. I felt the pattern shifting.

I thought about 'white coat hypertension' and realised that with a different attitude, it was fabulous evidence of the power of thought. I decided that even if I took my BP and it was high, if my thoughts could raise it, they could also reduce it. So I set myself a challenge.

Every day for the next seven days, I would adopt an attitude of relaxation and gratitude, and take my BP at home. I reminded myself that if there were any problems, I had a supportive GP and I could use medication for a short time until things improved. I was able to complete this task and after the first day, my BP was normal.

My GP was delighted to see my readings and wanted to know how I had managed it. I explained to that it was the power of the mind and a change in attitude. I have since started the ADHD medication and it has significantly helped me.

6

Helping People with Problems with Depression

Helping the Client to Understand and Deal with Depression

After anxiety, depression is the next most common emotional problem that people seek help for from ONEplus Therapy.[20] Again, many clients know very little about depression that will help them deal with their problems of depression and low mood. So here are some ideas that I have found useful to introduce into my conversation with clients that can help them understand and deal with depression.

- When people are non-clinically depressed, they tend to be depressed about a loss, a failure or an undeserved plight experienced by self or others.
- Such depression is based on a set of rigid and extreme attitudes that the person holds towards loss/failure/undeserved plight.
- The healthy alternative to depression is non-depressed sadness. This is based on a set of flexible and non-extreme attitudes that the person holds towards loss/failure/undeserved plight.
- Another way of looking at depression is to see that this emotion may be sociotropic or autonomous (Beck, Epstein & Harrison, 1983). When it is sociotopic in nature, the person is heavily invested in relationships and

---

[20] In this section, I will discuss what might be called non-clinical depression. This is depression that will respond to psychological intervention.

holds a set of rigid and extreme attitudes towards loss, failure or undeserved plight with respect to these relationships. When it is autonomous in nature, the person is heavily invested in autonomy, personal achievement and control and holds a set of rigid and extreme attitudes towards loss, failure or undeserved plight with respect to these conditions.

- The healthy alternative to sociotropic and autonomous depression is sociotropic and autonomous non-depressed sadness. In both, the person holds a set of flexible and non-extreme attitudes towards loss/failure/undeserved plight.

- When a person is depressed, this affects their behaviour. They tend to withdraw into themself, become inactive and refrain from engaging in activities that they previously found pleasurable, and which gave them a sense of mastery. Part of helping clients with depression is to encourage them to help them become more active and re-engage with these mastery and pleasure activities. This may be best done before helping them with attitude change or afterwards. People who are sad, but not depressed tend to stay active.

- When a person is depressed, this affects their subsequent thinking. They tend to think that things are hopeless, and that they are helpless to deal with life. They also tend to engage in depressive rumination. Helping people deal with the depressed thinking accompanying their depressed behaviour involves first encouraging them to trace such thinking back to the rigid and extreme attitudes that are the root of their depressed feelings and then to examine them and help them change these attitudes to their flexible and non-extreme attitudinal counterparts. After you have done this, you are in a better position to help them stand back, deal with their hopeless and helpless thinking and help them to disengage from depressive rumination. This is where mindfulness can be particularly helpful.

It is important to bear in mind that a person must be reasonably active to engage in such cognitive techniques. If they are not, you first need to help them to become more behaviourally active.

Transcript of My Work with a Person with a Problem with Depression

Therapist – Volunteer:	Windy – Margaret
Venue:	Private session that took place on 03/08/23 arranged via Onlinevents
Time:	40 minutes 57 secs

Windy: So, Margaret, what is your understanding of the purpose of our conversation today?

Margaret: It is to explore the subject of depression, which I know personally very well, and to see what can be achieved within a single session to mitigating that.

Windy: So, I'm going to make use of the pre-session questionnaire if that's OK with you.[21]

Margaret: Of course.

Windy: What struck me at the start, if I could start with that, you said at the very beginning that you're feeling grief for a life that could've been different.

Margaret: Yes.

---

[21] Here, I am referring to the pre-session questionnaire that I send out to clients to help them to prepare for the session. I invite them to send me their completed so that I can get a sense of their thinking before the session (see Chapter 3).

Windy: How would you have liked it to have been different?

Margaret: … The difficulty has always been, as I said I'm not officially diagnosed but 100% certain that I have a level of neurodivergence, is that part of the depression or pretty much all of it has been feeling slightly out of sync with the world … not understanding when things haven't gone well, genuinely lacking understanding of why people have been annoyed or what have you, particularly when I was younger. How hard it has been to forge a way in the world and … what little patience there was coming my way sometimes when I did struggle. And … [*pause*], now at my age, having finally realised what the issue may well have been all along – well, has been all along with 'out of syncness', is that, knowing that that was the case, not just for my own personal understanding of why things just didn't seem to go right for me and the constant, 'Well, it's just you: you're crap. Whatever it is, it's always your fault.'

Windy: Was that your voice to you or was that somebody else's voice to you?

Margaret: Both. It began with other voices and became my own. That understanding and that acknowledgement from external to me that would've perhaps brought me a little bit more patience and understanding from others, I've no idea what difference it would've made, obviously, because you can't tell. But I suspect it would probably have made a huge difference to my self-esteem and the years under which I have been diagnosed with depression, which has never gone away.

Windy: Are those two things linked?

Margaret: Yes, very definitely.

Windy: What if you had good self-esteem now, it was in place? What difference would that make to you going forward?

[Here, I want to help Margaret consider the possibility that she could hold a constructive attitude towards herself in face of others' negative attitudes towards her and that doing so might be useful for her.]

Margaret: … *[Long pause]* It would make it more possible for me to stride out and do some of the things that I want to do without the voice that is inherently part of me now telling me, 'What's the point because you'll fail anyway?'

Windy: What are some of those things?

Margaret: Well, one of the things I'm training to be is a psychotherapist, which is how I got onto Onlinevents and went to the Pluralistic conference and what have you. I have … a deep mistrust of the medical model, having been on the receiving end of it and received no benefit of it apart from a little symptom control. And I would very much like to, not only extend my hand to help those who've gone through similar/going through difficulties, but also to have a bigger voice in saying, 'Don't ask what's wrong with me. Asked what's happened to me' mode.

Windy: Yes. It sounds like to me, even though you've got this voice saying, 'You're crap and you're bound to fail,' it hasn't stopped you from taking a path forward.

[I want to underscore Margaret's achievement despite her negative attitude towards herself.]

Margaret: No, it hasn't. That's been quite recent. That's been fairly recent. I've been blessed now, I've been married to a good man for 10–12 years who's been in my corner, which has helped because my family have been supportive in their own way but their own way is very negative; it's a people-pleasing way of looking at the world: that you need to behave and be in a certain way so that other people will look favourably upon you, rather than you're good enough anyway and stuff 'em. Obviously, that's a very simplistic ... setting out of both, but I have had very little ... of the 'you're good at what you do', 'you've got a lot of good qualities', this, that and the other. The only thing that has ever been concentrated on throughout my entire life until recently is what could be better, not what is already pretty good. So that 'what could be better' has been the entire focus for many years.

Windy: And what mindset would you like to take forward in your life, then?

[Here, I am indicating that Margaret has a choice concerning which attitude towards herself that she can take forward in her life.]

Margaret: It's a bit of a weird one because I'm kind of feeling as if I'm in a bit of a transitory period. I'm going to sound completely bipolar now, but I vary from day to day as to whether I think, 'Sod it, I can do what I want. The only person holding me back is me and there's no reason for that,' and there are other days when I think, 'Well, how many times are you going to try this before you finally?' What I would like to be able to do is to maintain ... leaving that voice behind that says ... 'You can't do this. You will fail. You will screw it up. You always have.' You always get to a certain point, which I now understand is classic neurodivergent trait, that you'll push for promotion, you'll get to a certain point 'cos you know that you can do a good job and, when you get there, you don't want it; it all falls apart.

Windy: You'd like to leave that voice behind you?

Margaret: I would like to leave that voice behind me.

Windy: Do you have an image that goes along with that? The image that came to my mind is you getting off a train and the voice is still on the train and the train goes off, and the voice is still on the train but you're leaving it behind.

[Because I do not see clear images myself, working with imagery in ONEplus Therapy does not come naturally to me, so it was surprising to me that I had this image while talking to Margaret. I shared this with her and it was gratifying that she found it helpful.]

Margaret: That's a pretty good image, actually. I didn't have a visualisation of it. I'm guessing the closest I've come to it when I have thought about it is almost the effect of pretty much what this is: I've got my earphones in at the moment because the sound isn't brilliant on this computer, so I've got my earphones in, to the fact where you just, 'OK, no, I'm just going to hear what's happening now, what's real. I don't care what's happening over there. That's nothing to do with me.' That was the closest I'd come to when I put the earphones on and block out what's irrelevant and just concentrate on what matters.

Windy: Yeah. It's interesting, the various possibilities that we have to do in therapy with these voices. There's that kind of thing: 'Well, it's going to be there.' Generally, we're not very good, as human beings, of eradicating things that we don't like because, when we try to eradicate them, they're like hydra-headed beasts: they come back with two heads. So, trying to get rid of things that are not there. I'm just wondering what other effective ways you've had in the past that's helped you to deal with that voice.

[Here, I am doing two things. First, I am making the general point that attempting to eradicate experiences like voices is generally not helpful to people. I think I could have also or instead asked Margaret about her experiences of trying to get rid of her own negative voices. Second, I am asking her what effective ways she has found of dealing with these voices. The latter is a common strategy in ONEplus Therapy – see Chapter 3.]

Margaret: There was a time in my life when I blotted it out with alcohol. I stopped short of being an alcoholic, but I was starting to become reliant on it to shut the voice up enough to let me sleep, because I've always struggled with anxiety, which again is another neurodivergent thing. And … *[pause]* pharmacology – better living through chemistry has formed a big part of it.

Windy: Better living through chemistry?

Margaret: Antidepressants, anti-anxiety medication. Not recreational drugs, sadly. Maybe they would help, who knows. But, no, I've not gone down that path.

Windy: Are you on any medication now?

Margaret: Literally about ten days ago I started taking Sertraline again. I'm a year out, potentially, from getting my neurodivergent assessment because there's such a long waiting list; I've been waiting for over a year already.

Windy: Through the NHS?

Margaret: Yeah, I can't afford to go private for it. So, the medications that might help the ADHD side of it, which will help towards shutting down some of the voices as well because the focus will hopefully come back, is a long way off, and I was getting anxious and tearful again. So, I started taking Sertraline about ten days ago. I had previously been on Venlafaxine for nine years ... which I was not happy about. I came off it at my own decision, 'cos that's all that was offered apart from CBT which has its place, but for somebody who has now discovered they've got ADHD, giving them something else to do that they're going to fail at is not helpful. So, it actually was more of a problem to me being referred for that than it was helpful.

Windy: Yeah.

Margaret: So I started to do my own research and ended up going down the path of, 'OK, I'm going to learn how to do this for myself,' and then decided that I'd sign up to learn how to help other people with it.

Windy: Right, OK. Would you be interested in looking at possible ways of responding to that voice when it comes up?

[I am aware that Margaret has not come up with any effective ways of responding to her negative voice, so I ask her if she is interested in considering some ways. I prefer to get the client's agreement before proceeding with such matters.]

Margaret: Absolutely.

Windy: So, I'm going to offer you Dryden's Invitation Technique.

[I created this technique which comes from an REBT mindset – see Chapter 4.]

Margaret: OK.

Windy: It goes something like this: when you have a voice like that just give me an example of that voice?

Margaret: … I've been trying to look for some part-time work 'cos my mum and dad are elderly and I need to be available for them. And, when I've been trying to look for part-time work the … type of thing that is available that does the sort of hours I can manage, the voice in my head says, 'What's the point in applying? You couldn't do it anyway.'

Windy: OK. And does that voice have a source? Is it another person or a part of you?

Margaret: It's part of me.

Windy: Do you give that a name, that part of you?

Margaret: ... My [indistinct] refers to it as Part X. But, no, I don't identify it by a name. Well, not one I'm going to repeat in polite company anyway.

Windy: Listen, you are in polite company, but this is psychotherapy: you can say what you like.

[*I want to give Margaret permission to be authentic.*]

Margaret: OK. Well, when I realise what is happening and what is there, I just say, 'Oh, it's you again, you fucker.'

Windy: Let's call it The Fucker.

Margaret: OK.

Windy: So, The Fucker comes in – and I'll use my technique – and what does The Fucker call you?

Margaret: It doesn't, really. Just 'you'.

Windy: The Fucker comes on and says, 'OK, I invite you to think of yourself as somebody who's not going to succeed at this, so there's no point in trying.' So that's the invitation, right?

Margaret: It is, yeah.

Windy: Many years ago, did you ever get invites to weddings and stuff?

Margaret: Oh gosh, yeah.

Windy: Certainly, in my day there was an RSVP card. It said, 'Thank you for your invitation for us to appear at the wedding of Blah and Blah.' And there was a reply box saying, 'I accept,' or, 'I decline.' So Dryden's Invitation Technique goes like this: The Fucker says to you, 'I invite you to think of yourself as somebody where there is no point in even trying this 'cos you're going to fail,' and you then say, 'Well, thank you very much for that invitation,' and then you can either accept or decline. What would you decide to do?

Margaret: Well, decline regularly, I would hope.

Windy: 'And the reason I'm declining is,' what's the reason?

Margaret: … [*Long pause*] 'You're talking bollocks,' probably.

Windy: Fine, that's it. 'You're talking bollocks.' That's all we need: 'You're talking bollocks.' Then you proceed along the lines you want to. So that technique indicates that you're not going to stop this voice but it's a part of you that's inviting you. Your power is to accept or decline. You decline and you decline for a reason, and then you back up your reason with action. Now, the voice still may be there but then you could say, 'OK, I've already declined that.' It's a bit like somebody saying, 'No, come to the wedding. Come to the wedding. Come to the wedding,' and you say, 'No, I'm not even going to answer that because I've declined it. So I'm going to let them do that until they stop.'

Margaret: It's kind of a refusal to engage.

Windy: That's right. You can't stop it from starting. You can't stop it from being there. But it's like a child:

if you ignore it, eventually it will go away. I wonder what you think of that, of taking that forward.

Margaret: I'll certainly give it a try, because what I've been trying to do, which is almost reason with it and remind and actually say, 'OK, you know where that's coming from, you know the history behind that voice and you know what part of you its leaning on now, which is the 'still struggling with the world', which menopause blew completely out of the water – I became a deranged idiot when that happened, which has made it far worse than it ever has been before. So, what I have been trying to do is saying, 'Well, you know the history, you know why you're struggling at the moment, you know why you think you can't do these things, you know what an effort it will make to even try. So, of course you're going to try and talk yourself out of it before you start,' and trying to rationalise it.

Windy: What's the purpose of that?

Margaret: The purpose of what?

Windy: Of that reasoning?

Margaret: ... I guess the same purpose as actually just turning round and saying, 'No.' The fact that you're actually, instead of refusing to engage and saying, 'Well, that's bollocks,' I'm trying to persuade myself, through rationalisation, that that voice is wrong rather than just refusing to engage with it.

Windy: Yeah. I mean, I would say the voice, for whatever reason, is a part of you that comes from your experience and, yeah, you could have it as part of the reason: 'It's bollocks. I know where you come from. I'm not going to let you stop me. Off I go.' But my point is that you need to back it up with action and recognise that the voice – it's a bit like, I call it, if you look into a light and you close your eyes, you see the after image of a light.

[*Here, my intention is to integrate some of what Margaret has already done, but to encourage her not to engage with the negative voice. This shows of the influence of Acceptance and Commitment Therapy on my work (Flaxman et al., 2011).*]

Margaret: Yeah.

Windy: And that's going to be there for a while until it goes away. If you keep looking at the light, you're just going to re-engage with it. So, part of that, using the Dryden's Invitation Technique, is saying, 'That voice is still going to be in my mind for a while but I'm not going to feed it. I'm just going to say, 'OK, I know where you come from,' and then you can use the train image: 'OK, bye bye.' But the voice will come back until it doesn't.

Margaret: Yeah. It's going to be a diminish rather than a gone, isn't it?

Windy: Right, exactly. And the important thing is we can say there are two parts of you: one is self-critical, the other one is self-affirming, and the idea of which part of you wins in that struggle and that is the one you feed.[22]

Margaret: The one you feed.

---

[22] See:
https://en.wikipedia.org/wiki/Two_Wolves#:~:text=The%20legend%20is%20a%20story,%22whichever%20one%20you%20feed%22 (accessed 07/12/23).

Windy: That's right. So, we want you to starve the voice, not try to get rid of it but not give it any more attention that it needs and feed the other voice through action. Even if you go forward, because you have done – you've not said, 'Look, there's no point being a psychotherapist because what's the point? You're going to fail anyway.' You're being a psychotherapist. What you are doing now is helping you.

Margaret: Yes, it has helped.

Windy: So, continue to do that. And other things that you do, being mindful that there may be something neurodivergent that needs to be incorporated into the picture.

Margaret: Yeah. It's been frustrating that there's been such a long wait for that after ... taking 55 years to come to the realisation that there might be something there. But I guess on the self-affirming side, one thing that one of my more recent friends said to me was the fact that – obviously, OK, when I was a kid girls didn't get it, girls were never considered to be neurodivergent in any way, shape or form, it was a boys' thing – was that it's taken so long for it to be even occurred to me and never occurred to anybody else, because (1) I mask well and (2) I've been good enough at what I do for it not to be obvious. I've just underperformed my potential, as I've been told many times and been told I was lazy because of it. So, it's nice to know that that's not the reason why, but it also means that, again, I suppose the frustration is that, if it had been recognised, I might have achieved more than I have. And that's part of the grief I was talking about: that there are missed opportunities. But ... not a lot I can do about that now, is there? So, it's just what you do next that matters.

Windy: That's right. If you had volunteered for unhealthy regret, we would've been talking about you revisiting that until you drove yourself crazy, but you're not. So, you haven't done that. And the only thing that you can do is to learn from that and to capitalise on things that are important to you in the present. And it sounds like training to be a psychotherapist, this wish to address with other people certain things that people have gotten wrong with you, it sounds like you're on a pathway of something important to you. And the voice will have an opinion, but you can accept or decline the invitation. By the way, who determines your view?

[Here, I indicate to Margaret that she is not stuck in trying to change the past but that she has used the past to pursue an important path for herself.]

Margaret: … *[Long pause]* Well, I do, but it's heavily influenced by what I perceive from everybody around me.

Windy: Yeah, that's right. Now, some of the time you'll be right and some of the time you'll be wrong because that's what happens. But the point is, in a way it doesn't matter because, if you hold onto what's important to you, you can say, 'Look, I'm sorry that you got that view of me, but my view of me is somebody that, at this point in time, I know what's important to me and I'm going forward on that. I may fail, I may pass, but I can't predict that. But I'm going forward with self-acceptance, not self-rejection.'

Margaret: Yeah. It's kind of tough having been a people-pleaser all my life to actually now try and draw that line.

Windy: But I don't want to stop you being a person-pleaser. The question is which person are you going to please?

Margaret: Yeah, and there has always got to be boundaries there. You can be flexible to – I was going to say things I don't say to myself that I do say to other people is that there's a big difference between flexibility and being a doormat.

Windy: That's right. So, if you can actually say, 'Yes, basically I'm going to please me. I'm the person that I need to please at this point, because I'm a person, I'm a pleaser and I'm a person-pleaser, why not please myself?' And that's what you're doing. You're really saying, 'I'm pleasing myself by going forward.' Yes, you can please other people with flexibility, which means that, 'I don't have to be a doormat. If I don't want to do this then I'm not doing it.'

Margaret: Yeah. I'm not very good at that sometimes. 'No' is a hard word for me. But I recognise that now which I didn't before.

Windy: Is that wrapped up with depression at all?

Margaret: Yeah.... [*Pause*]

Windy: Would you like to spend a little bit of time on that now?

[*Here I invite her to follow the track that emerged from our conversation. Doing so is typical of my ONEplus Therapy practice.*]

Margaret: Yeah, sure. It's all been wrapped up with approval, I think.

Windy: Give me an instance of how this gets played out to your detriment?

[*Working with specific examples is also typical in ONEplus Therapy.*]

Margaret: ... [*Pause*] When I've been a bit doormatty is ... well, the most recent one was, I have stepchildren, was being told by one of my stepchildren what day they were going to come and spend time in my home. Not asked, told.

Windy: How old are they?

Margaret: Late 20s, 30s. They're not kids. But it happened to be a day when I was doing an online course. I'm upstairs in one of the rooms now but it wasn't available when that was happening, so it would be downstairs. And I was told by their mum, my husband, they knew I was doing a course or 'something' and that they just shut the door on me. And I let it go.

Windy: And what would you have preferred to have said?

Margaret: What I would have preferred to have said is ... 'Hang on a cotton-picking minute,' or words to that effect, 'yes, you want to come and see your dad, that's absolutely fine, but you can do it when my course has finished.'

Windy: OK. And, so what attitude do you think you'd have needed to have enabled you to have done that?

Margaret: … [*Long pause*] I would guess a stronger belief in the moment that what was important to me on that day was just as important, if not more so because it was happening in my home, than what they wanted.

Windy: And you need your stepdaughter's approval or not?

Margaret: … Yes, I often feel I need everyone's approval…. But I don't, no. In reality I don't.

Windy: If you had done the following, for example, and this is something to aim for based on the experience and extracting from this, if you recognise that, when you're put in that position, your first tendency is to say yes because it's coming from the idea that, 'I need this person's approval.' And then you say, 'OK, fine, that's my first response. I need to give myself some time. So, what I'll say to this person is, 'I'll get back to you on that one.' You're not saying no, you're not saying yes, 'I'll get back to you on that one.' So you come off the call and then you go into your own space and say, 'OK now, I don't need this person's approval. It's not convenient. So, therefore, I'm going to go back into the space and say, 'I understand that you want to see your dad, but it's not convenient for me. I'd like to make it another time,' or something like that. Having taken into that idea, 'I don't need the person's approval and their disapproval is not affecting the way I view myself. I'm the same person whether they approve of me or whether they do not approve of me.' If you were able to practise that would that make a difference to you going forward?

Margaret: Yes, if I'm in a situation where I can do that pullback. The one I quoted to you, she was standing in front of me at the time because we were out walking the dog.

Windy: OK.

Margaret: But the idea behind that, yes. I mean, on this particular instance, they'd obviously discussed it between themselves, and I was kind of presented with a fait accompli to my face, which made it a little bit harder to do anything more than stutter and go, 'Oh, OK.' But the principle of what you're saying is absolutely right.

Windy: But you can stutter and say, 'We'll discuss it when we get home.'

Margaret: Yes. That would never have occurred to me.

Windy: That's right. So, the thing that may well be useful to take away from this on this point is, whenever you're asked anything like that, always give yourself some time because your natural tendency is to say yes because that need for approval has come up. So, get used to say, 'Let me revisit this. I'll come back to you on that one.' Because I think you do need to give yourself some time, otherwise you get caught in the moment.

[I would have preferred to ask Margaret what she could take away from the example we discussed rather than telling her.]

Margaret: Yeah, that happens … quite a lot. I'm not very good when I'm put on the spot.

Windy: OK. So let's rehearse that. Surprisingly, I'm your stepdaughter. We're out with the dogs. So let's see how it goes.

[*While rehearsing a solution is an integral part of ONEplus Therapy and I am pleased to have had the opportunity to do so with Margaret, it would have better if I had asked her first if rehearsing the solution would be beneficial for her before proceeding.*]

Margaret: OK.

Windy: By the way, what does she call you?

Margaret: She calls me Margaret.

Windy: 'Margaret, I was talking to my dad and it's been decided I'm coming round on x day. Is that alright with you?'

Margaret: 'Well, I have got something going on that day, so let me just check out the logistics and come back to you.'

Windy: OK. How does that seem?

Margaret: That seems very reasonable. It's not an unreasonable response. It's not a negative. It's an 'OK, let me look at that.'

Windy: Right. And then, when you do look at it and then you decide that it's not convenient, what would you say to her?'

Margaret: On this particular occasion it was Father's Day. So I'd say, 'I know you want to see your dad on

Father's Day, but I have got this online training which I can't miss. So can we arrange the time to be when that's finished, please, so that I can take part in the visit as well and you will still spend time with your dad?'

Windy: Can I make a suggestion there? Rather than, 'Can we?' just say, 'I would like us to do this.' How does that sound to you?

Margaret: Yes, it's a bit more assertive, isn't it?

Windy: And you're taking control. You're not asking the question of her; you're just saying, 'Look, this would suit everybody.'

Margaret: Yeah, this way everybody's covered.

Windy: Yeah, OK. Now, if you'd done that, what do you think that would've done for you?

Margaret: ... [*Pause*] Assuming a different time ... worked for them, because I have no idea, then I would've felt ... [*pause*] pretty good about it.

Windy: Yeah, OK. And what about if the timing wasn't good for them but you were still going to do your online course because it was part of what's important to you?

Margaret: ... [*Pause*] Well, I wouldn't have told them not to come because it was Father's Day. Any other day I might've done but not that day. But at least it would've been clear ... that what I was doing was important to me and they were ... making ... that more complicated for me than it needed to be. There might've been a little bit more appreciation or consideration.

Windy: Yeah. Did you attend the course?

Margaret: Oh yes, I did. There was no way I was missing it.

Windy: Exactly: 'No way I was missing it.' So, I think what that shows you is, initially when you're in a situation your tendency is to say yes, and therefore you need to give yourself some time to think it through. Then you can say, 'No, this is important to me. I know it's important to you. Let's see if we can work something out.' 'I'm taking control,' rather than responding.

[*Again, it would have been better for me to ask Margaret for her takeaway rather than giving it to her.*]

Margaret: That's a good point.

Windy: Let me ask you a question, Margaret, are you worth doing this for?

Margaret: ... [*Long pause*] Yes, most of the time.

Windy: I'm sorry, what?

Margaret: Yes.

Windy: What do you mean 'most of the time'? You mean there are times when you're not worth doing it for?

Margaret: There are times when I don't feel very worth anything.

Windy: Right, but that's a feeling based on what?

Margaret: … [*Pause*] Yeah, the voice.

Windy: That's right.

Margaret: And history.

Windy: So that's going to come up on those occasions. You say, 'I know where it comes from. I'm not going to accept and I'm not going to feed the voice.'

> [*What I am doing here is to help Margaret to identify obstacles to self-affirming behaviour and how she could address them. Again, it would have been better if I encouraged to voice her own way of addressing them rather than voicing it for her.*]

Margaret: Yeah.

Windy: Now, you said that you weren't expecting much from one session.

Margaret: Yes, that's true, I did say that.

Windy: Are you getting what you expected?

Margaret: … I wasn't entirely sure what to expect, but I am getting … more than I expected because, having been to therapy before, talking therapies before, as you say, it does tend to be more of a longwinded, for want of a better expression, and also, from the person-centred point of view, there's very little interaction with the person that you're talking to, which doesn't work well for me. I need interaction. I need a discussion.

Windy: If I hadn't just rebranded my therapy to ONEplus Therapy, you've just helped me to see a great line: This is not longwinded therapy, this is short Windy therapy.

Margaret: Yes, that would be a great tagline.

Windy: Why don't you summarise what we've discussed today?

Margaret: Discussed the way to deal with the voice when it pops up and says, 'Don't bother doing that, you're useless. It won't happen anyway.' Decline to engage and keep declining to engage and doing stuff anyway until it just shuts up or speaks so infrequently it's hardly worth worrying about. And, when being put into a situation where the people-pleasing and need for external validation and what have you thrusts itself at me, to find a way to take a step, take a moment and evaluate, 'Actually, is this going to be an issue for me? And, if so, we'll find a way round it or we just don't do it,' rather than automatically giving in and going along with everything, which, again, then makes me worse, like I'm not worth bothering about.

Windy: Yeah, but that's your conclusion. You can remind yourself, 'I am worth bothering about whether or not I'm getting what I want,' because being able to speak your mind doesn't mean that you always get what you want.

Margaret: At least other people know that you've got an alternate viewpoint and you make it clear that something isn't entirely convenient for you, but you are actually … [*pause*] doing what the other person wants for the greater good, even if it's inconvenient or uncomfortable for you.

Windy: Now, I see both of these as skills to be practised. Internalisation comes through practise of these skills. Is that something that you think that you might be able to practise going forward?

Margaret: ... Yes. Yes, definitely. The voice might take a little bit longer because I don't notice it's there sometimes until afterwards, and then I think, 'Oh, OK.' But the actual keeping it in front of mind to not give an instant response when being pushed to do something or being presented with a fait accompli, to actually take that moment and go, 'Actually, do I really want to do this?' or, 'Is this really going to work for me?' or in some cases, 'What do you think you are?' to actually take that moment instead of just instantly caving, yes, I need to do that.

Windy: Yeah, and you also may need to think about, 'Well, what are the signs that The Fucker has been activated?'

Margaret: ... [*Pause*] Yeah. It gets so ingrained sometimes, doesn't it, that you don't realise that you're reacting to it.... So, I'm guessing that a lot of it is going to be – I'm quite self-deprecating, as you may have noticed, and that's probably a sign that it's lurking there all the time.

Windy: When you find yourself thinking self-depreciating thoughts, then you can look for The Fucker.

Margaret: Yeah. It's an ugly little shit anyway. I've got a vision of him: he's a squat, little ugly thing.

Windy: One of the things that I do, Margaret, is, when I come to write things up in the book, I give the chapter a title. At the moment: 'Looking for The Fucker' or, 'Looking and Dealing with The Fucker'. Who knows?

Margaret: Yeah. Ugly little git anyway.

Windy: Indeed. Is there anything else you want to say before we finish?

Margaret: No, I don't think so, other than thank you for the opportunity to meet and talk with you because it's been great.

Windy: My pleasure. Thank you for giving me the opportunity of meeting you and I wish you well in your career as a psychotherapist.

Margaret: Thank you very much. Lovely to meet you.

Windy: OK, bye-bye.

Margaret: Bye.

Margaret's Reflections on the Session: 30/11/23

I was unsure what to expect from the session, and a little apprehensive, but hopeful. I was hopeful that the session would help me break through the roadblock I had reached in my progress but I will admit to a little scepticism as to how one session could actually achieve this.

It is always difficult to open up to someone new, who you know only, in this case, by reputation and previous works but Windy made this possible very quickly and even knowing that the session was part of research with a view to publication, I did not feel unsafe and had confidence that I could be open and honest.

During the session I felt heard and supported. The questions asked and gentle challenges to my statements pushed me to reflection and self-analysis, to reconsider established thought patterns without being aggressive or triggering a defensive response. Whilst there were challenges to these statements and thought patterns, they were not in any way judgemental, there was no implication that I was 'wrong', simply that I should take a moment to look at them and understand that there was a possibility that they were the result of many external factors internalised, but not necessarily 'truth'.

I have always been quite reflective, but the session with Windy gave me new directions to take this in. The use of imagery to describe the techniques he provided me with made it easier to take these on board and to apply them to various scenarios outside of the examples that we discussed. In particular, the image of a train leaving with the unhelpful thoughts and feelings on board, their voices becoming fainter and fainter, struck me very vividly. Playing that over in my mind later I had an image of me helping a ranting figure on to a train, all the while saying, 'yes, yes, that's all very interesting, hmm yeah ok then, time for you to go now' then shutting the door and waving them off, with less than the usual complement of five fingers! It made me chuckle, and it still does.

The other scenario of ways to take a step back to avoid feeling railroaded into compliance with what suits others but is a difficulty to me has been very useful, but I confess is harder to practice and I still cave more than I am happy with. However, the difference is that now I recognise it and the instances are becoming fewer – I take that as a win overall.

In conclusion, despite it being a relatively short encounter I can honestly say that the session has given me ammunition and tactics for the fight, and although a few individual battles may not go entirely my way, I have the confidence now that the war will be won. As a bonus, I can amuse myself endlessly by putting people/thoughts/feelings onto a train and waving them off with a suitable salute. For that, Windy, I thank you!

7

Helping People with Problems with Guilt

Helping the Client to Understand and Deal with Guilt

Here are some ideas that I have found useful to introduce into my conversation with clients that can help them understand and deal with guilt.

- When a person experiences guilt, they hold a rigid and self-devaluation attitude towards one or more of the following adversities: (i) I have broken my moral code (a sin of commission); (ii) I have failed to live up to my moral code (a sin of omission); (iii) hurting others (e.g. 'I absolutely should not have hurt my parents' feelings, and I am a bad person for doing so'). When the person feels guilt, behaviourally, they will punish themself and beg for rather than ask for forgiveness. Guilt will also inhibit assertive behaviour. Cognitively, the person will engage in guilt-related rumination and take too much responsibility than is warranted for their behaviour and assign others who were involved too little responsibility than is warranted.
- The healthy alternative to guilt is guilt-free remorse.[23]
- When the person experiences guilt-free remorse about the same adversities, then they hold a flexible attitude

---

[23] We lack universally accepted terms to describe healthy negative emotions (HNEs). Thus, what I will do in this book is refer to the terms that I typically use. However, in ONEplus Therapy, using terms that make more sense to clients is vital, and if a client does not resonate with a particular HNE term, I suggest that you employ the term that does resonate with them.

128

and an attitude of unconditional self-acceptance towards these adversities (e.g. 'I really wish I had not hurt my parents' feelings, but sadly I am not immune from doing so and neither do I have to have such immunity. I am not bad for doing so; rather, I am a complex, unique and fallible human being who acted badly on this occasion, but capable of acting well'). When the person feels guilt-free remorse, behaviourally, they might take a penalty for their behaviour, but will not punish themself. They will ask for but will not beg for forgiveness. They will be able to assert themself. Cognitively, the person will take the appropriate amount of responsibility for their behaviour and assign the appropriate amount of responsibility to others who were involved. They will not engage in guilt-based rumination.

- If the person is interested, I will help them change their rigid/extreme attitudes to their flexible/non-extreme counterparts and help them think and act in ways that will support the development of these attitudes.

Transcript of My Work with a Person with a Problem with Guilt

Therapist – Volunteer:	Windy – Jane
Venue:	Private session that took place on 04/08/23, arranged via Onlinevents
Time:	45 minutes 07 secs

Windy: So, what's your understanding of the purpose of our conversation today, Jane?

Jane: I guess my understanding is that I'm taking part in a one session therapy session to explore the theme of guilt for me around … my relationship with my brother, and that part of this session will be used for a book later on down the line.... [*Pause*] And, I guess, yeah, I'm guessing part of it is about how a one therapy session can work, I guess.

Windy: Yeah, or not.

Jane: Or not, sure.

Windy: We shall see. Now, before we start, I think, because it is a single session, we want to be focused. If I need to interrupt you, how can I best do that?

[*Asking the person for permission to interrupt them and how best to do this is a typical early intervention in ONEplus Therapy which I do not always remember to do. But I do so here.*]

Jane: Good question.... [*Pause*] Maybe just hold up your hand, maybe.

Windy: Like that?

Jane: Yeah, that would be fine.

Windy: OK, fine, I'll do that.

Jane: A visual will help me.

Windy: So, you say on here[24] that the kind of help that you most wanted is some help expressing your feelings about the issue. Is that right?

Jane: Yeah, I would say so.

---

[24] I am referring to the pre-session questionnaire that I sent Jane and which she returned to me prior to the session.

Windy: What do you hope expressing your feelings would lead to?

Jane: … Peace? Or … maybe a better understanding or maybe some internal resolution, maybe.

Windy: I want to be clear about what I'm going to be doing and what I'm not going to be doing. ONEplus Therapy is about helping you to get the help that you want, not the help that I think you may need. So, let's be clear that what I'm not going to do, then, is I'm not going to necessarily give you my take on guilt, because you're not wanting that. If you change your mind, you can let me know. But it's really about being able to express your feelings and, as a result of expressing your feelings, you hope what?

[While the most common help that people seek from ONEplus Therapy is solution-based help, this is not universally the case and it is important that I offer Jane the help that she wants not the help that I think she needs (Dryden, 2025).]

Jane: … [*Long pause*] I think, in part, actually it would just be nice to share it somewhere, because at the moment it feels like it's someone else's story and I'm trying to protect my brother in some sense, which interests me it's going to go in a book, so that's quite curious.

Windy: The point is, if you feel that at any point that you don't want to participate in this project later on, or even during the session you might say, 'Actually, I don't want to do this,' that'll be fine. So, it's almost like, as you talk, you recognise that this could actually be out there. Even though names will be changed, stories might be recognised.

[Given what Jane has said, I wanted to make it clear that she can opt out of the project at any time.]

Jane: Yeah. I'm quite liking the fact that I don't think any of my family will tend to read any therapy-based books.

Windy: So, nobody in your family's an avid reader of psychotherapy books?

Jane: No. Just me.

Windy: So why don't you start with where you need to start?

Jane: Where do I need to start? ... Actually, I probably need to start with a bit of a pre-warning that, although I know the difference between guilt and shame, they might merge a little bit as I talk, maybe, so feel free to ... point that out if that's happening.

Windy: Sorry, point what out?

Jane: If I'm veering away from guilt into an area of shame.

Windy: OK. You want me to do that?

Jane: I think so, yeah, because they are two very different things and, whilst they interlink in parts, I'm happy to talk about either.

Windy: Alright.

Jane: But I guess we're here for the guilt part.

Windy: That's right. Fine, I'll do that.

[This is a good example of the client and therapist agreeing on a focus for the session.]

Jane: So my ... brother is four-to-five years older than me. He is my parents' biological son. I'm adopted. ... *[Pause]* And a lot of our childhood was spent ... just doing our own thing. Both my parents worked very hard in the helping professions... *[pause]* and were rarely ever there together; were usually alternating in their parenting. So, there was usually only ever one parent present. Rarely did we ever have babysitters or anything like that. I would stay with my grandparents in the summer quite a bit when my brother got a bit older and refused to be my third parent for a bit. My grandparents helped out a bit more.

But I think probably the guilt comes from a realisation, probably through my own therapy and my journey as a therapist, that there was a lot of parentification for him, so there was a lot of having to cook me dinner. He'd be 14 and I'd be 10. Maybe it's normal stuff, I'm not sure, but I kind of look back and think, well, he should've been doing teenage boy things, not parenting me and having to look after his little sister.

Windy: Who gave him that role, by the way?

Jane: Well, my parents, I guess. They ... bought a house that was too big for them that they had to pay for. They worked long hours. My mum would work nights, my dad would work days and they would try and cross over in time but there were, from my memory, quite a few instances frequently where my mum would have to leave to go to work and my dad hadn't gotten home yet, whether there was something he had to hang around for. So, it meant that mum would prep whatever was for dinner and leave it on the side for my brother to make for us. It's not just that but there were lots of things. I just felt he was ... [*pause*] maybe used as a bit of an extra parent at points. And I had a lot of medical issues growing up.... I had to go to the hospital quite a lot for checkups and things when I was younger, and I ... just get a sense that there was quite a lot of resentment towards me when we were younger.

Windy: Did he have to take you to hospital?

Jane: No, but I guess it took time out of my parents' – my parents were already overworking, very busy.

Windy: Right, and then they focused on you because you were ill, and there was the sense that that was another area where your brother may have missed out. He missed out on growing up to be a teenager and he missed out on some parental focus because they were off attending to you.

Jane: Attending to checkups. I'm sure they did get the odd bit of quality time together, but it rarely happened, even for me. From what I remember there wasn't much attunement. They were always tired and burnt out from childhood and we were a bit of a burden, not in the sense of, 'Oh crap, why have we got these children?' but it was very much, 'I'm exhausted. Can you please just stop. Go away. Just give me five minutes.' That's my understanding of that side of things.

Windy: And they bought this house before they adopted you or afterwards?

Jane: Before, yeah. So, I think they'd moved into it when my brother was maybe a year or two old. I think he was still a very young baby. My mum particularly went through early menopause. It was a hereditary thing in the family.

Windy: So, they wanted more children but they couldn't have them.

Jane: Wanted more children, couldn't have them. And I do think there was a period when my mum was probably actually quite depressed. So, this would've been around about when he was about two, three, four. And I joined them when I was two, so he would've been about six by that point. So, he would've had six years of being the only child, potentially with a year or two with a depressed mother. And then I arrived stealing his toys and being a pain in the backside.

Because I have quite an interest in attachment and early development and developmental trauma and things like that, I got interested in that period or thinking about what that must've been like for him at that point. He was actually diagnosed with hyperactivity as a child, which now would be diagnosed as ADHD and, if he were to be assessed, I'm pretty sure he would be … diagnosed with hyperactivity. But it definitely presents in low self-esteem, struggles to focus. He's very bright, very intelligent, incredibly clever, but really struggled at school and it just got worse through each school phase. By the time he'd left secondary school, he just I think was already self-medicating with drugs and … going out to parties, and then parties became big raves. It just … continued.

And I remember feeling quite frustrated with my parents for what felt like they weren't doing anything about it.

Windy: They weren't parenting him.

Jane: Yeah. In my mind, if that had been my child, even he was 18 or 40, I would want to sit him down and say, 'Right, come on, what's going on? What's happening?'

Windy: Take an interest, maybe some limits, yeah.

Jane: Sure, yeah. They were very good practically. If you broke a leg, they would know what to do, but emotionally not great. Both frightened of conflict ... to the point where my mum particularly would almost puppeteer in the family; if she had an issue with one person, she'd tell another person in the family knowing that that person would probably get it back to the person that needed to really hear it.

Windy: What did you call that? A puppeteer?

Jane: I called it puppeteering, yeah. Maybe that was a bit harsh. It's deflecting, isn't it? It's kind of a way to get the message to someone but it's diverted.

Windy: Indirectly, yeah, OK.

Jane: Indirect communication.... [*Pause*] Yeah, it's an orchestration, isn't it, of trying to get messages across the family without actually having to face the difficult conversation, I guess.... [*Pause*] Yeah, I don't know. The reason why this has all come about at the moment is... he's actually been with a partner for quite some time and they have a son together, my nephew, and ... his partner has her own ... concerns in terms of self-medication with alcohol and things like that.... And their relationship is just not very healthy at all.... He's a very angry person. He struggles to emotionally regulate his anger, which causes her anxiety, and her anxiety sets off his anger. It's not a great combo. And it all came to a head recently. Although I think there was some coercive control from her part, following him round the house and not giving him any space, and he very stupidly, instead of walking away and leaving the house, physically hit back.... She called the police.

Windy: When you say 'physically hit back', did she hit him?

Jane: I don't know. Not that I'm aware of.

Windy: So, he responded with physical.

Jane: Yeah. I don't know the full details of it. My parents have been quite protective about it, but I think it involved shoes and I don't know. But there had been another incident previous to this, recently as well – the catalyst was that he had actually, finally, at 39 gone to the GP to attempt to get an ADHD diagnosis and to maybe get some help and to try and begin to start that process and work out how he could get some support. He's not one for going to therapy.

Windy: Even when provided by his sister?

[An attempt at humour]

Jane: Well, I mean I can't provide therapy to him, but I could definitely refer him to someone or listen. For a few days he has kind of actively avoided me. If I go up to see my parents, he'll stay in his room, because he was living there for a while ... and just not wanting to. I think I've always been that kind of annoying child that's like, 'Oh, look at this elephant in the corner of the room. Let's talk about this,' and everybody's going, 'No, shh.'

Windy: So, you've always been the one to talk about issues and they've been the ones to want you to either shut you up or avoid issues.

Jane: Yeah. I like to point things out and say, 'Hey, shall we talk about this?' which of course not everyone wants to do ... and my brother in particular finds it very difficult to have [*indistinct*], if I'm honest. He finds it really difficult. So, he is currently serving four weeks in prison at the moment for the first time.

Windy: For the abuse?

Jane: Yeah. Which I've heard he's doing very well, completely sober, hasn't been drinking, no drugs and is very much going, 'This is horrible in here. I never want to be here again.' And I've spoken to him once and I'm going to visit him next week. But it's not the call that I thought I would get. There were many calls that I thought I would get that might involve my brother but not that one.... And, so I feel maybe a bit guilty because ... [*pause*] I don't condone his behaviour and I think it's disgusting, but I also love him and I'm worried about him and I'm worried that I haven't done enough, particularly as a sister and as a therapist.

Windy: If you had done enough, what would you have done? If you were able to say, 'Look, I'm satisfied that I've done enough,' what would that have looked like?

> [*Here I am working to bring some clarity concerning what Jane wished she had done that she did not do.*[25]]

Jane: ... [*Pause*] I think I would've ... probably need to overstep a boundary, to be a bit forceful maybe, which feels unnatural for me to do so 'cos I like to respect people's boundaries mostly. But ... he needed someone to kick the door in, metaphorically and probably in reality.

Windy: When did you come to that conclusion?

Jane: ... Since the news that he was going to prison, I think. It was always like, 'Hang on a second, how did we get to this point?'

Windy: So let me get this clear, you now think that, although you're a person who respects boundaries, that it would have been better, in hindsight, to have overstepped the boundary, kicked the door in and somehow presented a more ... 'in your face' type of response.

Jane: Yeah. Hindsight's a useful tool, isn't it? But, yeah.

Windy: At the time, what was guiding your behaviour was respect for boundaries.

Jane: Yeah ... possibly, yeah.

Windy: Well, what else could explain you choosing not to overstep the boundary?

---

[25] Not doing the right thing is one of the three things that people feel guilty. The other two are: doing the wrong thig and hurting someone.

Jane: Was that actually an excuse? Was it on the surface I'm respecting his boundaries but underneath I'm following the similar family communication process?

Windy: So, you're asking yourself, 'Although I am the kind of person who likes to point out elephants in rooms and discuss them, did I, on this occasion, join with my family in avoiding it?'

Jane: Yeah, and I think I have.

Windy: Right. And then, 'If I have done that, how am I going to think of myself?'

Jane: Yes. Yeah, this is where the guilt's coming in.

Windy: Yeah, and when you're in that guilty frame of mind, how do you think of yourself?

            [*This question is informed by REBT – see Chapter 4.*]

Jane: … [*Long pause*] Good question.... A bit like a failure, I think, like I've let him down.... [*Pause*] A bystander to abuse, interestingly. But, yeah, kind of, because avoidance can be abusive, I guess. Neglect can be definitely abusive. I feel like I've colluded with the family, unhealthy family narrative.

Windy: Well, let's suppose that, because your questioning of that it's not clear to you. What is clear to you is that you respect boundaries, you're wondering whether you're not taking a more proactive, let's put it that way, over-stepping-the-boundary type of approach, is a reflection of the fact that you respect boundaries or is it a reflection of a conclusion with a family ethos of avoidance. And I'm saying, if it was, let's suppose that temporarily, if it is a collusion, you then think of yourself as a failure when you feel guilty? Is that what you're saying?

Jane: Mmm [yes] ... yeah. I think I like to be the rebel sometimes.

Windy: The rebel?

Jane: Yeah. I think if I see something and I don't think it makes sense or I don't think it's right, I will say something. But, yeah, I didn't do it on this occasion, probably because it's family. In some respects, I did keep a boundary – I kept a boundary of the ethos which was to avoid.

Windy: Well, yeah. In a way, that's a different kind of boundary, isn't it? The other one is a respectful boundary and this one is an avoidant boundary.

[*Here, I am aware that Jane indicated at the outset that she wanted to express her feelings, gain some deeper understanding of what is going on and achieve some internal resolution. I am trying to keep these things in mind when working with her. It might have been better at this point to see what help has priority for her and focus on that.*]

Jane: Yeah.

Windy: So, it's a question of, 'How am I going to think of myself for acting or not acting in a way that I wish I had?'

Jane: … [*Pause*] Several years ago I probably would've felt a lot of shame around it, but what popped into my head was, 'It's OK. You're a human.'

Windy: Just now, you mean?

Jane: Yeah.

[*Jane's 'It's OK. You're human' comment gives me an opportunity to help her achieve the internal resolution that she is seeking.*]

Windy: And being human means what in this situation?

Jane: Imperfect.

Windy: And not living up to, I guess, your standard for yourself of, in this case, doing what may have proved to be the right thing – I say 'may have proved' because we don't know; if you had overstepped a boundary who knows how he would've responded, but it's a question of, 'Do I go the route of saying, 'I'm a failure for having failed,' or do I step back and say, 'Yeah, I did get drawn into the ethos. I'm human. That's what humans do and I'm part of that.' When you take that, stepping back it and looking at it like that, what impact does that have on you?

[*It is a part of my ONEplus Therapy practice that I like to outline options for clients concerning how they wish to go forward. These options, here, are based on what Jane has been saying.*]

Jane: … [*Pause*] It sends my mind into two different ways. There's like a rescuer and a persecutor going on, because there's a part that's saying, 'Yeah, that's OK. It's alright,' and then there's another part that sends me off in another direction and says, 'But … [*pause*] your parents are kind of frightened of his anger whereas you're not,' probably because growing up he was my bully. I have seen a lot of his anger.

Windy: Yeah. What's the persecuting bit in that?

Jane: Well, the persecutor bit says, 'You still have the bravery. Unlike your parents, who are actually quite frightened … doing the conflict bit, the difficult conversation of, "Are you going to get angry? How angry are you going to get?"' I don't have that bit with him. He doesn't scare me. His anger doesn't scare me in the same way that his anger does with my parents. So, I have the tools. My bravery was my tool to be able to kick the door open and say, 'Listen, we need to talk.'

Windy: But what's the persecuting bit of you saying about the fact that you failed to do what you had it in your repertoire to do? You had it in your repertoire, you're not scared of his anger, you had it in your repertoire to maybe take a more proactive stance and you didn't do that. So, I'm still struggling to hear the persecuting bit of that because we're assuming that that happened and all those are facts. Where's the persecution in that?

Jane: … [*Pause*] Well, the persecution is, 'You should've done more. You should've done better.'

Windy: Let me just stop there a minute. What was the second word there?

[Jane's response has given me an opportunity to bring my REBT perspective to the work.]

Jane: Should. It's my least favourite word and I'm always throwing it out of therapy sessions.

Windy: Is that a good should or not a good should?

Jane: I don't think should is ever good. You either want to or you don't.

Windy: If I say to you, 'Look, you really should go and read Professor Dryden's latest book on single-session therapy,' that's a good should, isn't it?

Jane: Sure.

Windy: You've got the persecuting should.

Jane: Yeah.

Windy: The question is how do you deal with the persecuting should?

Jane: Tell it to do one, yeah.

[This is Jane's pithily expressed solution to her 'persecutory' should.]

Windy: Tell it to do one, right.

Jane: More often than not I'm like, 'OK, that's nice.'

Windy: So, if you can recognise then that there is a part of you that recognises that you didn't act in a way that you wished you had, bravely going in there and

	boldly going where your family feared to go type of thing.
Jane:	Yeah.
Windy:	That's the other thing, isn't it? That's what you wanted to talk about. But the idea is, yeah, it would be nice if you had done that but you're going to tell the persecuting part of you when it's shoulding all over you to do one.
Jane:	Yeah. Essentially, it's … an opportunity for learning with anything. OK, yeah, maybe I could've done more … and … I can do that now, and he has reached out for support for the first time directly to me.
Windy:	Is this the episode when he brought his son along or was it another episode?
Jane:	No. So that's been really recently since he's been in prison. He phoned me directly, which he never does … ever, unless he's in real trouble, and just said, 'I've had a lot of time to think in here. It's vile in here. And, actually, I'm going to be sorting myself out.' And I said, 'I'll support you. I'll come and visit you, we'll sit down and we'll talk it through and I will support you to do that.'
Windy:	Do you remember Question 8 on my pre-session questionnaire? It was the last question.
Jane:	I ticked all the boxes, yeah.
Windy:	Well, initially you did until I said, 'No, you can't do all of that stuff. Hold on a minute.' The reason I put that is in single-session therapy I don't know the

help that you want; I need to find out what help you want. The only way I can do that is to ask you what help you want. And I'm wondering if there's something you can take from that with your brother.

[*I am using the question on my pre-session questionnaire which asks the client to nominate the main type of help they want from the session to suggest to Jane that she could ask her brother what help he wants from her.*]

Jane: … Well, helping him to get in touch with his feelings as well.

Windy: No, I'm talking about maybe asking him, 'OK, Brother, what help can I provide for you? What help would you find most helpful?' 'cos you don't know.

Jane: No, I don't know.

Windy: The danger may be that you might be bringing in concepts of what you think is going to be helpful, but maybe you can take a leaf out of the single-session therapy playbook where it says, 'No, I don't know what's going to be helpful. He can tell me and then I can maybe offer that if I think it's not going to make things worse.'

Jane: Yeah. It's providing him his autonomy and agency, isn't it?

Windy: Something that you value.

[*Encouraging a person to see that a potential solution is consistent with their values helps make that solution attractive to the person.*]

Jane: Yeah.

Windy: Something that you value and maybe that will also help you to sort the rescuing bit, because, when you rescue, you think that you know what the other person wants, and you jump in. So maybe this will help you with that, to stand back and say, 'Look, Brother, of course I'll help you, but what would you find most helpful from me?' and if he says, 'I don't know,' then you can give him some options. This is why I have that on the form. It says, 'These are the options that I can offer you.'

Jane: Yeah, that's really helpful, because I think that was the bit that I was also worried about next week going to visit him. I had every intention of saying, 'What's your plan? What do you want? How can I support you with it?' but, as far as that, if he'd said, 'I don't know,' I didn't want to project any of my opinions around what I think he should do.

Windy: Yeah, but maybe giving him some options to think about.

Jane: Yeah, sure, 'cos there are several options for him to choose, actually.

Windy: Yeah, and you may need to be clear that, if he wants something that you're not prepared to give, to be clear about that as well, maybe.

Jane: Yeah. A difficulty for me is the worry that he'll fob it all off or say, 'Yeah, sure, I'll take the support,' and then not.

Windy: But let's suppose that. Let's suppose in technical terms he's gone from the precontemplation stage of

	change into contemplation and says, 'Oh, I think I might need help. Let's talk about that,' and let's suppose you offer him that and he then scurries back into precontemplation. Let's suppose that. Now, what's the issue about that for you?
Jane:	... [*Pause*] That the cycle will continue and that he'll just fall back into ... [*Long pause*] what he's been doing previously. I don't want to put that out into the ... ether, really, because I don't want that to be the reality for him at all.
Windy:	No, but, if that happens, what's your involvement and what's your responsibility? What are you responsible for and what are you not responsible for?
	[*Questions like 'What are you responsible for and what are you not responsible for?' and 'What are you in control of and what are you not in control of?' are important to ask where relevant in ONEplus Therapy.*]
Jane:	Well, perhaps that I ... offer him the understanding that ... whatever he decides to do, if he's not ready to do it at any point and he needs to go back into that precontemplation, but, if and when he decides he wants to step back into action and towards change, then I will be there to support him again.
Windy:	That's right. So, your responsibility is making it clear that you're going to be there for him. It's a bit like a little animal poking his head out and going back in, poking his head out: 'Is it safe yet? No, it's not safe yet. Well, let's see.' So, he knows, then, that whenever he's ready you're there.

Jane: Yeah. I think he finds the idea of change difficult. Who doesn't? But there's something about the strife and the difficulty and the struggle of trying to make change and more actually sticking with it. It's the maintenance part of the change cycle that he really....

Windy: Do you know much about your birth parents?

Jane: I do, yes. I'm in reunion with my birth family, not with my birth parents but with my maternal family – so my grandmother and my uncles and aunts and my cousins.

Windy: Have you picked up anything from them about their tendency to deal with conflict? Are they avoidant? Are they more like you?

Jane: They're more like me. They're very open.

Windy: So, I think there's a biological tendency or an inherent tendency that I think your brother's got that you don't. In a way, I think he's struggling with that.

Jane: Yeah. Also, I had a very good two years from nought to two with foster parents who were incredibly attentive and very loving. Whereas my adoptive mum very much struggled to show warmth.

Windy: So, even if you had broken a boundary and gone in then and got stuck in....

Jane: He would've hated it. He would've told me to F off and keep my nose out, probably.

Windy: He would've told you to do one.

Jane: He would've, yeah, exactly. That's my fantasy, isn't it, that he would've done that. And maybe he would've. I don't know.

Windy: Yeah.

Jane: Potentially. And I don't know what's gone on between my parents and him. I don't know the conversations that have gone on and whether he's told them to do one. Who knows? Yeah. ... [*Pause*] What we have is the present and it's what we can do going forward, isn't it? You can't change what's happened.

Windy: So, based on what we've spoken about today, how would you like to move forward with this?

        [*I am picking up on a very constructive statement made by Jane to move into action planning.*]

Jane: ... [*Pause*] With as much as openness and compassion and patience as possible, I think, keeping my ... [*pause*] opinions to one side and giving him his autonomy and his agency to decide what he wants to do. It's his life.

Windy: And, if you make another mistake and the persecuted part of you starts 'shoulding' all over you, what then?

Jane: Then I will tell it to do one and say, 'You're not being very helpful right now.' Yeah.

Windy: One of the things that I like to do when the transcripts are in and I've thought about it, I like to give the transcript titles. At the moment I'm thinking about the title: 'Telling the Persecuting Part of Myself to Do One When It Shoulds on Me'.

Jane: Absolutely. Yeah, definitely. The word 'should' used to be very much in my vocabulary when I was younger before I did my training, before I did my therapy. And I promised myself that I would throw it out of the window.

Windy: But that's another should, isn't it? 'I shouldn't use the word should!'

Jane: Yeah, exactly. I think, when it comes to family, all those old dynamics creep back in.

Windy: Yeah, and that's why you may need to be extra vigilant for those 'shoulds' when it comes to your family for all kinds of reasons.

Jane: Yeah.

Windy: But it sounds like, just talking to you, and you've been through a tremendous period of growth and development, that you can do that; you can actually take that and look out for it and be vigilant. It's great to tell that part of you to do one. That's very vivid. So, I'm wondering what you're going to take away from this that is going to make it feel like, 'I'm glad I came to talk about this because I'm taking away' what?

[*The focus on takeaways at the end of a ONEplus Therapy session is very common.*]

Jane: I think, actually, it kind of goes back to the bit that existed for me before this all came about, was that I was trying to step out of my family role of being the container for everybody's emotions and the problem-solver and the one that fixes things and helps to communicate between the family.... That I can actually return to not having to do that. I felt like I've been pulled into it in the last month or two because of what's happened. And there was this real urgency, initially, to be like, 'Oh my goodness, I need to do something.' And then I was like, 'Whoa, hold on a minute.'

Windy: That's right. You've just introduced the other relatives in the 'should' family: the 'have to' and the 'need to'.

Jane: Yeah, and it's a horrible feeling because it's all part of that drama triangle: that rescuer role that feels like they've got to suddenly step in and rescue the situation and make it better for everyone. Actually, what needs to happen is that I need to allow myself to put myself first and keep that present. And that it's OK if my family are in chaos. I do not need to rescue them.

Windy: No. In fact, if you don't, it will be interesting to see what happens to their own natural tendency. Will they avoid chaos? Who knows?

Jane: No, because I think that's kind of what's been happening. I've been stepping out of that role for the last five years maybe and ... my parents are on anti-depressants and a brother in prison, which I never thought I would say out loud.

Windy: And, if you'd have stepped in, they would have not been on anti-depressants and he wouldn't have been in prison.

Jane: Yeah. No, probably not.

Windy: Is there anything you want to say that you haven't said yet or anything you want to ask before we finish?

[This is a typical question asked at the end of a ONEplus or single-session therapy session. It is designed to effect a satisfactory closure to the session.]

Jane: No. I'm aware of time as well. I don't think there's anything in particular that I have left to ask or anything like that. It's been nice to be able to mull it over, actually.

Windy: Good.

Jane: I've got good, strong, supportive friends. I was quite nervous about talking to a complete stranger about it, strangely, even though....

Windy: Sure. I understand what you're saying.

Jane: But it's been nice, thank you.

Windy: So I'll write to you in about three months and you can provide a reflection on the session and what came afterwards for you, OK?

Jane: Lovely. Yep, that's great.

Windy: OK, Jane, take care.

Jane: Thanks very much, Windy.

Jane's Reflections on the Session: 01/12/23

I was nervous going into the session with Windy. I felt as though I was in some way betraying my family by speaking about the maladaptive family dynamics to someone not 'on the inside'. On reflection, I realise, in part, this is what I've been conditioned to do, to keep secrets, to keep up the pretence and the presentation of a 'sturdy ship' to others, when in fact, there are gaping holes in the hull and some crew members are dangling upside down from the sails, feet caught in the ropes unable to save themselves whilst others sit around drinking mead and eating cheese.

My experience of my ONEplus Therapy session with Windy gave me a chance to air some of my anxieties and guilt around my relationship with my brother. I was not sure what to expect from the session and I had reservations about how helpful one session would be for what felt like a complex sibling history.

The contracting provided by Windy at the beginning of the session helped create trust early on. I was offered a sense of agency and autonomy around conducting the session together. I was given clear instructions about what the session 'was' and what it 'wasn't'; this helped with aligning my thoughts and helped cut through the fodder to get to the core of what I wanted to bring to the session.

Having grown up in a household with inconsistent and, at times, chaotic parenting, I found myself initially hesitant about Windy's presentation and demeanour. He was neither warm nor cold, neither soft nor harsh in either nature, assertiveness, or boundary setting. I was able to quickly realise that my brain and nervous system were confusing unfamiliarity with danger and Windy's consistency helped me to quickly regulate and settle into the session.

I was able to take from the session a reminder to myself that I did not need to step back into the rescuer role, a role that I have often felt I needed to take upon myself due to my parents' avoidance and lack of attuned and available parenting. I could also, even with hindsight, be forgiving towards myself for colluding with the family's avoidant tendencies towards my brother's distress. My ego did not need to believe it had such importance.

The session allowed me to sit with and confront the guilt I hold for my brother, but furthermore, to remind myself it is also not my guilt to be holding. My perspective on my childhood has always been that my older brother suffered a degree of parentification due to my parents' inability to be present both physically and emotionally for both of us. This is because a lot of the parentification had been around 'childminding' me when he 'should' be enjoying his teenage years. For some reason, I had felt that by existing, it was, therefore, my fault. I realise, on reflection, that even the idea of this continues to collude with my parents' avoidance and inability to take personal responsibility to confront the 'elephant in the room', both in childhood and still now in adulthood.

8

Helping People with Problems with Unhealthy Regret

Helping the Client to Understand and Deal with Unhealthy Regret

Here are some ideas that I have found useful to introduce into my conversation with clients that can help them deal with unhealthy regret (Dryden, 2023b).

- When a person experiences unhealthy regret, they hold a rigid and extreme attitude towards one of the following two adversities: (i) I acted in a way that I wish I hadn't and (ii) I failed to act in a way that I wish I had (e.g. 'I did not take that job when it was offered to me years ago and I absolutely should have done so. It's terrible that I turned that job down').
- When a person holds such a rigid and extreme attitude, they think their life would have been much better if they had chosen differently. They also engage in what I call unhealthy regret-related rumination. In their mind, they try to undo what they did or what they did not do but fail. However, such failure leads to more rumination. They also keep searching in their mind for a good enough reason to explain their past decision but fail to find it. Rather than give up these pursuits, they keep trying to find answers that will satisfy them through such rumination. Both of these ruminative strategies are doomed to fail because rigid and extreme attitudes underpin such thinking.

- The healthy alternative to unhealthy regret is healthy regret.
- When a person experiences healthy regret, they hold a flexible and non-extreme attitude towards the same two adversities: (i) I acted in a way that I wish I hadn't and (ii) I failed to act in a way that I wish I had (e.g. 'I did not take that job when it was offered to me years ago. I wish I had done so, but that does not mean that I absolutely should have done so. It's unfortunate that I turned that job down, but not terrible').
- When a person holds this flexible and non-extreme attitude, they think their life may have been much better if they had chosen differently, but they also recognise that it could have been worse, or it may have made no difference. They tend not to engage in rumination. They recognise that their past action (or inaction) was due to how they thought then and that there is no way to undo that now. All they can do now is learn from that experience and use that learning to guide their future decisions.
- If the person is interested, I will help them change their rigid/extreme attitudes to their flexible/non-extreme counterparts and help them think and act in ways that will support the development of these attitudes.

Transcript of My Work with a Person with a Problem with Unhealthy Regret

Therapist – Volunteer:	Windy – Libby
Venue:	Private session that took place on 11/08/23 arranged via Onlinevents
Time:	42 minutes 50 secs

Windy: So, Libby, from your perspective what's your understanding of the purpose of our conversation this morning?

Libby: So, it is a session, a voluntary session which will be recorded and then the transcript will be sent to me, and it'll be used in the production of a book.

Windy: Right, OK. That's the nuts and bolts of it, but how about for you? What's the purpose of the conversation for you?

Libby: It's around regret.

Windy: And what would you like to achieve at the end of the session that would make volunteering worthwhile for you?

[*I often ask about a client's goal for the session in this way*]

Libby: … Just to have another maybe little piece or understanding. It's not that I expect that it's going to be completely resolved, but it's just maybe having another insight into it that will make it easier to deal with.

Windy: So, like a step towards something.

> [*I sometimes describe the goals of ONEplus Therapy as helping the client begin to address an issue rather than resolving the issue. Occasionally the issue does get resolved but this should not be the agreed goal as it is generally unrealistic.*]

Libby: Yeah.

Windy: Do you have a vision of what the problem would be like if it was completely resolved?

> [*I call this the problem-related goal as opposed to the session goal – see Chapter 3.*]

Libby: … Yeah, that I wouldn't get so triggered easily … that I wouldn't go into the negative mind spiral.

Windy: Right. That's interesting the way you answer it because you answer it as, if I was going to a train station and the guy asked me where I'd like to go to and I said, 'Well, I don't want to go to Southend or I don't want to go to Clacton.' So, you're clear about where you don't want to be.

Libby: OK, yes.

Windy: But are you clear about where you do want to be? We're talking about something which is obviously of great importance to you. By the way, is it OK if I refer to your form as we go?

Libby: Yeah.

Windy: OK. So, I'm just wondering, 'cos it's easier to head for something if you know where you're heading for.

[Libby has given me a problem-related goal which is the absence of an unhealthy state. I respond by asking her for a problem-related goal which is the presence of a healthy state.]

Libby: Yes.

Windy: You have a vision of where you don't want to be rather than where you do want to be.

Libby: Yes.

Windy: So, if we put those things together and say, look, this is a very important issue for you when you look back. And, if I can name it, on your form it's not having children. And, so we have to find something which indicates that this is of great importance to you but you don't want to go into a spiral. By the way, how much does this issue affect your life now?

Libby: … I wake up on most mornings with that spiral going round in my head and the ifs and all of that. And it affects my contact … in social situations.

Windy: In what way?

Libby: I will avoid situations if I can that will involve other mothers or involve conversations around children or … *[pause]* you know, anything that might trigger I will try and avoid those situations.

Windy: And has that avoidance helped you in the long term do you think or not?

Libby: … I think it has helped and I can choose. It's not like I avoid these situations all the time because it's not possible to avoid it all the time, but at least I feel like I have more space around it and I can make a choice.

Windy: So, avoidance for you, the important thing about that is that you have space and a choice.

Libby: Yeah.

Windy: If you were to, for example, take the goal of waking up in the morning, what would be a way of thinking and feeling that would indicate that, 'Yeah, this is important to me but I'm not going to go into a spiral,' what would you have to think and feel about not having children that would characterise that, do you think?

Libby: I guess thinking and feeling how lucky I am in what I have got.

Windy: Right, OK.

Libby: As opposed to focusing on what I haven't got.

Windy: What about both?

Libby: OK.

Windy: Is it OK, as we go, for me to give you my take on certain things? Would you welcome that?

          [While in ONEplus Therapy, it is important to work with the person's knowledge, strengths, capabilities etc, sometimes it is important for the therapist to offer their perspective on matters under discussion.

> *This is particularly the case when the person could, in the therapist's opinion, benefit from a professional understanding of the issue at hand. This is the therapist offering their expertise without adopting the stance of THE expert.*]

Libby: Yeah.

Windy: The trouble with counting your blessings, so to speak, it doesn't help you cope with a loss.

Libby: Yes.

Windy: So, we need to help you to cope with loss and then count your blessings.

Libby: OK, yeah.

Windy: Rather than dealing with the loss by counting your blessings, so to speak.

> *[In this recent exchange, what I am doing is taking the client's solution of 'counting their blessings' and adding to it – count your blessings AND deal with the loss.]*

Libby: OK.

Windy: I think it's unrealistic to expect you, after all these times, of waking up and not thinking about that you don't have children. Is that the thought that you have? What thought do you wake up with? I'm curious.

Libby: … *[Pause]* I guess imagining what it might have been like. So, I suppose regretting what I don't have in that sense. Maybe it's sometimes around my friends who have children and … I guess imagining how their lives are and how they're different. And … those loss of connections as well.

Windy: So that's the bit which, in a way, I think it is a loss. There's nothing that you can say, or I can say. We can count blessings, we can do what you like, but the reality is that you don't have children, you really wished you did, and you regret not having children. Feel free to say anything or not say anything, because we are recording it, but may I ask is there any reason that you don't have children? Was it any physical thing or anything like that?

Libby: Yeah…. It just took me a long time to meet somebody, and it was really important … for me – I didn't have a father growing up, so it was really important for me to have a secure … stable relationship with a father figure. And it just took me a long time to meet somebody. I had to do a lot of work on myself first to sort a few things out. So, I was quite late meeting somebody.

Windy: By late you mean?

Libby: Yeah, late 40s.

Windy: You were late 40s before you met somebody?

Libby: Yeah. Well, I've had relationships, but they weren't….

Windy: It sounds to me like it's almost like you were looking for a partner who's going to be a good father.

Libby: Yeah.

Windy: Rather than a partner.

Libby: Well, yes, that's interesting you put it that way.... Yeah.... And yet I found a partner that's a loving, very beautiful partner. He's not a father.

Windy: No. When you got together and became a partnership was it already too late or did you try? What was the context that we're talking about?

Libby: Yeah. I mean, we spoke about it. He already had two grown-up children. So, he wasn't exactly completely there, but it was like he was willing to try if it was something that I wanted.

Windy: Right. And it was.

Libby: Yes. And we tried and it didn't happen.

Windy: So, if I can just get clear in my mind the context of that, because of the issues with your father it was really important for you to have children but it's very important to you to have children with a secure base, both with a loving mother and a good and secure father.

[*I have found it useful in dealing with unhealthy regret to understand the context of the person's regret (Dryden, 2023b).*]

Libby: Yeah.

Windy: And it took you quite a while. You had partners but they didn't meet both those criteria. And, when you did meet your current partner, it was late in the day.

Libby: Yeah.

Windy: And, as a result of that, although you got the context and it could've happened, but it didn't happen. So, what do you regret in that scenario?

Libby: ... [*Long pause*] I regret that ... [*pause*] we didn't try more things.... [*Long pause*] It was kind of we were allowing it to happen more naturally, but we really needed probably to have intervention.

Windy: And at what point did you realise that?

Libby: ... [*Pause*] I think probably from the outset but, I don't know, I think there was confusion for me as well. There was a lot of conflicting things happening for me. So, there was worry because I was older.... [*Pause*] And I think I was also still conflicted whether I'd be a good mother or not. So, I was kind of one foot in, one foot out. I was finding it very conflictual, and yet there was a really strong part of me that wanted it, but then there was a part of me that was hesitating.

Windy: So, it sounds like at the time you were both thinking about both natural ways of bringing a child into the world and more external interventions, if you like. Although that was being discussed, you didn't, as a couple, decide to go down that route. Did you eventually decide to go down that route or what?

Libby: No.

Windy: Was there a reason why you decided that you didn't want to go down that route?

Libby: ... I think I was frightened.... [*Pause*] My husband wasn't really completely committed either. He had sort of said, it was kind of like, 'If you want to have the child....'

Windy: It sounds like that, if the two of you were both gung-ho about this, then you may have decided to actually seek external intervention, if I can use that terminology.

Libby: Yeah.

Windy: Am I hearing that right?

Libby: Yeah. And ... he suggested it as well. My husband had suggested it and..., I don't know. There's just that part of me.

Windy: So, you were both conflicted.

Libby: Yeah.

Windy: And, so that level of conflict led you to keep trying, as I say, the natural way. And you regret that now.

Libby: Yeah.

Windy: Interesting that, when I asked you what you regretted, what you didn't say. What didn't you say?

Libby: ... [*Long pause*] I didn't say I regretted not trying more things.

Windy: No, what you didn't say, 'I regretted not trying with one of these other partners.' That's not something you regret.

Libby: No.

Windy: So, as the course of your life unfolded, that you were clear that you were only going to have children with somebody who was a good partner and a secure father.

Libby: Yeah.

Windy: It turned out that you met that person later than you hoped and, when you met him and decided to go into exploring the possibility of having children and acting on that, you were both conflictual.

Libby: Yeah.

Windy: That led you to choosing to go the more 'let nature take its course' kind of thing rather than 'Let's really explore the external intervention.' He suggested it but it was in the context of him being not wholly signed up for the project anyway.

Libby: Yeah.

Windy: When he suggested it, you were still conflictual.

Libby: Yeah.

Windy: Concerned about whether you would be good. So that was the reality.

Libby: Yeah.

Windy: And that reality has led you to the situation where you are now, which is that you don't have children and that you wish you did.

Libby: Yeah.

[*Here I am making sure I have understood the full picture of the context of Libby's 'inaction' – if I can call it that – and that she confirms my understanding. I will return to this understanding later.*]

Windy: Now, what part of your going into – what did you call it when you start to think in the morning? You used a particular word. It begins with S,[26] I think.

Libby: … [*Long pause*] Well, I mentioned going around in my head.

Windy: Yeah, so you're ruminating.

Libby: Yeah.

Windy: So, what if you could experience the loss without the rumination? How would that be for you?

Libby: That's interesting…. Yeah.

Windy: And what would that sound like if you were to experience the loss without the rumination?

Libby: I think I would acknowledge the loss and feel it rather than talking around in my head.

Windy: So, you'd feel the loss.

Libby: Yeah.

Windy: And what about all these 'if onlys': 'If only I did this, if only we'd done that' – what about that? How would you respond to that?

---

26 The word I was looking for but could not find was 'spiral'.

Libby: … [*Pause*] 'Well, we're here now. I can't change any of that.'

Windy: That's right. Sadly, we can't. I often say to people when I'm talking about unhealthy regret, I'm quite happy to put your name down on the waiting list for the TARDIS, Dr Who's time-travelling machine.

Libby: Yes.

Windy: So, based on what we did know now, we'd go back with that knowledge and you and your partner would actually choose to take – well, who knows. We don't know what you would actually choose, as a matter of fact, but let's assume that you would choose some external intervention. If you chose to do that, if we had the TARDIS, what do you think would've happened with this external intervention?

Libby: Well, we could be still sitting here having the same discussion and maybe there would've been a sense that, 'OK, well, we tried. We tried everything.' Do you know what I mean? … Maybe it could've been put to rest a bit easier. I don't know.

Windy: That's right. There's a sense that at least, and that is the kind of sense in unhealthy regret: the idea that, 'I could then look at myself in the mirror and say, "Look, I tried everything."'

Libby: Yeah.

Windy: Now you can look at yourself in the mirror and actually say, 'Look, we tried naturally. But the reason why we didn't try everything is because I was conflicted and he was conflicted. That was the reality.'

[*My intention here is to encourage Libby to look at the situation she was in then while taking into account all the factors that were present at the time – see Dryden (2023b).*]

Libby: Yeah.

Windy: And I'm going to use a different use of the word 'should': that should have happened because it did.

Libby: … [*Pause*] OK, you need to explain that. Sorry.

Windy: Well, what should you get if you take two particles of hydrogen and one of oxygen? You get water, right?

Libby: Yeah.

Windy: You should get water because all the conditions are right to get water. So, all I'm saying is all the conditions were in place for you to do exactly what you did at the time. And this part of you which says, 'But we should've done more,' is based on what happened later put into the past.

Libby: Yeah, I hear what you're saying.

Windy: So, one of the things you can say is, 'Look, yeah, I really regret the loss. I need to feel the loss. And we did what we did because of what we were thinking at the time. We couldn't have done anything else at the time.'

Libby: Yeah…. [*Pause*] Yeah, that's true.

Windy: Could you imagine waking up and having that as a different way forward from what you do now, which is you wake up, you go straight into rumination rather than to experience the loss and to acknowledge the reality of what you did based on all the conditions that we've talked about: his conflict, your conflict, your decision to do it naturally, neither of you were gung ho about it? So, if your gung ho'ness was the H_2 and his gung ho'ness was the O and you put that together, you would've got a different outcome. But we didn't have those components in the situation.

Libby: Yeah, true.

Windy: Now how would you put that in your own words?

Libby: … [*Long pause*] Well, I mean, it is interesting, the chemical equation about it.… [*Pause*] It's almost like, instead of using the word conflict, maybe we could use the word confusion, maybe, or something like that. So, it's kind of like confusion plus confusion.

Windy: That's right. Confusion plus confusion equals nonaction.

Libby: Yes.

Windy: And, when you look back and say, 'I wish we would've done more interventions,' that would've involved you both being gung-ho about it.

Libby: Yeah.

Windy: But the reality is confusion plus confusion equals a decision to actually have a child naturally.

Libby: Yeah.

Windy: That was what was happening at the time. I think that's an excellent way of putting it.

[*This equation is a short-hand way of expressing what was happening at the time for Libby.*]

Libby: Yeah. And it's kind of like, because we couldn't, either of us ... it's like we handed the decision over to nature.

Windy: Yeah. Right. Let nature decide.

Libby: Yeah, exactly.

Windy: Yeah. Healthy regret is saying, 'Yeah, I wish we didn't do that, but we did.' It's not a question of regret. It's about loss, about loss of not having a child. It's what you don't have. Regret is more about what you did or actually what you didn't do in this case. And I think what you're doing is you're trying to solve the problem of loss by solving the regret problem. And it ain't gonna do it. You've got to solve both. And I'm saying you can solve the regret problem by, 'We're in the situation of confusion plus confusion equals let nature decide. That's the reality that we're in. But now, OK, let me just accept that, but now let me get on with the business of actually grieving the fact that I don't have children.' And that's painful. There's nothing that I can say.

I always refer to my mother on these occasions. When I was an adult visiting her, I was a bit early and I found her crying. I said, 'What's wrong?' She said, 'Oh no, every day I remember my mother and I have about a ten- or fifteen-minute cry because I miss her,' and then I get on with my day,' she said.

Libby: OK, yeah.

Windy: I think you've got work to do on dealing with loss.

[I am making the point that Libby does not allow herself to feel the healthy pain of not having children. She is trying to count her blessings which is fine but does not help her to deal with her loss.]

Libby: ... *[Pause]* Yeah, I think that there's loss ... underneath that loss that hasn't been dealt with.

Windy: Yeah, OK. Now, this is not the place to do that.

Libby: No, I know that.

Windy: How do you feel about finding out that there is loss underneath the loss so that you do need to find a space to deal with it? How do you feel about that?

Libby: Yeah. It's interesting because it's like a thing I know but maybe we know it for other people sometimes. They often talk about grief is like it sits on top of other grief.... So, it's often not a grief on its own. It's an accumulation.

Windy: Sure.

Libby: So maybe I'm starting in the wrong place.

Windy: Yeah. Having made that realisation, does that lead you to decide to do anything about that realisation?

Libby: Yeah.

Windy: What's that?

Libby: ... *[Pause]* Yeah, I suppose just to work on acknowledging ... the grief that's there.

Windy: Yeah. And I think that's important. And that isn't going to be done by you counting your blessings. It's not going to be done by you even dealing with your unhealthy regret problem, which I think will facilitate that 'cos I think the ruminative unhealthy grief stops you from the realisation which you now realise. I think, maybe if I've done nothing else to do, it's to help you to deal with the regret to the extent to which you now realise that there's loss to deal with. How would you feel about our session if that's all we did?

Libby: Yeah. There's almost a part of me that wants to understand a little bit more how you would define unhealthy regret.

Windy: It's about keep on going back and saying, 'I should've done this. If only I'd done that. Why didn't I do that?' It's a refusal to acknowledge the 'confusion plus confusion equals let nature decide' reality.

Libby: Yeah.

Windy: It's also based on the idea that, 'If we had gone, and clarity plus clarity equals external intervention, then it would've turned out OK. We would've had one or two lovely children.' So, there's a tendency to think, in unhealthy regret, that the road not travelled would've led to a great conclusion, and the road travelled leads to a worse conclusion.

Libby: Yes.

Windy: We don't know that, exactly. We haven't explored that with you, but sometimes there is self-

	recrimination: 'I'm an idiot for not doing this,' or, 'I'm a fool.' I don't know whether you have that.
Libby:	Yeah.
Windy:	So, what form does your self-recrimination take?
	[*Here, I am faced with the choice of going into this related area or remain with the agreed focus. In retrospect, I could have asked Libby whether she wanted to deal with this rather than decide for myself.*]
Libby:	… [*Long pause*] It sounds like a weird expression to use, but kind of man up, if you know what I mean; that I couldn't just take the courage in my hands and just do it.
Windy:	Yeah.
Libby:	That I was somehow weak or indecisive, almost allowing my history to impact me.
Windy:	Yeah. So, you were weak, you were indecisive and you were dominated by your history.
Libby:	Yeah.
Windy:	What do you do for a living?
Libby:	I'm a psychotherapist.
Windy:	So, if a client told you this, what would you think of her in this case: a similar background, same dynamic and they started saying, 'Well, I'm weak and indecisive and I shouldn't have allowed my history to dominate this'? Would you say to her,

'Yeah, you're right there. You are weak and indecisive. You should've manned up'? Is that what you'd say to her?

Libby: No.

Windy: Would you think it and not say it?

Libby: No.

Windy: What would you say to the client?

Libby: I think I would acknowledge that that's where she was at that moment and that was the feelings that she was having, and she could only really operate or she could only respond to what she was feeling at the time. She couldn't change it.

Windy: Would you encourage her to accept herself for that and to show herself some compassion?

Libby: Yeah.

Windy: Now, what would happen, Libby, if you took that attitude and applied to the woman in the mirror? What would that be like?

Libby: … [*Pause*] Yes, it would be novel.

Windy: You're not used to that?

Libby: No.

Windy: I think, actually, that that attitude of self-acceptance and self-compassion are skills. They're based on an attitude, as we say, but they're skills. We need to practise them and be aware of obstacles that may come up. But can you imagine yourself practising those skills? I'm not suggesting you look in the mirror, but that would be a part of your dealing with grief and saying, 'Confusion plus confusion equals letting nature decide. I wish I was more "strong", but I wasn't. I'm an ordinary, fallible human being and I'm prey to the same things as my clients are because we are all part of this big community called human beings and there's no special rule for Libby,' unless you want to have a special rule for Libby.

Libby: Yeah.... I mean, there was a lot of stress as well.... My brother died a few months after we got married and it was very stressful.

Windy: As we get more details of the context, I would urge you to also build that in as a way of actually saying, 'Look, these were the pressures on me. There were external pressures and internal pressures.'

[Libby is providing details of more relevant factors that were impinging on her and her partner at the time. I acknowledge this and encourage Libby to factor these in for herself.]

Libby: Yeah.... *[Pause]* So I need to be kinder to myself. Yeah.

Windy: Yeah. And I think, if you're kinder to yourself in that way by understanding the context and actually recognising that you're not weak and indecisive and a victim of your past, but you're an ordinary human being who was struggling in that situation, and you've got strengths and weaknesses like everybody else and we're all affected by our past. At times they are going to come up and saying, 'I shouldn't have done that. I should've manned up.'

It's not going to change anything but it's only going to add self-recrimination. I can't see how self-recrimination is going to help you to deal with your loss, can you?

Libby: No.

Windy: It's only going to interfere, I think, with dealing with your loss because now, rather than focusing on your loss, you're focusing on what a weak, indecisive individual you are. You're not over there, you're over here.

Libby: Yeah … that's true.

Windy: Are there any other factors that we need to add to the context at the time?

Libby: Yeah. We got married and we went to a house with his two sons, so there was a lot of adjusting there as well. And I ruptured my Achilles tendon as well on honeymoon, so I was on crutches. And my normal thing would be to go out for a drive in the car; if I was a bit stressed, that would be my calming thing. So, I couldn't drive. So, there was a lot happening, yeah.

[*Even more factors!*]

Windy: With all that going on for both of you, I don't know how the two of you got together and said, 'Let's go and get some external intervention.'

Libby: Yes.

Windy: So, would you like to summarise where we are at the moment, Libby, what we've covered?

Libby: Yeah.... So we've looked at what unhealthy regret is. So, basically, it's about 'could have', 'should have' and you're basing that and I'm basing that on things that I would've inserted from the present into the past, which I can't do.... And it's about looking at what the equation was at the time. So it was confusion plus confusion, which basically couldn't make a decision in that regard and it was left up to nature.

Windy: Yeah, confusion based on internal conflict, external situations, physical situations that were going on.

Libby: Yeah.... It's about acknowledging grief rather than immediately going to all the things that I do have. It's maybe allowing the grief first and then being grateful for what I have.

Windy: Yeah.

Libby: And it's about self-compassion.... [*Pause*] I feel that's mostly what I got.

Windy: I would add something, just to add a bit of reality but a bitter pill, I think you're always going to have that twinge when you see people with kids. I think that's going to be there for you, but your twinge doesn't need to lead to you going down a rabbit hole. You can just accept the twinge and recognise that, 'Yes, I don't have kids and I really miss not having kids.'

Libby: Yeah.

Windy: So, what are you going to take away in particular that you might want to implement?

Libby: ... I think looking at the grief piece and maybe allowing that more.... And also, just knowing that that was the situation at the time and, given the same circumstances again, I couldn't have made a different decision. I would make a different decision if I could bring back stuff with me, but I can't.

Windy: Yeah, exactly.

Libby: So, knowing that. And I'm also managing ... [*pause*] this perfect outcome that could've happened, but I actually don't know that; that may not have happened either.

Windy: Yeah, exactly.

Libby: Yeah.... [*Pause*] So I think it's just giving it a little bit more context and a slightly different perspective, and that's kind of what I was hoping for: just to get a slightly different perspective on it.

Windy: Yeah, OK. So why don't you implement that, and I think that you can implement that a bit every morning when you get up and respond to it in a different way. I think you've been responding to it in a certain way. So, you might start off that way because it's habitual, but then you can say, 'Now, wait a minute, let me really practise this new way of actually looking at things,' and then we'll see what happens. And I'll write to you in a couple of months, and you can write a reflection for the book. Is there anything you want to say or ask that you would've wished you'd said or asked later on? You can ask now on this issue.

Libby: Yeah. Maybe just to go back over, because it's interesting when we talk about unhealthy regret and healthy regret? It almost feels like regret is not a good thing in itself.

Windy: Well, no. It's just saying, 'I wish I had done that, but I didn't have to, but I still wish I had.' Every morning I wake up and I wish I had hair. Nothing wrong with the wish. So don't try to get rid of the wish. I think what you've done in the past a little bit is to use avoidance to try to solve the feelings. And I think it helps in the immediate term but it doesn't help going forward. I don't think there's anything wrong with saying, 'Yeah, I wish I was stronger at that time but I didn't have to be. And, actually, looking back at it, there's no way I could've been, but I still wish.' There's nothing wrong with the wish.

[I am glad to have had the opportunity at the end to clarify that regret can be healthy as well as unhealthy]

Libby: Yeah. So is that what you are describing then as healthy regret?

Windy: Yeah.

Libby: So it's OK to have had the wish.

Windy: Yeah, 'I wish I took this case but I now realise that there's no chance that I could've done.'

Libby: Yeah.

Windy: As opposed to, 'Oh, if only I'd done that and if only I'd done this,' that kind of thing.

Libby: Yeah.

Windy: We don't want to turn you into Édith Piaf: 'Non, je ne regrette rien.'

Libby: Yes.

Windy: Because I don't think that's healthy either.

Libby: Yeah.... [*Pause*] Yes, I know what you mean. It's denying as well.

Windy: That's right, yeah. And, certainly with grief, there's a period of dealing with grief that is denying, but that's not the main way to deal with grief.

Libby: Yeah.

Windy: So lovely to meet you. In a couple of days I'll send you the recording. It will be through something called pCloud download link. Check all your folders because sometimes it goes into junk. Then you've got to download it within a week otherwise it disappears. Then you can listen to yourself and then draw whatever you draw from it, OK?

Libby: OK. Thank you.

Windy: All the best, bye-bye.

Libby's Reflections on the Session: 30/11/23

What My Experience Was in Having the Session

I was familiar with Windy Dryden's work and I was curious to experience it in action. Commencing the session felt strange as there was only a brief time to build a connection. At the beginning of the session, it felt like Windy was trying to find a way in and the going was slow initially. Once he found a gap it seemed to proceed quite quickly.

What Difference It Made

The structuring of the questions really helped me to understand how I was viewing the situation. It helped to give me some distance and, thus a different perspective.

'Do you have a vision of what the problem would be like if it was completely resolved?'

I had not initially realised that I had framed my wish in the negative. Windy helped me to see this. My initial goal for the session was to have another little piece or understanding that might make the regret a little easier to deal with. The question really helped me to reflect on the future and what I am looking for rather than ruminating in the past. I found it helpful to hear my own voice speaking affirmatively. It gave me a sense of control rather than feeling controlled by my thoughts about it.

There were certainly new insights around my decision-making or rather lack of decision-making. It has helped give me a new perspective, and I am less hard on myself. It is as though I can forgive myself for what I didn't know at the time. It was good to be heard and be supported in feeling the loss and not just dismissing it. Realising that I was also dismissing my own loss and my ruminating was a way not to feel my sorrow. Windy helped me see the possibility of both holding the sadness of the loss and the gratitude for what I have. It was not necessary to force myself to feel a particular way but rather the importance of acknowledging the loss before I could look at the gratitude.

It was also interesting to distinguish between healthy regret and unhealthy regret. It is not about getting rid of the wish or the desire but rather acknowledging the wish. It very much helped me to understand that avoidance is another way of rejecting my feelings. Overall, all the sense I took away was one of self-compassion for where I was at the time, and even if I could go back I could not have done it any differently.

On rereading the transcript, I was surprised to see that I had referred to 'other mothers' as though I myself was one. There was a realisation that I am a mother and I have been mothering perhaps not in the traditional sense but yet it is there. It is interesting to see the Freudian slip.

What I Have Taken from the Session

Even in one session, you can pull some threads in your original story enough to imagine other possibilities.

9

Helping People with Problems with Shame

Helping the Client to Understand and Deal with Shame

Here are some ideas that I have found useful to introduce into my conversation with clients that can help them deal with shame.

- When a person experiences shame, they hold a rigid and self-devaluation attitude towards one or more of the following adversities: (i) I have fallen very short of my ideal, usually in a social context and (ii) Others have judged me negatively when I have fallen short of my ideal (e.g. 'I said something silly in a work presentation which I absolutely should not have done. There is something wrong with me.'). Behaviourally, when the person experiences shame, they will tend to hide away from others and avoid situations where they may experience this emotion. Cognitively, the person will tend to overestimate the amount and extent of the negative evaluation they will get from others and will engage in shame-based rumination.
- The healthy alternative to shame is shame-free disappointment.
- When the person experiences shame-free disappointment about the same adversities, then they hold a flexible attitude and an attitude of unconditional self-acceptance towards these adversities (e.g. 'I really wish I had not said something silly in a work presentation, but that does not mean that I absolutely should not have done so. There may have been something wrong with what I said, but

there is nothing wrong with me. I am a fallible human capable of acting in many ways'). Behaviourally, when the person experiences shame-free disappointment, they will face others rather than hide away from them. Cognitively, the person will make realistic inferences about the amount and extent of negative evaluations they will get from others, but will not engage in shame-based rumination.

- Again, if the person is interested, I will help them change their rigid/extreme attitudes to their flexible/non-extreme counterparts and help them think and act in ways that will support the development of these attitudes.

Transcript of My Work with a Person with a Problem with Shame

Therapist – Volunteer:	Windy – Robert
Venue:	Private session that took place on 11/08/23 arranged via Onlinevents
Time:	48 minutes 52 secs

Windy: So, Robert, what's your understanding of the purpose of our conversation today?

Robert: Yeah, so I know you're developing a new therapy and you're writing a book on it, but the purpose of our conversation is to explore a particular emotion. I think I said shame, I said for myself, and, I don't know, explore it and see where we get to, I guess.

Windy: And where would you like to get to at the end of the session?

Robert: Yeah, as I said in the bit of the sheet you sent me, I think I've given my job and background and stuff – I do an awful lot of time thinking about it and trying to work it out and all that, so I don't feel as though I need to do loads of that, although a different perspective's always good. It's much more about is there some ... way that helps me deal with it better, I suppose, or find a different solution to the problem.

Windy: Why don't you, really in a nutshell if you can, describe the problem and maybe give an example that might illustrate it, and we can start from there. Does that make sense?

[My preference in ONEplus Therapy is work with an example of the person's nominated problem.]

Robert: Yeah.

Windy: Incidentally, if I need to interrupt you to keep us focused, how can I best do that?

Robert: Just interrupt me. I can handle it.

Windy: Is that alright with you?

Robert: Yeah, yeah, yeah, it's fine.

Windy: If go off beam you can interrupt me as well.

Robert: OK. So the problem, shame, I always find it hard to put a label on anything because anything's more complex than just one label, isn't it? But, if I was to summarise what I'm talking about when I say that, it's kind of a sense of something being wrong, something being bad I'd even say. I know that's quite a common way to describe it, but that's how it feels.

Windy: Something wrong and bad with what?

Robert: Within me ... like I'm carrying around almost or that's it's inside me, and it's been there ... really for as long as I can remember, like even when little.... The way I sense it more than anything is, I remember when I was little or whenever I was on my own, I always felt this kind of unsettledness and anxiety about myself, but it's always in comparison to other people and it always plays out in relationships with other people. And I don't want it to sound like, 'Oh, he's a 39-year-old and he's still stuck at something when he was little,' it's just I go back to that because it's been there that long.

Windy: Yeah, OK. And what is this thing within you that is bad, do you think?

Robert: Yeah, so, as I say, I've done a lot of thinking about it. I'd guess that my mum was really unwell when I was younger, like mentally, like suicidal at times, and there was a lot of upheaval in the family. There was a lot of pressures, like money problems and stuff. And I think I probably internalised a lot of that. That would be my best guess.

Windy: And, if you were to articulate what it is you internalise, what would that be?

Robert: I think there was a definite sense of unhappiness and having to walk on eggshells and I'd say depression and ... danger as well – you never knew when things were going to erupt and things like that. And I think maybe I took a lot of responsibility for that.

Windy: Meaning what?

Robert: ... [*Pause*] Yeah, no, that's a really good question. ... I jump to maybe I thought it was my fault, but I'm not entirely sure that's the case.... [*Pause*] Maybe ... I didn't think it was my fault but maybe I felt as though I deserved it in some way.

Windy: Deserved it because?

Robert: ... [*Pause*] Because the two children that came ahead of me, my two siblings that are older than me, they seem to have had a much better experience of being parented and seemed to do much better at school and were really well talked about and thought about.... It was only me that the seeming problems came.

Windy: Yeah. And therefore what did you conclude about yourself, do you think?

Robert: ... [*Long pause*] In some way I'm bad. In some way I'm ... naughty.

Windy: In the moral sense?

Robert: I think behaviour. And people see it. I think I carried that with me for an awful long time.

Windy: People see what?

Robert: ... It's almost like, when I walked in a room I'd expect people to ... 'Oh, he's going to be trouble,' that sort of thing. And it actually happened. Well, I don't know if it exactly happened like that, but it's the way you remember things, isn't it? I remember, when in primary school, my mum saying to me ...

[*pause*] 'The teachers have said to me that you're very different to the other two.' I don't entirely know what that was about still, but I instantly took that as, 'They think I'm trouble.'

Windy: Yeah, and, 'They think I'm trouble, they're wrong,' or, 'They think I'm trouble, they're right'?

Robert: ... [*Pause*] A bit of both, if I'm honest. They think I'm trouble.

Windy: Which bit is related to shame?

Robert: Definitely the bit that ... they're right. They're correct.

Windy: And who made that conclusion?

Robert: ... [*Pause*] But, actually, can I just come back on that, because I think they're both related to shame in a way, 'cos even the bit of me that fought for myself, I then felt as though I was wrong to do that, 'cos often I'd get angry ... and then I'd get negative repercussions about that. So both of them. Whatever I did led to me perceiving....

Windy: That what?

Robert: ... This is what I'm struggling to get to.... [*Long pause*] If I'm honest with you, Windy, I'm struggling to think of the words. It's more of an emotional kind of response. I can feel it. I'm struggling to put it into words.... [*Pause*] It's ... a real sadness.

Windy: Yeah. I'd be interested to hear how you think of shame and then I can tell you how I think of shame and see if we're on the same page. You volunteered under the heading 'shame', so it must have resonated with you. You didn't choose guilt.

[*However, I was thinking just before, 'This sounds more like guilt than shame.'*]

Robert: No.

Windy: You chose shame. So, I'm just curious about how you think of shame, so we can find out what that is.

Robert: So, in my mind, shame is ... [*pause*] a sense of ... having done something wrong or something being wrong with you. It's like ... society based. I think I often experience that in terms of relations with others, and I think that my idea of that comes from thinking about evolution. I think the purpose of it is to maybe maintain your place within a tribe or that, if you've done something wrong, it's best to hide it away and keep it hidden than it is to share it, because that might get you kicked out of the tribe in some way.

Windy: And, if you were kicked out of the tribe?

Robert: ... Well, it can be very vulnerable-making, very dangerous because you're all on your own. In the past, it was probably even more so important to ... strengthen numbers.

Windy: Let me tell you how I think about shame because I think we may be talking about two different things. I don't know. For me, shame is about two things: one is a sense of one has a standard for oneself and that one falls very short of that; and then there is a sense that one is either defective, small or diminished or disgusting. Then there's a sense of, because of that, then one has to hide away because if other people saw the same thing they would make the same evaluation. So quite often shame is involved of you putting into the minds of others how you think about yourself.

So, I think, in a way, the difference between my definition and yours is that yours, you were struggling to articulate, and maybe 'cos it's not there, a sense of 'I am,' whereas in mine it's 'I'm defective, I'm disgusting, I'm diminished. There's something wrong with me as a person: defective.'

Robert: … [*Long pause*] Yeah. No, but I don't think we're a million miles away from each other because I think there is something there, I just don't know how to put it into words, because … all my problems in relationships, not romantic relationships, I just mean with friendships and stuff like that, network and all that … it's always come from a sense of, 'They don't like me. They're going to be talking behind my back.' And, in my mind, that's got to come from a sense of, 'Well, there's got to be a reason for that,' but I just don't know maybe what it is.

Windy: Have you ever been able to draw it, draw a view of yourself that matches that experience?

Robert: I remember when I was much younger I used to draw pictures and leave them in books around the house and maybe hope that someone would see them… and, yeah, they were always very kind of … [*Long pause*] – this is what I was trying to depict in the picture, I don't know how to describe what the picture actually looked like, but to me what I was trying to get across was just the confusion of it and the feeling of really not being understood and ... [*pause*] the anger I felt towards me.

Windy: From whom?

Robert: ... [*Long pause*] Probably from everyone, really, apart from a select few, particularly relationships where I feel really close to I didn't experience that, but any other relationship I would.

Windy: Right. So it's almost a sense of, 'He's trouble. He's an outsider? Different?' that kind of thing?

Robert: Yeah.

Windy: I'm aware that that's my language.

Robert: ... [*Long pause*] Yeah, there's definitely something in there about, 'He's different to us.'

Windy: Different not in a good way.

Robert: ... [*Long pause*] Definitely not in a good way in how it left me perceiving things. ... [*Pause*] Different? ... [*Long pause*] My mind's gone blank a little bit there.... [*Long pause*] If I'm honest with you, I don't know where my mind's going but it's struggling to go there a bit.... [*Pause*] Different – I don't know, this is just instinct response, but different like, 'We need to attack him in some way.'

Windy: Yeah. 'We need to attack him because'?

Robert: ... 'Because he's a threat to us.'

Windy: Yeah.

Robert: … [*Long pause*] 'He hurts us.'

Windy: 'He hurts us,' right. So, in a way, there's a sense of being quite powerful in that difference.

Robert: Yeah.

Windy: Somebody almost like an alien who's going to be threatening you in that sense. Is that more like it, like an alien, like somebody who's different, who's going to be threatening?

Robert: Just to check, when I say … 'He's different, he's a threat, he's going to attack us,' I'm saying they're perceiving that about me. That's what I think they're perceiving about me.

Windy: Yeah. They're doing that because of something.

Robert: Yeah.

Windy: They could say, 'He's different, he's a threat, so let's get to know him. Let's see if we can bring him into the fold.' But you're not saying. It's almost like a pushing out, not bringing in.

Robert: Yeah, and I think you just hit the nail on the head a little bit. 'He's uncontrollable…. [*Pause*] If we did get close to him, we can't … shape him. He's out of control.'

Windy: Right. And to what extent did you think that you took that upon yourself as a way that you see yourself going forward?

[In this case, because my view of shame that it involves a self-judgement, I wanted to discover to

what extent Robert has internalised the view that he thinks others had of him as being difficult, threatening and uncontrollable and believes this about himself when he experiences shame.]

Robert: Hugely. I think ... it shaped probably ... if not everything, most things ... and still does.

Windy: So, 'He's a threat to us, he's going to be uncontrollable.' Let's see how this plays out in everyday life in a specific situation, see if we can go from that here to the present, see if it makes sense. Have you got a specific situation in which it plays out? You mentioned work.

[*I aware that Robert and I have been talking in general terms. I wanted to shift the level of the conversation to a level of greater specificity so that we can see how these general factors play out in daily life for Robert.*]

Robert: Yeah. Team meetings, straight away.... [*Pause*] I probably manage OK in most areas of work, but team meetings I find them extremely difficult, and they're all done online, which I think for me makes them even harder.

Windy: Right. So, let's just take an experience where this is relevant. Have you got one in mind?

Robert: So, yeah, let's say if we're discussing an idea for the team, for instance – it could be anything really – and I speak up and I share my thoughts.... [*Pause*] Well, I very quickly perceive, 'Oh, they don't like that I've spoke up or they're offended.'

Windy: What leads you to conclude that?

Robert: … [*Pause*] Maybe someone doesn't like my idea or maybe someone questions it. If I'm honest, on a bad day it could even be just that they try and shape it a bit more and all that sort of stuff. Most days I'm quite fine with that stuff, but on a bad day it could even just be what could be seen from the outside as probably a healthy conversation could leave me to perceiving, 'Oh, they've seen me back in that position again.'

Windy: Back in what position again?

Robert: Of being seen as trouble, that I'm trying to upset the system, that I can't just toe the line like they want me to.

Windy: OK. How have you dealt with that view of yourself before?

[*Here, I am looking to see how Robert has dealt with this issues previously so I can encourage him to take from these attempts helpful strategies and let go of unhelpful ones.*]

Robert: … In all honesty, in good and bad ways, probably. In the past more bad ways. When I was younger, I became very angry a lot of the time. In primary school and stuff I used to fight all the time. But to be honest, that really worked. It was a really effective strategy because it gave me a way to protect myself. But then, as I got older, other people got bigger than me but also I realised that it wasn't very good socially. So, I lost that strategy, and it left me with not many other effective strategies. I think, when I was younger, I think I went into a deep depression, really, for a long time. I really did. It was really tough, and that led me to being a victim of bullying and stuff 'cos I just had no defences, well no self-esteem so I was an easy target.

Windy: What do you think you would've done if you'd have been able to bring that self to the situation, the fighting self we might call it? What do you think would've happened there?

Robert: ... [*Pause*] Well, obviously I could've physically fought a couple of people, might've helped a little bit. But, if it was a more mature way of asserting myself, I think I could've.... You see, I didn't. I chose froze.

Windy: Right, but what could you have done?

Robert: I could've ... told people for a start. I didn't tell anyone. I just put up with it for months. So, I didn't get any help but I also didn't challenge it.

Windy: What didn't you challenge?

Robert: 'Cos a lot of the time it was very verbal, the bullying. I didn't challenge any of that. I'd just freeze and not say anything.

Windy: So, there's challenging, there's fighting in a mature way, in a sense. What else have you tried to deal with this feeling that we're calling shame?

Robert: ... [*Pause*] More lately, I've ... really focused on my role as a new father. I've got a four-year-old and a one-year-old. And as a husband as well. I've really focused on that and tried to build my self-esteem through that, which has been effective.

Windy: By saying what?

Robert: … By saying what? Well, one of the receptionists at work said I was the most anxious father-to-be she'd ever seen, and the reason for that was 'cos I truly believed that … I wasn't capable and whatever led to me getting bullied and feeling the way I did, I believed that that would happen to my children. And therefore, I'm able to tell myself now, 'Look, it hasn't happened. You've got two very healthy and happy children that are doing really well.'

Windy: Right. And how has that helped your sense of shame?

Robert: … [*Long pause*] It has helped it because…. [*Long pause*] I suppose it offers a challenge against this instinct that there's something wrong with me and maybe a foundation as well to be almost stronger from.

Windy: OK. So, when you start thinking that, 'There's something wrong with me,' you counter it by?

Robert: … [*Long pause*] Yeah, thinking about my children. They come to my mind instantly and how happy they make me and how well they're doing. The other thing I've done as well is challenged myself to do things that really scare me or that have felt impossible to do before. So, I think I wrote in the bit that I'm scared of heights, so I challenged myself to do a bungee jump.

Windy: Where did you do that?

Robert: In Manchester off a crane over a lake.

Windy: OK.

Robert: But the point about that is, whenever I've really struggled....

Windy: Can you see that?

[*I am showing Robert a picture of me doing a bungee jump. Showing that we both had done a similar jump was my way of showing him that he is part of something.*]

Robert: Is that you? You've done it?

Windy: In Queenstown in New Zealand.

Robert: It's unbelievable, isn't it?

Windy: It's fantastic. Unfortunately, I wanted to do a 300. I got high pressure in my eye and they said, 'Don't do it,' so I missed out on that experience. I'll let you do it for me. I think what you're doing will help you in part, because I think what you're doing is you're correcting that and saying, 'Look, there are other parts of me and these are: I'm courageous, I'm a good father 'cos look how my kids are turning out.' And that's fine, I wouldn't suggest that you stop doing that. But it's not going to help you necessarily with this more primitive sense that, 'He's an outsider. There's something wrong with him. We've got to be scared of him.' And you're saying, 'Well, I don't want to reconfirm that, so I'll do nothing. I'll stay silent.'

Robert: Yeah.

Windy: And I think you bring that to team meetings. It's almost like, 'Either I stay silent or it's almost like, "No, wait a minute, then they'll see me as a troublemaker, and they will be right about me," as opposed to, "and they would be wrong about me because, yeah, I have the capacity to cause trouble, but I've also got the capacity to fit in.'"

Robert: ... [*Long pause*] I'm just thinking about that, yeah. You're absolutely right. It's emotional, having this conversation, it really is because I don't ever talk about this with anyone, really. But just to say, though, it's so hard to live with. It really is. I'm so good at masking it and hiding it, but it's so painful when I experience myself as difficult. If I'm honest, when I think about me as a father, I'm really proud and really confident that ... generally, the decisions I make and my values, everything, are probably somewhere near where they need to be.

[*While I said that there is nothing wrong with Robert being courageous and focus on him being a good father, I do make the point that these things don't address the source of his shame which is his self-judgement that there is something wrong with him.*]

Windy: Sure. Do you see this?

[*I am showing Robert a wooden letter 'I' with different coloured dots.*[27]]

Robert: Yeah.

---

[27] This is a wooden letter 'I' with many different coloured dots representing the different aspects of a person. The therapeutic purpose is to encourage the client to view themselves as a complex, fallible human being, and that specific aspects of themselves cannot legitimately define them as a person. This is particularly applicable to issues of shame which involve the person giving themselves a global negative rating such as, 'I am defective' 'There is something wrong with me' or 'I am not good enough'.

Windy: What do you see?

Robert: … Well, initially I've seen an 'I' and now it's loads of little circle dots.

Windy: OK. So, this is you as a whole and these are all of your myriad of different aspects. And I think that what you've learnt through your experiences, early experiences, etc., etc., that somehow either, 'Yeah, I can be trouble, that's that little bit, and therefore that's me,' or, 'That somebody sees me as trouble as a whole and they're right.' So, I think that you can be trouble in the sense that anybody can be trouble and be seen to be trouble, if you assert yourself. One of the most common words that was said about me when people, mainly from a person-centred stance, see me do counselling is that I'm blunt. Yeah, well, I have that capacity. Does it define me? No. And I think you've learnt, through your experiences, that these things have defined you as opposed to that you, in a sense, can't be defined like that because you're far too complex, but you have the capacity to be trouble like everybody else. You've got the capacity to be wild like everybody else. Now, I'm just wondering if that resonates with you in any way.

Robert: Yeah, no, it's really powerful. Emotionally it's really powerful. I'm just sitting with that.… What came to my mind, Windy, if it's OK to share, by doing that I'm then giving them all the power.

Windy: Yeah, that's right. In a sense, shame is about being small and hiding. So, by giving them the power, you unwittingly maintain the problem.

Robert: Can you explain that a little bit more?

Windy: Well, if you give them the power, then you've got to protect yourself from them, and a way of protecting yourself is staying silent, not fighting your corner, because fighting your corner means being seen as trouble, and being seen as trouble means that you're this sort of weird outsider that is a threat and needs to be watched out for, as opposed to, 'Yeah, I can be trouble, but I'm part of the human race. I'm not this strange being outside.' That's a very powerful sense for you, I guess, 'I'm this trouble and I'm this outsider who can be a threat and I have to be controlled. I don't want to be that, so I'll give up entirely. I'll just take it.'

Robert: Well, the opposite of it is, 'cos sometimes I feel stronger, so it's almost like I've got one of two pathways and neither of them leads to a good place. I'll either go quiet and I'll become small, which is the most common one, but now again I'll be like, 'No, right, I'm going to fight them.'

Windy: Well, yes, and listen to your language: 'fight them' as opposed to 'stand up for myself'.

Robert: OK, yeah. Yeah.

Windy: You see, it's almost like you see people as adversaries and either you stay silent from them or you can fight them, as opposed to saying, 'No, actually, I don't have to do either. They're human like me and, even though I've got these two different aspects that I keep going, I need to practise more the standing up for myself, even though I've got these, "I'll fight" or "I'd better stay quiet", in the background.'

Robert: Yeah.

Windy: Because I think they are quite powerful, they're habitual ways, they're going to come up. One way you can actually do is imagine yourself, even though you've got these two bits of you, you could actually tone them down a bit. You can't eradicate them, because, if we try to eradicate parts of ourselves, they come up even more. So, you can tone them down a little bit and say, 'OK, now I'm going to assert myself even though there's these two bits of me still in the background.' How do you think of doing that?

[Here, I make the point that Robert's shame-based ways of viewing himself and others are habitual and that rather than try to eradicate them, he can respond to them by taking assertive action while accepting the existence of the habitual responses.]

Robert: How would I think about doing it?

Windy: Yeah. I mean, what do you think about doing that?

Robert: I think it's really helpful. There's a little bit about me, maybe a little bit of shame now or something that's kicking in: 'I work as a psychologist myself; I should know this stuff.'

Windy: Here's my response to that. You're a human being first and you're a psychologist 993rd.

Robert: Yeah.

Windy: My mother used to say that to me. I used to come in and she'd be angry and say, 'And you're a psychologist?'

Robert: It's really tough to look at yourself, isn't it?

Windy: Actually, you know something, you're not a psychologist. You work in the role of psychology.

Robert: Yeah.

Windy: It doesn't define you unless you choose to let it.

Robert: ... But what do I think about it? I think that's ... really helpful. It's almost like you've got those two pathways and then you've got this middle way that can be developed and learnt. Not getting rid of those two 'cos I don't want to get rid of them because, to be honest, I've probably needed them at certain points in my life.

Windy: Right, yeah. For a while you actually got people away from you. I don't know how you did it, but by being scary or this troublemaker. And the other one you probably did disappear into the ground and stayed a bit invisible. So, yeah, they have their places, but the space in the middle is a space for you to come and say, 'Actually, I'm going to rework to give birth to a new view of myself who's a human being connected to other people. I don't have to fight people. I can hold my ground and say, "Well, OK, you believe that but I'll believe this. Can we agree to differ?"'

[My goal here is to help Robert develop a non-shame-based mindset which he can rehearse (see later).]

Robert: ... That's really good to think about.... *[Pause]* I'm just trying to articulate what's going on for me. But it's almost like that shame reducing in itself the fact that, because when you hold onto this badness, you believe it's intrinsic in you and it sums up everything about you, whereas what we're saying is ... no, there might these bits of you that maybe experience that or identify with that ... [*pause*] so you might be trouble in some ways, you might be difficult in some ways, but you can also be creative and inventive and motivated and determined and become someone that actually changes yourself as well.

Windy: That's the whole package. This is you in all of your complexity, you see. I think you've learnt to define yourself as being trouble on the outside, somebody who has to be watched because they are potentially a threat. And I can understand the context in which you develop that.

Robert: Yeah.

Windy: And changing that's going to be difficult because that's how you've viewed yourself and acted. But it's quite possible to actually, as I say, give birth to a new way forward for yourself while recognising that these two things are still going to be there but you could say, 'OK, fine, I'm not an outsider. I can come and speak up and not be invisible. I can hold my ground.' One of the things you can do is to rehearse that before meetings to get yourself into that frame of mind before meetings. Part of what I'm talking about is an attitude, but there's a practice element to it. You could actually see yourself going forward into meetings with that way of viewing yourself.

Let's give you an opportunity to practise that. When's your next team meeting on Zoom?

Robert: So, it will be about three weeks from now.

Windy: So, how would you practise getting into this mindset ahead of the meeting? How would you do that?

Robert: ... [*Long pause*] I think, in some way, probably in my mind. I could draw it out as well but I'm quite capable of doing this stuff just in my mind. Just being really mindful. Well, really articulating to myself, actually, not just being mindful, like really articulating it, the three different positions. I think first of all I'd do the old two parts of myself first and maybe what they're about, maybe why they're there, because I think it's really important to understand that they've got a purpose and they're not just there out of some abnormality.... So, yeah, and almost say to myself, 'I understand how important they are but I want to move on from them. I want to develop on from them.' And then I'd probably, yeah ... start thinking more about, 'OK, so what do I want to do that's different to that?' I'd probably think about that 'i' that you just brought up – so what dot of that do I want to make bigger?

Windy: Have you got a mobile phone?

Robert: Yeah.

Windy: Do you want to take a picture?

         [*I am inviting Robert to take a picture of the wooden 'I' with multicoloured dots.*]

Robert: Yeah, could do.... [*Long pause*] There you go.... So, yeah, what dot in that would I want to make bigger? ... [*Pause*] And I think, in doing that, I'd know that... [*pause*], by emphasising another aspect, I'd probably be making those two other aspects smaller, which also, even just thinking about it, it's a bit sad. It feels a bit scary because they've been a pain for a long time but, I don't know, they've been with me for a long time as well.

Windy: Yeah, right. You can't get rid of them, first of all, but by acknowledging that they're there and recognising that they had a purpose, you can start to give them their rightful place in the update that is Robert.

Robert: … Yeah. And then I'd really want to focus, but I wouldn't want loads; like one or two main points so I can hold them in mind quite easily.

Windy: Sure, absolutely.

Robert: What is this new part of me going to do? Do you want me to go on?

Windy: Can you see yourself, for example, in a team meeting expressing a view, having it challenged and maybe saying, 'I understand where you're coming from but I'm still holding this, I still believe this,' rather than wanting to fight them or to stay silent?

Robert: … I think it will be a real challenge because I've done it for so long and it's so powerful…. [*Pause*] Let me just think. I honestly believe, when I work with clients myself, it's the uncertainty and the question marks around things that causes all the problems. It's not the being able to do it or change or the anxiety that goes with it. Actually, sorry, I'll change that. I think it's the uncertainties and the question marks that lead to the anxiety that make us not be able to change or be too scared to face it. So, whilst mapping it out like that and having that model of the third version, almost like developing a new way of being in the world ... [*pause*] yeah, it changes things remarkably just by knowing that's going on, if that makes sense.

Windy: Right, sure.

Robert: So having a model of it, I suppose.

Windy: Yeah. And thinking about the behavioural and the thinking elements of that in a meeting and allowing the feelings to be there, 'cos the feelings are going to change last. I don't know if you ever do that in your work, but often I say that think of thinking, behaviour, feeling as a three-dog greyhound race – the trap goes up, the thinking comes up, the behaviour comes up and you're starting to think in new ways and behave in new ways and, at some point, the trap of feeling comes up and starts to move. So, I encourage people to do things and think new ways and let the feelings catch up in their own time, because they will.

[*I often use this greyhound race scenario to indicate that emotional change is slow to start but will catch up, if the person persists with the linked behavioural and cognitive change.*]

Robert: OK, right. I think the real challenge for me will come when ... [*pause*] people respond to that. I think that's where, yeah, the challenge is. So, I might be able to put myself into that going into the meeting. It's when I'm reading the faces, and I might be totally misreading them, but in my mind, 'Oh, they look angry at me' or 'They look unhappy at me.'

Windy: Yeah, OK, but you could say, 'No matter how they look I'm still going to hold to the third way.'

Robert: ... [*Long pause*]

Windy: Did you ever see *The Dam Busters*?

Robert: Yeah, I did.

Windy: They're going through this narrow passage; the Germans are attacking but they're focused on their task: they're focused on dropping the bomb. So, they won't say, 'Oh, the Germans are firing at us. Let's go home. Let's go back.' No. They say, 'OK, they're firing at us. Fine. We don't like that. It would be nice if they didn't, but they are. Let's concentrate on our goal.' And you can actually have your own Dam Busters moment by recognising, 'Yes, I can't read faces. They could be angry, some of them, but let 'em be. I'm focused on my goal, which is speak my mind, hold my piece, stand my ground.'

Robert: I suppose the reason that's such a difficult and powerful thing for me is because probably – we won't go into it all, but when this was conceived, this problem, it was probably very important for me to not upset people and be aware if I was potentially doing that.

Windy: Of course. I don't want to trivialise it, but that was then, and this is now.

Robert: There's another bit as well to that, Windy, though, 'cos ... I suppose it comes back to that though, but what's more important for me than anything in the world now is what type of father am I being, what type of role model am I being.

Windy: Right.

Robert: So, if I let these Germans who are firing at me scare me and define me, I'm going to stop what I'm doing and just go back home because they're not very happy with me, but what message is that going to give to my kids?

Windy: That's right, yeah. And what message do you want to give to your kids?

Robert: ... [*Long pause*] Do not let ... [*long pause*] people that don't really know you or don't really understand you define how you see yourself. You need to define yourself and through people that you trust.

Windy: Even though it's difficult to do that going forward.

Robert: That's massively difficult and a challenge, but ... it's about building that resilience, that foundation within yourself, and you do that by, both within yourself, by challenging yourself.

Windy: That's the bit you can bring your bungee jump self, because you can do it even though you're scared, right?

Robert: Yeah.

Windy: So, you can hold your ground even though you're scared.

Robert: … [*Pause*] But also being able to recognise whose opinion it is worth paying attention to.

Windy: Exactly. So, we have to finish in a minute, so do you want to quickly summarise what we've done and what you're going to take away from this?

Robert: … [*Long pause*] Well, we've kind of come up with a rough definition of shame. I think it's a bit different between us both, but these things can be sometimes. But it made sense to me anyway, what I've experienced…. And … from that, we've looked at … how I experience that, how it's played out in my life, both maybe in the past but also in the present. And then … [*pause*] it's been really helpful to think about that I've become almost too entrenched in these certain aspects of myself, and I'm made up of many aspects. And, actually, maybe I struggle to hold onto it, but I've already proven that to myself in many ways…. [*Pause*] And the importance of taking my own messages that I'm trying to instil in my kids, taking them on myself as well in terms of, 'Why am I letting these people define me and why am I being … shaped into … withdrawing and shutting down because of my perception of people's reactions, which might have absolutely nothing to do with me anyway?'

Windy: 'And my perception of myself in the face of their presumed reactions.'

Robert: Yeah. Just that importance of … looking at the things I am getting right: being a father, being a husband. It takes a lot of guts to even keep going and keep challenging yourself and keep trying. I'm doing all that. I'm not getting it right all the time but I'm certainly trying.

Windy: And you can bring that into the team meetings as well. OK. So, have you got what you'd come for?

Robert: … Yeah, definitely. Oh yeah, it's given me, which is what I asked for, isn't it, it's been helpful to think through it. I think we always have to do that to some extent, but having a different way to attempt to reduce it in the future.

Windy: Lovely, OK. So, I'll send you the recording later. It's been great to meet you.

Robert: Thank you very much, Windy. It's been great to meet you as well.

Windy: OK then. All the best, bye-bye.

Robert: Thank you, bye.

Robert's Reflections on the Session: 22/11/23

Honestly, I was so keen to volunteer that I didn't fully take the time to consider my common emotional problem. This is not to suggest that I was not struggling, just that I was uncertain with which emotion in particular. Following my selection, I do remember feeling uneasy and wondering whether I would be 'found out'. The emotion I had chosen was shame.

For the next few weeks, I was excited as I have been a fan of Windy's work since training, plus the realisation that he is also a fellow counselling psychologist just made this more special. Upon meeting Windy I remember thinking how I perceived him instantly as more forthright than I had anticipated. I am aware this might just have been due to my anxiety and anyway is probably a useful, if not necessary, skill in the art of particularly short-term therapy. I like to think of myself as open-minded and flexible though, and quickly decided to go with it. I was very aware that this was a one-off encounter, which meant I felt pressure to put aside anxieties around trust and just accept the other as well-intentioned. Rather than this making the process more difficult though, I think it actually made it easier, as I did not have the time to ruminate and instead simply focused on the issue I had come for assistance with.

In the session I remember feeling heard, understood and challenged (the latter being really important to me). Though it has taken listening to the recording to really begin to appreciate and understand the journey we had covered in such a short time. The initial discussion about our different perspectives on shame has proved really beneficial. Although I remember at the time, paradoxically, feeling ashamed due to my earlier outlined insecurities around this as my defined difficulty. Now when I think of this discussion, it helps me recognise my need to define my problems more accurately, as to not do so is likely intensifying my anxieties. At another point in our encounter, I shared how I struggle to speak up in work meetings as it leads me to perceive others think I am difficult, a trouble causer and that this defines me as a colleague. Windy's explanation of how actually this is just an aspect of my multi-faceted persona, using his wooden coloured 'I', I experienced as very powerful and is probably the element of our work that has most stuck with me.

It is now around three months since our session, and of course, life moves on, with new and old problems making themselves known to lesser and more degrees. When I recall the session with Windy, I feel positive and hold it as a memory for which I am glad I volunteered. I think the experience has changed a small part of me for the better, and I would summarise this as challenging my relational model when it comes to feeling heard, supported and helped. I guess I always believed it was trust that enabled personality transformation but now I wonder whether my focus on trust might sometimes just be getting in the way.

10

Helping People with Problems with Unhealthy Anger

Helping the Client to Understand and Deal with Unhealthy Anger

Here are some ideas that I have found useful to introduce into my conversation with clients that can help them understand and deal with unhealthy anger.

- When a person experiences unhealthy anger, they hold a rigid and extreme attitude towards one or more of the following adversities: (i) Another person (or you, yourself) has transgressed an important personal rule; (ii) Another person has disrespected you; and (iii) You have been frustrated in your pursuit towards (e.g. 'You put me down in public which you absolutely should not have done. You are bad for doing so'). When you experience unhealthy anger, you feel like attacking the object of your anger and engage in revenge-based rumination.
- The healthy alternative to unhealthy anger is healthy anger.
- When the person experiences healthy anger about the same adversities, then they hold a flexible attitude and a non-extreme attitude towards these adversities (e.g. 'I really wish you had not put me down in public, but this does not mean that you absolutely should not have done so. What you did was bad, but you are not a bad person. You are a fallible human being who did the wrong thing'). When you experience healthy anger, you want to assert yourself with the other rather than attack them and you don't engage in revenge-based rumination.

214

- Again, if the person is interested, I will help them change their rigid/extreme attitudes to their flexible/non-extreme counterparts and help them think and act in ways that will support the development of these attitudes.

Transcript of My Work with a Person with a Problem with Unhealthy Anger

Therapist – Volunteer:	Windy – Tab
Venue:	Private session that took place on 18/08/23 arranged via Onlinevents
Time:	41 minutes 37 secs

Windy: So, Tab, did I ask you what name you want to be known as in the book?

Tab: Tab's fine. I don't mind it being mine.

Windy: You can always change it if you want to do that later. So what's your understanding, Tab, of the purpose of our conversation today?

Tab: I know I picked about underlying anger issues and exploring how that would be looked at in a single session.

Windy: OK, fine. What do you hope to achieve as a result of our discussion today?

Tab: I suppose it's almost getting a bit of insight into perhaps the things that I struggle with. Almost that knowing that what I'm dealing with at the moment is like a normal response from how I've dealt with anger before or perhaps how that emotion's been shown to me. A way to manage it better, ultimately, I think, even if it's just not to solve anything as such because it's still an emotion that I want to feel. It's more just how I manage it in general.

Windy: Yeah. I make a distinction which, if you're interested in, later on I can discuss it if it comes up between healthy and unhealthy anger.

[*I make this distinction at the outset so that we can make use of it later, if necessary.*]

Tab: Yeah.

Windy: For example, Martin Luther King had healthy anger. It wasn't necessarily going to feel, 'Oh well, there's injustice. That's unfortunate.' But he channelled that feeling into constructive behaviour. So, you've given me an interesting breakdown of things with one exception: I don't know what you get angry about.

Tab: Yeah. It's one of those things, it's quite broad. I feel like, to me, it wasn't since I started looking at anger being more than just anger, it was the build up from being annoyed, irritated, frustrated, and exploring that as a rage. Understanding that rage as almost like the last level of it. And I think, ultimately, it's always been anger that's been the one feeling and emotion that I haven't seemed to, I guess, accept maybe and not know how to express that in a way that is perhaps socially acceptable.

So it's various things. It could be as little as day-to-day things of getting annoyed slightly that the trains are busy. For me, it's not like just a little frustration. It's like, oh gosh, I can feel it within me.

Windy: We can talk about the trains if you like and I can help you to deal with that or are there any other situations that you do say, 'Well, look, if I could really deal productively with that situation, then that would be a useful thing to take away from the session'?

[Here, I am inviting Tab to choose a focus for the session.]

Tab: I would say it perhaps links strongly to a little bit with procrastination and how I use my time when I don't have anything to do. That's a big one for me where it does consume me and then I just feel like I'm in this pit bubbling away. It's any second I'm just going to lose it.

Windy: And what happens if you lose it?

Tab: Well, this is the part where I'm stuck with because growing up I know whenever I had that sort of frustration or aggressive side, I guess, I would always be quite physical, like throwing things at people or lashing out and doing stuff like that. Obviously, as an adult I don't want to be doing that.

Windy: What do you do for a living?

Tab: So, I am a therapist on the outside and then I've started as a pastoral tutor at a college.

Windy: You could be known as the Angry Throwing Therapist.

Tab: Yeah. It's that typical thing where I'm saying to people about anger is something, if you suppress it and push it down, it's still there underneath. It's like that volcano that's just about to erupt.

Windy: And do you ever throw things now?

Tab: I don't.... I suppose, instead of intentionally throwing something, it will be like slamming a book down quite hard or perhaps pushing a door a bit more, so it slams instead of just shuts.

Windy: What do those actions do for you?

Tab: It feels like there's some kind of release, I guess, because it's almost that energy of needing to just get something out.

Windy: Right. And you want to change that as well or what?

Tab: … I guess it's like … doing it in a way that I know isn't going to, perhaps I suppose being around other people, being that shocking, 'Oh my gosh.'

Windy: So, you don't mind doing it for yourself, if you're around yourself, but you just don't want to show that side to others?

Tab: Yeah. I mean, towards myself there's been a few times that I can think of where I have had that moment of just, I don't know, ripping pictures down off a wall or I've just had that, it's a bit like a tantrum.

Windy: Yeah. That's a sign of unhealthy anger, when you want to destroy things, you want to throw things, break things. I think you've probably grown up learning to control that a little bit 'cos you're not doing it that much. There's still that feeling as if you want to.

Tab: Yeah.

Windy: So that's what we call an action tendency and, even though you don't act on it, you feel as if you want to. That, for me, is a sign that the anger is unhealthy.

              [*I wish I had asked Tab if she agreed with me about this. Not doing so is an error.*]

Tab: Yeah.

Windy: So you mentioned procrastination. By the way, are we talking about anger towards self or anger towards others? What do you struggle with the most?

Tab: I think it ultimately is towards myself because, to use the example of procrastination, even today having this session, so since I've woke up I've had that like, it's not that I have to get stuff done today. It's almost like, 'Actually, it would be helpful if I got this blog post finished' or 'Maybe if I'd done this and that' and I don't and I just sit there. It's that kind of critical talk comes into mind where it's like, 'Tab, what are you doing? You're just sitting there wasting hours.' Then that starts the boiling process of it just really is that. It's almost like I can see versions of me shouting at myself going, 'Come on, you need to get with it. You need to do this and do that.' And I suppose to not inflict any of that kind of destroying or harm to myself, that's when it goes outwards. That's when it is I need to do things like punch a pillow or go outside.

Windy: The first episode which you mentioned, which is the train, you're not involved in running the trains but you're still getting angry about that. But the main thing is you want to deal with your anger towards yourself. Maybe, if we have some time, we can circle back and help you to deal with the train type situation. So, there you are, you're procrastinating, you're putting things off that you want to do at a particular time. So, what are you angry about at that point?

Tab: I think I'm angry because I know I can just do it and I know that in the short term it will save me stress, it will save me even more frustration to just get things done, or actually I suppose that I want to do them.

Windy: Yeah, OK. So, you're getting angry because you're not acting in the way that you want to, right?

Tab: Yeah, 'cos it doesn't feel like an unrealistic expectation. I think days where I've been at work it's whether it's that difference of like you go to work, you have to be working, it's not like you can just say, 'Well, I'll do this later,' and whatnot. So, I think it's more those days where I have that flexibility.

Windy: Yeah. It sounds like you want to do things that you want to do and, when you notice that you're not, you start to get critical of yourself and then get angry at yourself.

Tab: Yeah.

Windy: How have you tried to deal with that kind of situation before, Tab?

[*This is a typical ONEplus Therapy question concerning the person's previous attempt to solve the problem.*]

Tab: I think, ultimately, it's been trying to be compassionate towards myself.

Windy: How does that sound on this occasion: there you are procrastinating, getting angry at yourself, how does self-compassion sound for you?

Tab: For me, it's more saying, 'Today obviously you're not feeling in the right mindset' or 'The day's not finished yet so you don't know if actually something might be achieved by the end of it', and checking in if there's any expectations going on there.

Windy: Expectations about what?

Tab: About me and what I should be doing.

Windy: Well, there is. You want to do the piece of work.

Tab: Yeah.

Windy: So, that's clear. So, it sounds like you're trying to, through your compassion, to indicate that there's time later to do it. Does that help you with your anger?

Tab: It can sometimes because I think it will be things, for example, if I have had quite a busy beginning of the week, for example, and it gets to Thursday or Friday and I think, 'Well, it's not like I've done nothing all week and I'm allowed to have a day to do nothing or do whatever.' That comes across. And I think it's more that time where it's been several days in a row that I'm like I've still put something off.

Windy: It's more repetitive when you've put off things not one day, which you could say, 'Well, I'll do it later,' and then later comes and you still haven't done it and then later comes and you still haven't done it. At that point do you get angry with yourself rather than compassion?

Tab: Yeah.

Windy: And how else have you tried to deal with that more repetitive putting off?

[*I meant to ask how else Tab has dealt with her anger.*]

Tab: I've tried things like, because I used to be a very big list-maker, some of the lists that I look back on I think I don't even think people can do that in a week, let alone living with everything else that goes on in life, meeting your basic needs as well. So what I used to do was sit down and go, 'Right, here's everything that I wanna do,' but then I'd scale it back. So I'd almost pick even one thing to do a day, so it didn't feel like so much pressure. And then it was like, if I did do that one thing and I was still like, 'Oh, let's go onto the next thing,' I'm feeling with it, I'm feeling that motivation. That felt a lot more rewarding rather than having a list of say five or six things on it and not getting anything done.

Windy: Right. But how has making a list helped you with the situation that we're talking about, which is when you get angry with yourself because you continue to put off something that you want to do?

[*I get back on track here by asking Tab how making a list has helped her with her anger rather than her procrastination.*]

Tab: I don't think it has helped me because it's almost a reminder. I feel like it's the same thing that I write out. So, I'm just reminding myself of something that I haven't achieved yet and I fall into that, 'Are you really going to do it? Is there any point writing it?'

Windy: Right. One thing it sounds like you don't do is to try to figure out why you're procrastinating in the first place. You're getting angry with yourself for procrastinating rather than standing back and saying, 'I wonder what's going on for me that I'm putting it off?' And that is a typical thing, that you never get to that, because you're getting angry at yourself.

So let me give you my take, if you're interested.

Tab: Yes

[*I think I could have given more weight to this invitation. My 'take' as discussed in Chapter 4 is based on ideas from Rational Emotive Behaviour Therapy.*]

Windy: You start off with a perfectly healthy desire, which is, 'I really want to do this. I really don't want to be putting this off anymore.' So that's fine. Then you tell me which of the following two attitudes, because there's only two attitudes that are possible and realistic in that situation: a flexible one or a rigid one. The flexible one says, 'Look, of course I really want to get this done and it is annoying that I can't. However, I don't have to do what I want to do because there's obviously something stopping me and I need to find out what that is. Therefore, I'm having a problem and I'd better accept the fact that I've got the problem. I don't have to be problem free.' Now, the rigid one says almost like bullshit: 'You want to do it? Do it. You have to do it. You have to do it.' Now, which attitude do you think drives your anger towards yourself?

Tab: I can confidently say the second one. Yeah.

Windy: I agree with you, Tab. How would you feel if you really believed the first one?

Tab: … I guess calmer … and I guess … it would feel like I'm connecting more with myself. It's not that voice that's criticising. It's more what's going on for me behind that.

Windy: Yeah. You're still not doing what you want to do, but you're recognising, 'OK, there's something going on here. I don't have to do what I want to do. There's a blockage here and I need to find out what that blockage is.' That's what often procrastination is. So, what you end up by doing is being very creative, Tab – this is not unique to you, this is part of the human condition – you start off with one problem, procrastination, and now you're giving yourself a second problem, anger. Buy one get one free. Now, in order to get to the point where you could then stand back and say, 'What the hell's going on? What am I avoiding?' in order to do that which anger's going to help you to do that: the healthy, nondemanding, flexible anger or the rigid, demanding, inflexible anger?

Tab: Yeah, the healthy one, for sure.

Windy: How would you put that into your own words?

Tab: ... [*Pause*] It's a much more understanding anger.

Windy: No, how would you put the attitude into your own words? I wasn't being clear enough.

Tab: ... [*Long pause*] I'm not too sure.... [*Pause*] It is that compassion I feel, that attitude of ... just holding a bit of space for you and having that breather, I guess. Instead of going from zero to a hundred, it's much more of a, 'Hey, what's going on?'

Windy: Yeah, and a recognition that you don't always have to do what you want to do.

Tab: Yeah. When you said then about what am I avoiding, why am I avoiding it, I've never thought to ask myself that.

[*The danger in situations like this is that the therapist switches from Tab's anger – the agreed focus – to her problem with procrastination*]

Windy: No, of course not, because you're angry with yourself. You don't get to ask yourself that question. And that's one of the reasons why, with the anger that we're talking about, it doesn't help you to solve problems. It creates a second problem other than helping you to solve the first problem. You could then go on and ask yourself, once you got into that state of mind, and then you can add the compassion: 'Yeah, I've got a problem. I'm like millions of other people with procrastination.' Do you know my joke about procrastination?

Tab: No.

Windy: I've written a book on overcoming procrastination. It's my best seller but least read book. 'But it's on my bedside table!'

Tab: It is funny, because I'm at my parents', the book I've brought away with me is about procrastination. It's one of those 'Get motivated in five steps'.

Windy: Yeah, and that's good, but, in order to transition to that, so to speak, you need to deal with that gap between what you want to do and what you're doing. You've got a problem, you're getting angry with yourself for having the problem. That creates a second problem. You never get back to solving the first problem. So, if you could really say, 'Yeah, I've got a problem and that's the reality. I don't have to be problem-free, for God's sake. I'm like other people. Now, let me just accept that and now figure out what am I avoiding.'

              The other thing you mentioned which struck me,[28] and now I understand it a little bit better, is that you're talking about impulsive behaviour about money?

Tab: Yeah. So that's something that I definitely recognise when I'm in that … I suppose it's a little bit of a self-blame and, like I said, that critical voice comes in. When I have the energy and what I've said before about that bubbling … I almost feel like that's an act of destroying something. It's not destroying something physically but it's destroying my bank account.

---

[28] I am referring to one of Tab's responses on the pre-session questionnaire I sent her.

Windy: OK, so give me an example of that so I can understand it better, if you find that useful to do?

[I make this shift and wish I hadn't because I am not sure I have sufficiently helped Tab develop an attitude-based solution to her unhealthy anger problem in the example she provided when she procrastinates.]

Tab: Yeah. So I think it was a thing. So I quit my job back in April or May simply for the fact of having a bit of a nervous breakdown. So I was left in a position where money was going to be tight for the foreseeable future as far as I was aware. But I remember I still acted as if nothing had happened or I didn't take into account, 'OK, I need to start budgeting a bit better. I need to be careful with where my money is going.' And I just felt a bit reckless, I guess, that reckless impulsiveness where I'd go up town, spend nearly £100 on stuff, come back and I'd just sit there and be like, 'What the fuck have you done?' It was like I was telling myself off.... Again, I just remember sitting there, getting so emotional. It wasn't coming out but there was a screaming in my head. It's like I could vision myself just going wild, having that ultimate outburst, the fact that I've been so careless at a time when it's really not. It's going to impact that.

Windy: And then what happened? What did you do?

Tab: Most times when I've had that angry outburst, I've then just sat there, felt a bit sorry for myself and then got on with it. And I remember returning all the stuff the next day 'cos I was like, 'I can't have it.'

Windy: The other thing to look at with anger is, although if we look at the episode, did you feel like throwing things?

Tab: Yeah.

Windy: And did you?

Tab: No, I didn't.

Windy: So how quickly did you calm yourself down?

Tab: … I'd say maybe in like, all round, an hour from going from that sitting back down.

Windy: So, even if you do nothing with that anger, you give yourself – I know in an hour, if you're really angry, you could do a lot of damage, but we don't think we're talking about that kind of anger. So, even if you did nothing about that, it's like a process, isn't it? And it sounds a little bit like the procrastination: you're into what I call the mode of an ostrich – 'I have a problem, I don't want to think about it. I need to distract myself about it. I'm feeling bad. I want to feel good. How do I feel good? Retail therapy.' You go off, you buy these things, then you come back and say, 'What the fuck have I done?' basically, 'And I should not have done it.'

Tab: Yeah.

Windy: Now, at that point, how could you be flexible about what you did so you don't even have to have an hour of that unhealthy anger?

[I am helping Tab to generalise from the anger-related procrastination example to this one

concerning her unhealthy anger related to her impulsive buying.]

Tab: ... [*Pause*] I guess perhaps ask myself ... not why I've done it but almost ... that checking again about what else has been going on. What was I thinking of when I was going around and getting it. But now I realise and I've bought the stuff, what can I do? What choice do I have?

Windy: Right, but you still need to deal with the mismatch between what you did and what you would've preferred to have done in that situation. You see there's a mismatch, in the same way with procrastination there's a mismatch between what you want, which is to get on with things and not have a problem with it, and the reality which is you're not; you're procrastinating. So, there's a mismatch again. You have an idea of how you would like to deal with the situation, which was what in this case? How would you have liked to have handled it instead of spending?

Tab: ... Do something different with that energy. Not put it on a debit card.

Windy: OK, fine, to deal with that in a different way. You see the mismatch between what you wanted to do, and what you did?

Tab: Yeah.

Windy: And you're basically saying, 'I shouldn't have done this. I should've done that,' but in a rigid, absolute way, not, 'Yeah, I really wish I had done that, but I didn't because I acted in a way that I did, what was going through my mind at the time. Let me accept myself for that' – this is where self-acceptance comes into it – 'let me then bring in self-compassion – what else was going on? How can I understand this?' And, again, I think you were dealing with things in a very human way, which is why I always say Charles Darwin was wrong: we're not descended from the apes, we're descended from the ostrich – a great tendency to bury our heads in the sand and then we come up and go, 'Where's the shopping? Let's go shopping. I've got to make myself feel better about this,' as opposed to, 'No. OK, that's what I did. Fine. That's the reality. I don't have to be different.' Then you could go back and actually have a look at what else was going on and then, 'Well, I do need to deal with this original problem,' which you've gotten further away from, haven't you?

Tab: Yeah.

Windy: Do you see the similarity between the two situations?

Tab: Yeah.

Windy: Now, the one thing that I want to help you with that you mentioned that we haven't yet got to, and that is I call anger, the type that you're talking about, the Porsche of emotions. Do you know why?

Tab: Why?

Windy: Because you can go from 0 to 60 in a split second. So, you need to become good, in my view, of actually recognising the beginnings of an episode, because when you're at 60 this flexible thinking is going out the window. It's not going to do it. So, what's the first sign for you that you're beginning to get angry?

Tab: It's definitely … feeling impatient with things, being short with others.`

Windy: And where do you experience that?

Tab: Mainly at home with my flatmate.

Windy: No, in your body?

[*That's what happens when you ask an unclear question!*]

Tab: It's always my arms and my hand and sometimes in my chest.

Windy: But the arms. Any particular: left, right?

Tab: No, both of them.

Windy: What's the feeling?

Tab: Very tense.

Windy: OK, 'I'm getting tense.' I'm going to give you something which my mentor, Albert Ellis, suggests, which is based on what we're talking about. At that point you can ask yourself, 'What am I demanding? What am I saying has to happen, either in the world or in my behaviour?' Do you think you need to stand back in order to do that, literally stand back, or how you can respond to that initial tension to give yourself an opportunity to get into that thinking mode?

Tab: Often, I find it's leaving the space that I'm in for a moment, because it gets physically out of there to then be like, 'What's going on?'

Windy: OK, fine. So, ask the question and then recognise you've got two choices: 'Am I saying I have to do this or I want to do this but I don't have to? If I'm saying I have to do that,' what could you then do to get yourself into that more flexible frame of mind?

Tab: Remind myself that that's coming from that sort of rigid place, and I haven't reached 60 yet so I still have that flexibility to change that.

Windy: Yeah, 'I don't have to do what I want to do. But, because I want to do it, let's see what I need to attend to.' Now, when I asked you where you experienced it, you said in the flat. Who do you live with?

Tab: I live with … my friend who used to be my partner. It's a very complicated environment.

Windy: Which we ain't got time to get into. Is it a him or her?

Tab: It's a him … and I think I've always been the more emotionally expressive one, but, even with that anger, it's still been one I've tried to keep private.

Windy: So, what do you get angry with respect to him?

Tab: Oh gosh! Doing things like doing the washing up and expecting around of applause like it's a big achievement, where I'll probably spend at least a couple of hours a day cleaning. It's that indifference, if that's the right word to use, of doing more than he does but not feeling like I can get annoyed at him because he's the one that pays the bills and everything. So, it feels like that imbalance.

Windy: Right. So, one dynamic is that you recognise that you do more than him and, when he does something, there's this round of applause expecting. Is that what you get angry about, the fact that he wants that round of applause even though you do more?

Tab: Yeah, and I think it's more like as well not seeing what I do. I feel like I have to justify my days. That's something I get angry about.

Windy: Because he sits you down and says to you, 'Justify your day?' or what?

Tab: No. It is, 'How's your day been?' and I know if I've had a day of just sitting there putting things off, getting wound up, I feel almost a bit of shame.

Windy: And how do you handle that shame?

Tab: I lie a little bit and I say, 'Oh, I've done this, I've done that,' I think of all these very small tasks and make them seem really elaborate to then get that, 'Oh, that's really good.'

Windy: Do you also get angry towards him for asking you?

Tab: I have before when it has been very consistent, where I've done that, 'Why do you bother asking me when you know I haven't worked or you know I haven't been out?' kind of thing.

Windy: So, if we were to look at the schema that we've talked about here, in terms of when you get angry towards him, what's the mismatch between the way he is and the way you want him to be?

Tab: ... [*Long pause*] I don't know. I feel like it's like when you're trying to make someone something they're not and you can't change that, and I don't have that. Our behaviours are different, so, even if I wanted him to be a certain way, he's not going to be.

Windy: Right. And do you remind yourself of that when you're getting angry or not, when he does a plate and turns round and says, 'Look what I've done!'?

Tab: I do get a bit sarcastic, which again is a form of being....

Windy: It doesn't sound like anger is playing too much of an issue at home in your flat, even though when I said to you where do you feel it most you said, 'In the flat.' But, as we look at it, we're not talking about the same kind.

Tab: No. It does feel a bit more gentle.

Windy: So, are there any situations that we can discuss where, if you went away and we didn't discuss it, you would say, 'I missed an opportunity to discuss this,' what would that 'this' be with respect to anger?

Tab: ... [*Long pause*] I'm also not too sure. I can't pinpoint an exact thing. I suppose at the moment one thing I've continued to hold that anger about is the situation with, like I said, my flatmate who used to be my partner, who's no longer my partner, who has put me in a position where I have to move out. And

I've started a job in the last month, I have no savings, so I'm fully dependent on this person.... I just feel that anger's towards me, towards my actions, my behaviour. That's what I'm ultimately angry with at the moment, things that I can't change but have impacted me presently now.

Windy: Right. Let me see if I understand that. You have to move out, you're in a situation whereby you've just started a job but you don't have the financial capacity to move out?

Tab: Yeah.

Windy: And what are you angry about in that situation?

Tab: Because the reason why I don't have the financial funds is due to leaving that job that I mentioned in April. It took me from end of March until mid-June to find another one. So that's five months with no income, no financial freedom.

Windy: That's tough, yeah, right.

Tab: And it ultimately makes me angry at leaving the job, even though I knew I couldn't....

Windy: Angry at yourself?

Tab: Yeah.

Windy: So, you're angry at yourself for leaving a job because of the consequences of leaving the job.

Tab: Yeah.

Windy:	So, it sounds like to me that you're saying, 'I wish I could've seen then what I see now.' And are you saying, 'And therefore that's the way it absolutely should've been. I absolutely should've been able to see that,' or are you saying, 'Yeah, that would've been nice, but, unfortunately, there's no reason why I have to do that. I don't have that capacity as a human being, but I wish I had'? Which kind of anger are we talking about?
Tab:	Yeah, I should've seen it.
Windy:	Well, that's a great trick, isn't it? 'I should've been able to do then what I know now.' And, again, that's a rigid should. How would a flexible attitude sound like when you look and wished, because there's nothing wrong with the wish? It would be nice. I get up in the morning and say, 'I wish I had hair,' but I don't. I don't have to have it but it would be nice to have it. So how would it play out for you when you look back and say, 'I wish I knew then what I know now'?
Tab:	It would sound like me saying, 'I wish I knew then what I know now,' but at that time I was putting myself first. I was looking after myself mentally. I was in pure survival mode and I couldn't have predicted we'd have got to this stage. And, again, it's almost like there's no rush.
Windy:	Again, if you really spot that anger, ask yourself what you're demanding, step back, see your choice between that rigid attitude and a more flexible attitude. Put the flexible attitude in your own words and then process it with the help of some self-compassion thrown in, if you want. That's fine. That will help you again. So, it's about really looking at

anything when you start to get angry, ask yourself that question: 'What am I demanding?' It sounds like more of yourself than other people. Yeah, you can get angry at the train timetable, but it's mainly about yourself.

Tab: Yeah.

Windy: OK, do you want to summarise, Tab, what we've talked about and then we can talk about what you're going to take away?

Tab: Yeah. I think it's ultimately been exploring what kind of anger I have and really identifying that difference between the rigid and the flexible. That's something I never really took into account. Exploring the different areas that affect me and actually realising how much it's internal and not external. And just the times that I need to ask myself what I am demanding and having that check-in ultimately, which is something I've never done.

Windy: Yeah and utilise the more physical signs in your arms that something is brewing that you need to pay attention to vis-à-vis anger.

Tab: Yeah, definitely.

Windy: Before we finish is there anything that you want to say that you wished you may have said later or asked that you wished you may have asked later? Anything you want to cover?

Tab: No. I think it's opened my mind up to a little bit of a, 'OK, we've got some stuff to consider going forward.'

Windy: Yeah, and that's what single-session therapy is about. It's not about the end of something. It's opening up something that you can take ahead with you. Excellent. I will be in touch. I will send you the recording tonight, so look out for an email from pCloud. Check all your folders and download it quickly because after a week they get rid of it.

Tab: Awesome. Thank you. Bye.

          [*This session shows, I think how an attitude-based solution can help someone with unhealthy anger when what they had tried before was not providing an adequate solution to the problem.*]

Tab's Reflections on the Session: 29/11/23

As I have started different therapies before I never really know what to expect or how I will feel in the session. Windy was able to create a space and addressed my responses in a way, that I was able to just continue unravelling the layers of my frustration and anger. I was quite hesitant into being able to get much out from the session but the way it was cultivated and how Windy engaged with myself I felt like it was more than I've said in years to anyone. For it being an emotion, I've normally felt shame around and in how I 'manage' it, it was nice to be given that space to be challenged but also have explained the difference between ways of thinking – being self-critical, etc.

I think the part where Windy said about having a problem, then getting angry because of that and creating a second problem was something that stayed with me for a while. I felt I was able to identify quicker when I was starting the unhealthy desire of getting too much done and then getting worked up also with not starting. The difference has been made through questioning. When I notice myself getting worked up that self-blame voice being present, I ask myself what am I trying to avoid here? And, if it's coming from that rigid place. If I feel I must do something making sure I can allow in that acceptance and compassion after if it doesn't get done and be okay with that. Towards the end of the session, I mentioned about the anger towards my ex-partner who I was due to be moving out from and have now. Even with exploring this momentarily in the session and the recognition of 'justifying your day' that for sure used to be like lighting the match to the fire of being asked 'what have you been up to today?'. Since moving out, although the stress has come with it I feel as though I've left some of that rigid thinking behind, I feel a lot more open and accepting to things not going accordingly to plan, and also having the understanding of I can't see the future and know all that's to come, and that's OK!

11

Helping People with Problems with Hurt

Helping the Client to Understand and Deal with Hurt

Here are some ideas that I have found useful to introduce into my conversation with clients that can help them understand and deal with hurt.

- When a person experiences hurt, they hold a rigid and extreme attitude towards one of the following adversities: (i) Another person whom you value is less invested in your relationship with them than you are; (ii) Another person whom you value has let you down or betrayed you, and you think that you are undeserving of such treatment (e.g. 'My best friend doesn't care about me as much as I care about her because she went out with another friend and did not invite me. She must care about me as much as I care about her, and it is terrible that she doesn't'). When you experience hurt. You tend to sulk and engage in hurt-based rumination.
- The healthy alternative to hurt is hurt-free sorrow.
- When the person experiences hurt-free sorrow about the same adversities, they hold a flexible and non-extreme attitude towards these adversities (e.g. 'I really wish my best friend cares about me as much as I care about her, but sadly she does not have to do so. It is bad that she doesn't but not terrible.' When you experience hurt-free sorrow, you want to discuss how you feel with the other rather than sulk and you don't engage in hurt-based rumination.

240

- Once again, if the person is interested, I will help them change their rigid/extreme attitudes to their flexible/non-extreme counterparts and help them think and act in ways that will support the development of these attitudes.

Transcript of My Work with a Person with a Problem with Hurt

Therapist – Volunteer:	Windy – Anna
Venue:	Private session that took place on 07/08/23 arranged via Onlinevents
Time:	48 minutes 14 secs

Windy: So, Anna, what is your understanding of the purpose of our conversation today?

Anna: I guess my understanding is that I will explore the issue with you, that hopefully I will have some kind of insight from that which I ... already have insight but it would be great to have another person's insight. Ideally, it would help me cope with the feeling of hurt when it arises better than I do, not that I cope with it that badly, but an internal sensation is what I have, and I would like to be able to get through that and recover from it quickly and not particularly act out on the hurt should I feel it.

Windy: OK. So, you say that you have been dealing with it yourself. By the way, is it OK if I refer to your pre-session form?

Anna: Yeah, totally.

Windy: One other thing, this is about being focused so, if I need to interrupt you, Anna, what's the best way that I can do that from your perspective?

Anna: By just suddenly start talking and, if I keep talking, saying, 'May I say something?' It's fine.

Windy: 'May I say something,' OK.

Anna: I'm quite longwinded, so please do interrupt me.

Windy: Well, I'm a short Windy. OK, so you were saying that you have received some help through therapy.

Anna: I've had a lot of therapy in my days.

Windy: So, I'm just wondering what's your understanding of the factors that make up your hurt and how have you been successful so far in dealing with it?

[*Here I am checking on Anna's understanding of hurt and what has helped her to deal effectively with it in the past.*]

Anna: Interestingly, the first thing I would say is that, when I was looking at the choice of things to choose for having a session with you, I looked at it, and I thought, 'hurt'. Then I thought, 'This is bizarre.' Even though hurt has been something I'm very familiar with, I never, in a sense, used that word in quite the way that really jumped out at me. So, since then I've been thinking about the various issues, I have around the theme of hurt, which in and of itself has been helpful, interestingly, the idea of naming it. So, in terms of me understanding what that's about, I'd say the most significant aspect of my life is probably my mother died when I was 13 years old and then the story after that for the next years of my adolescence was very much one of rejection and then abandonment and leaving the country and being very much on my own. And the way that I actually, I think took that on board was, 'There's something wrong with me.' And I think that, basically, when I'm feeling it, because by this age I generally don't feel jarred by stuff, but certain things feel like they really cut in, and that's stuff which is like rejection, basically. Rejection or being ignored.

So, especially since planning this session, I've been thinking about I really tried to boil it down myself, recognising this is single session, let's get to the point in a way.

Windy: Good, OK. So, what I call the adversity is rejection and being ignored. Are they the same for you or are they different?

Anna: … Good question. I think rejection is a bigger category. Being ignored. I'm sure I could think of other ways. Fear of rejection. But being ignored, or my perception of being ignored which is not necessarily that I am being ignored, but there are certain things when there is something where I feel, 'OK, they've passed me by. They're not interested. They're not looking.' What it kind of boils down to is, 'They don't like me,' and that feels extremely young. The bizarre thing is I don't walk around the world thinking, 'Oh, people don't like me.' I've had enough evidence that they do.

Windy: Yeah. So, is that the common linking between rejection and being ignored, that, 'This person doesn't like me'?

Anna: I think so, yeah, they don't like me.

Windy: So, what's hurtful about that?

Anna: … [*Pause*] Because I want to be liked. I guess because it's lack of inclusion, because it makes me feel alone. I was fairly catastrophically alone after my mother died. I mean, I really was abandoned. There was a sense of abandonment.

Windy: How old were you?

Anna: I was 13 when she died. I don't know how much you want. I'll do the history real fast, if you want, because it is really significant. So, my mother died, I had a father and a brother. My father was pretty much destroyed by the death of his wife, my mother. He then fairly quickly married another woman who was an alcoholic and violent and didn't really like the fact that there were these two kids around. So, they left. So, he and his new wife, my stepmother moved away and left me on my own. So, I was 16 years old and I was kind of homeless with no money. I'd sometimes go to visit and my stepmother would throw me out. So, I lived fairly alone, trying to make it through in a way. And then I left the country. So, I'm American but I left the United States and I came to Great Britain, where I have lived since, really.

Windy: What led you to make that decision?

Anna: Because I felt I had nothing to lose.

Windy: So, you came here on your own?

Anna: I came on my own. Interestingly enough, it's probably like almost 50 years ago today.

Windy: You sound quite resourceful.

[*Focusing on a person's strengths and inner resources is key in ONEplus Therapy. The therapist can ask the person directly for their strengths and infer them from their narrative.*]

Anna: I must be. I mean, I didn't feel it then. It's the sort of thing, in retrospect, one could think back and think that. So, I imagined to craft a life on my own from 19 years old.

Windy: Sure. So, you've actually built up a life from, shall we say the ashes of being left and abandoned.

Anna: Yeah.

Windy: That kind of thing. That's the background.

Anna: Yeah, that's the background.

Windy: So, through therapy, you said, and maybe other things, how have you tried to deal with the feelings of hurt that you've come to talk about?

Anna: Well, the first thing in therapy was to identify that there was anything that was wrong because I was very young. So, I first went to a group therapy thing in New York because that was kind of what people were doing at the time when I was, I think, 17, 18. The first thing I thought was, 'Gee, I feel bad.' Dumb as that might sound, I didn't even have those words. I didn't have the words of, 'Something bad has happened. I'm depressed. I'm down.' I just flopped around feeling like there was something really terribly wrong with me, and I didn't have any vocabulary because nobody had talked to me. This is like decades ago. This is before it was like, 'Well, Child, let's deal with the fact that your mother has died.' It was like, 'Get on with it.'

So, identifying that there was an issue, a lot of catharsis, a lot of crying over the years. The first proper ongoing therapy I did was Gestalt. So, a huge amount of catharsis, which only takes you so far, but which was useful to be in touch with. So that literally was very useful.

So, your question was what else have I done? What was your question, I'm sorry?

Windy: Not what have you done but what sort of strategies and what insights have you used?

Anna: Well, I would say it's more lately that I would be able to identify strategies, which is more, if I feel hurt now, what I'll think is, it'll be real bam, I mean, I'm quite a good one for identifying the feeling: 'Feeling hurt? OK, why? Because what was said? OK. Now let's try to think … why.' So, 'Calm down, think of something else' – not 'think of something else', 'think of something which is relevant', not distract.

Windy: OK. I think what I would find helpful is to have an example, a really good example.

[Anna is telling me about her experiences of feeling hurt in general terms. So, I ask her for a specific example.]

Anna: I could give you two examples, because, again, I've been thinking about this, because I reckon there are two different ways I feel hurt.

Windy: Well, let's take them one at a time, shall we?

Anna: Yeah, OK. So one is … to do with my husband and the other is to do with people in general, and I'll go for people in general first because it's kind of less hurtful, in a sense.

So, the other day I was in an online group where there were various people talking, and I was one of them. So, it was like people had made bids for the time, as it were, and I said, 'I've got something I'd like to talk about.' So I talked about it briefly, I talked about it a bit, whatever, and another person had also said that she wanted some time. So, I had maybe five or ten minutes of talking, and what it felt like, whether this is true or not, is another story, that people weren't actually interested in what I was saying, that they didn't like me, they didn't like my expression. All these people are English, and I'm not. And some of this is accrued around being a foreigner in a way that it didn't to start with. So, I thought, 'OK, I'm too loud, I'm too something. They're all much more.' So, I go into a thing.

Because what happened – sorry, I jumped – after I had said a little bit of my bid, it was like, 'Let's move on to the other person,' and I just felt absolutely wounded, totally silenced. I withdrew and I just thought, 'Yeah, they don't like me. I'm not English. I'm something. I'm too loud.' So then I went into a whole kind of thing, and then I thought, 'Oh yeah, I really recognise this. This is what I do. It's on-screen, so I can just sit here quietly and I can just think, 'Don't get into this, Anna. Don't go too far into this. Don't believe the story.' I had no reason to really think these people don't like me. But I was quiet, and I could feel the woundedness. Once upon a time and in a non-online thing, which was going to be ending in an hour, I might've walked away.

Windy: Right, so you stayed there.

Anna: I stayed.

Windy: And at what point did you move on from the hurt?

Anna: Ten, fifteen minutes later, I think, just a kind of thing about self-calming, self-soothing, talking myself through it. Also thinking, and this goes along with the withdrawal, so, even if all these people actually hate me, which is unlikely, what does it matter? I don't have to stay with my perceived, no doubt erroneous, take. And, even, in fact, they are a bit of, 'Well, we don't especially like your expression. We will close ranks towards one of our own,' I thought, 'There's other people in this world, I don't have to be here.' So that's withdrawal. So, then it goes right back to I left the United States, I don't have to be here, I can go.

Windy: So, it's almost like, 'I don't have to endure this. There is a route to escape.'

Anna: Yes, always. Always, always, always. I'm a big one for having the emotional bags packed by the door. I can leave on a dime.

Windy: Does that help deal with the problem, or does that help to maintain it?

Anna: Well, it has a rather big downside – not in that circumstance: I don't think I would suddenly say, 'Hey, what about me?' but the downside is that I withdraw, can shrivel up, and I don't stay for working something through, as it were. And, also, I'm not good at – it's not even conflict, it's like I don't ask for help.

Windy: Just taking that example, it seems that there was an element that you considered that you were being shut down or ignored. That meant that people didn't like you, you were too loud or whatever.

Anna: Yeah.

Windy: You then felt hurt. It sounded like a strong feeling, but you were able to stand back and recognise that this was a bit of a pattern for you and that it sounds like, in talking to yourself, you reminded yourself that, well, (1) 'What does it matter if they don't like me?' and (2) 'Will other people like you?' And, 'If it gets too bad, I can always leave.'

Anna: Yeah.

Windy: Is that accurate?

Anna: Yeah.

Windy: Would you like me to add my take and maybe suggest a few things that you might want to have a look at?

[*While, in my view, Anna is doing certain things that are helpful, I think that she can do more so, I asked her if she would like to hear my 'take' on the issue.*]

Anna: Why not? I don't want to lose the husband example.

Windy: No, OK. So what do you want to do first? Do you want to take the husband example and then we can come back?

Anna: Well, I'll follow your lead, actually.

Windy: No, I follow yours because this is what we do in single-session therapy: we follow the client's lead.

Anna: I'll go for husband thing because it's similar but has a slight twist on it.

Windy: And it might actually help me to get a more specific.

Anna: Yes.

Windy: OK, why don't you tell me about that?

Anna: OK. So, the husband thing actually is far more important in that this man is indeed my husband. So, therefore, he's a much more important relationship and I can't just decide to walk out the door. Well, I withdraw with him as well. So, I'll give you an example. So, again, this is a fairly ... banal example, but it stands in for other stuff as well, in a way. So, in common with many, he wants to get out the door in five seconds, whereas I want to do this and that and this and that before I go out the door, make sure I've got everything. And this is always a point of problem between us, in a sense, because I'm feeling like he's really passively angry at me, and he starts being a bit mean and will say things. I can't actually give an example. He'll be kind of snipey and I'll start to feel really ... thrown by that and anxious, which makes it harder for me to get it together to leave in the nice fashion I'd like to.

And what I recognised the other day, since this session and having the word 'hurt' kind of hurt, what I feel is hurt. So here I am, I'm just thinking, 'Right, I've got to get out the door,' and I think I have trouble getting out of doors; I mean, I think I have issues around. I mean, not hugely. So, I'm like, 'Do I have this? Do I have that?' And then when he starts, 'Come on, hurry up. There's something wrong with you. I want to go.'

Windy: Does he say that?

Anna: … What does he say? He might say something a bit more snipey, like… what did I say the other day? Oh yeah, I think he said, 'Right, I want to go,' and I said something like, 'Well, it'll take me five or ten minutes to get ready,' and he said, 'Well, that's a pity.' But, if that was the only statement that had ever been said, if there weren't years of history in this, then that was the snipe, but the snipe that encapsulated everything.

Windy: What meaning did you give the snipe?

Anna: Well, in this case, it is something like something's wrong with me. It just throws me off because his opinion of me is way more important.

Windy: Wait a minute, you think he's saying there's something wrong with you?

Anna: Yeah, he is saying there's something wrong with me 'cos his line is, 'Why can't you just get out the house? What's wrong? Look at me, I'm out in five minutes.'

Windy: So, you're reading the message that he's saying that there's something wrong with you. And then what?

Anna: OK, so I'm both hurt and angry. So that's the difference. With the general public people, as it were, I'm hurt and withdrawn and think, 'I can always get out if I have to.' With him, well, angry and then withdrawn. So, I won't get angry, I'll just feel really withdrawn, but I'll recognise I'm so angry, and I say nothing at that time.

Windy: What about the feeling of hurt there, then?

Anna: That's a hurt that's like in my throat. It's just right down my abdomen – I haven't been hit in the stomach, to be honest, so I don't know, but it feels like an impact. And then I feel really jarred. It's similar to the other one where I think, 'OK, shut down. They don't like me.' But, because it's him, then what I feel is, 'No, nothing's wrong with me,' so the hurt becomes anger, which is also problematic, but I don't act on the anger. I'm not all that angry as a person, but I feel hurt, and I do recognise that with him my anger is....

Windy: So angry at him for implying that there is something wrong with you?

Anna: ... Yes. I don't mind that he wants to leave in five minutes. I don't have a problem with that.

Windy: Let's just concentrate on the hurt in that because you were hurt and angry. It's almost like, 'How dare you think that there's something wrong with me?' But, if we focus on the hurt and if you speak from that emotion, what do you think the issue is there?

[Here, I am encouraging Anna to focus on hurt rather than anger, mainly because that what she said at the outset she wanted to focus on.]

Anna: OK, interestingly I'm thinking back. It's only more lately I've felt the anger. For years I just felt the hurt. We've been together a long time. When I was much younger I would just, 'I've done something wrong. He doesn't like me.' So, this is when I actually start to feel slightly tearful even speaking from this. It's like, 'He's going to go. I'm going to be on my own. Nobody likes me. Oh my God, what am I going to do? I can't bear this.'

Windy: OK. So, do you see the links? I think you're looking at the links anyway between the more general example and the more specific example.

Anna: Yeah.

Windy: Do you see any links when we focus on the hurt?

Anna: Links in what way do you mean? I'm just curious.

Windy: Well, what the meaning is that leads you to feel hurt.

Anna: I think the bottom line is they're going to go. I think, to cut right to the chase, the thing that makes me feel emotional talking to you is I'm going to be on my own. I'm going to be alone. And the travel to get there is, 'They don't like me. There's something wrong with me.' I mean, mainly now I don't actually, at this age, feel that there's anything all that wrong with me. I used to dreadfully feel, 'There's something really wrong with me. They're going to go.'

Windy: So, if you knew for sure that you would not be on your own in both of these, that you might be disliked in a more general example because you were, using your words, too loud and that your husband might think there's something wrong with you because you can't get out the door as quickly as he, but, if you were convinced in both of those, you knew that in both of those situations you would not be alone, just imagine that, what difference would that make to your feelings of hurt, if any?

Anna: Actually, it makes me feel very tearful just 'cos it's such a core issue. Yes, the idea of being alone – whoa! If I really, really, really could believe that, it would make a big difference, yes. And it's not even these people because it's a catastrophic, absolutely alone. It's not even, 'Oh, he'll leave me alone, they'll leave me alone.' It's that I'll be just alone.

Windy: Yes. So, if you knew that that wasn't gonna happen, what difference would that make to your feelings of hurt?

Anna: Well, just imagining it … much, much better…. Yeah.

Windy: It sounds like the real driving force of your hurt is the idea that you're going to be what you call catastrophically alone.

[*This is a good example of me working to get to the heart of the matter.*]

Anna: Yeah.

Windy: Of course, you wouldn't actually be alone in one sense, would you?

Anna: I don't know. You tell me.

Windy: Because you'd have yourself, wouldn't you?

Anna: Ah, OK. In that sense, yeah. And that is something which, at the beginning of all of this, when I was a kid I mean, I didn't have that sense. I was like blank to myself.

Windy: No.

Anna: And now, as an adult, I do have that sense, because there I am when I am feeling this stuff, thinking … in a nice way what I think is, 'Right, here I am, and here I am with you.' So yes. I feel myself with myself and I can actually really feel now, all these years later.

Windy: So I think it's a bit like almost getting to the end, 'cos you sound like you get to the bit which says, 'I'll be alone,' and then you say, 'Oh my God, that's terrible,' and then you stop at that point. You don't say, 'OK, then what would I do if I was alone?' with the examples that you've given anyway.

Anna: In my immediate freaked-out moment and the thing has just happened, then it's like an emergency repair job: 'Here I am with you. Let's try,' and I can actually feel myself soothing myself. But, in fact, the whole question about being alone, when I'm just idly thinking about catastrophic thoughts and I'm just idly thinking about stuff, getting older as well and seeing more people die around me that I'm aware of alone as a theme, as it were. So then I think about, if I was alone what would I do? But that's a slightly different thing, perhaps, than what we're talking about here.

Windy: I think that, as we look at your feelings of hurt, it's to do with your relationships with others – this idea that you shut down, that brings up the idea that, 'Maybe they don't like me.' The bit that I might add that might help you go forward in dealing with the hurt, I think you're still going to have that initial hurt and, incidentally, even if you did nothing, it sounds like it lasts for fifteen minutes, so, although it's painful at the time, you're able to do certain things to help it subside.

Anna: Well, with my husband it's a bigger deal because with him I don't just think, 'Yeah, hey, fine,' I sort of think like every time it happens it goes to a repository.

Windy: Well, maybe we should focus on the husband example, then, as that's more difficult for you to recover from.

Anna: It is.

Windy: So, I think that the one thing is it sounds like the idea that he thinks there's something wrong with you, what's hurtful about that?

Anna: Well, it's that he doesn't like me.

Windy: What's hurtful about that?

Anna: I want to be liked. This is my husband.

Windy: That's right, but, if I was going to add something there from my own perspective, I think there's a difference between holding an attitude which says, 'I want to be liked,' which is, on its own, perfectly reasonable, and either keeping that flexible or making it rigid. So, the flexible version would be, 'Look, of course I want him to like me. He doesn't always have to but I'd like it, and it does make a difference.' I think that, in a way, the healthy alternative is what I call sorrow, which is indicating the idea that, when we're not liked and we want to be liked, and when we're not included and we want to be included, it is a sorrowful experience. But, just to come back, the difference between at the time believing, 'I want to be liked but he doesn't always have to like me,' or, 'I want to be liked and therefore he does have to like me. And, if he doesn't, then I'm unlikeable,' because it sounds like initially you get to that point and it's not a million miles away to say, 'Well, if he doesn't like me, if I'm not likeable, then I'll be alone.'

[*Again, I wish that I had created more of a space where I asked Anna if she was interested in my perspective before going ahead and outlining it – which is informed by REBT (see Chapter 4).*]

Anna: Yeah.

Windy: It's almost like that jump. And I'm wondering if, at that point, the work that you need to do is twofold: one is it does matter to you that he likes you but does he always have to, is one question I'd suggest you put to yourself; and the other one is, 'If he doesn't like me, how can I accept myself? Can I accept myself when my husband doesn't like me?'

Anna: Interestingly, I feel now that in fact I really do accept myself even if in the moment it seems like he doesn't like me, or at other times even if he didn't really actually didn't like me. And, of course, then like is also how much are we talking like, how much are we talking love, how much are those related anyway?

Windy: It's the same principle in terms of the flexibility or not.

Anna: Yeah. Then he doesn't always have to like me. In a totally rational way what I can think is, going out the door as an example because I think that happened very soon after I knew I was going to be talking with you, so I thought, 'Here's one' – there are other examples, I'm sure, but I can't think of them. So, the idea that he doesn't have to like me, I could just think, 'Yeah, he's a guy.' It's interesting 'cos I do kind of think this already which is, 'Yeah, his family, they always run out the door and they always don't have their keys and their whatever,' and it's like, 'So what? I'm not like that.'

Windy: I think that's what you have to watch out for: the movement to the 'so what?'. It matters to you, because, if it didn't matter to you, we wouldn't be having this conversation.

Anna: True.

Windy: Do you want your husband to recognise that, yes, you have a difficulty maybe leaving home without getting irritated? You're looking for a different response from him.

Anna: Yeah, that's true, I am.

Windy: Yeah. And it would be really nice if you got that, but what I'm saying is, is that response from him necessary or not? If it's not necessary, it's still desirable.

Anna: Yeah, it feels desirable for sure.

Windy: Yeah, and that's fine. Wanting him to say, 'Yes, this is her. OK, I understand that.'

Anna: Yeah. It's interesting because what I also think it makes me think is I actually want him to say, 'I'm sorry I hurt you.' I actually want him to recognise that, when he says that, he's hurting me and he would say, 'Look, I just want to get out of the house. I'm sorry I said that. I'm sorry I hurt you,' and we're actually leaving the house now anyway.

Windy: Yeah, and it would be nice if he did that. It would be nice.

Anna: We could be waiting a long time.

Windy: We may be. So, the question is you've got things that matter to you. You want understanding, you want an apology. That would be nice. It is sad when you don't get it. I think that's what you're not holding onto: the fact that you've got perfectly reasonable desires. Coming back to the online thing, it's perfectly reasonable to want to have your time and it is sad, disappointing and sorrowful that you're not getting it.

Anna: I think the sorrow angle, that is in there, for sure. I wonder whether part of how that mixes in with aloneness as well is, when my mother died, I really was. The whole family – my brother, my father, me – were extremely on our own. There was no recognition of anything. It's not like other family members came and helped. We were on our own. Everybody was just in extreme grief and sorrow and with no help whatsoever. So, I wonder the sorrow idea, this kind of stuff now I can recognise that. I think the sorrow idea, I think I'm bad in the sense historically – if it touches back into something like that, then I think that the idea of sorrow is something that I do have, 'I'm not going to feel that. I'm off. I'm not going to feel that. I'm angry.'

Windy: Yeah, that's right. It sounds like, if you were to ask to choose between feeling angry or sorrowful, you'd choose angry because it's less painful for you.

Anna: Well, at this point talking to you, I'm actually much more inclined to think that sorrow is a better way forward, because that's what the depth of the problem is. My anger – in a way it's a big deal. The only thing about my anger is it's learned. I did used to feel sad and the anger just came up as eventually with my husband over other issues, not just leaving the house, when I would think, 'Agh,' and that felt better than, 'Oh.' It's the sorrow on my own which is the issue, the sorrow and nobody knows, and nobody cares.

Windy: Yeah, although, again, even if that were the case, we don't know, that you know and you care.

Anna: Yeah.

Windy: It's almost like the final backstop is saying, 'Well, look, even if I do get up on my own, I can still care for myself as I did when I was coming from America.' That's what I'm saying, you showed tremendous resources and strength. So, I think, if we get you in touch with that aspect of you and that also that you can care for yourself – it's nice when other people care for you, it's nice when they recognise things, but, if they don't, that is sorrowful, that is sad.

Anna: Yeah, I think a growth point for me would actually be to take this further and to think, 'OK, so why am I packaging my sorrow?' using the word which is a big category word, 'Why am I packaging it to this extent that I also think nobody wants to know?' because it's like how do I know that nobody wants to know?

Windy: Well, there are two types of hurt. I think we're talking about one. One is like, 'They don't like me. I'm not likeable.'

Anna: Right.

Windy: The other one is, 'They don't like me. I don't deserve this. Poor me.' I'm wondering if there's any of that type of hurt in your experience.

Anna: Well, poor me, certainly I used to feel poor me. I don't so much now.

Windy: Not now.

Anna: … Well, there is more of that in the online group. There was more of that there, for sure.

Windy: I'd recommend that the remedy to the poor me is to recognise that you are a non-poor person who's in a poor situation, rather than being a poor person for being in a poor situation.

Anna: Yes.

Windy: So, you're appraising the situation, you're not appraising yourself.

Anna: OK, yeah.

Windy: So, there are elements, particularly in terms of the more general thing, you might start off going to the idea that, 'I'm not likeable,' but I think you come away from that; you don't stay there.

Anna: I do now, absolutely….

Windy: No, exactly. But I think, with the husband example, if you could recognise that you are looking for certain things from him – understanding – and, if you don't get it, that is sad, but the question is you can ask yourself, 'Is it necessary for me or is it desirable but, on this occasion, not necessary?'

Anna: Well, I guess, the fact that I've kept on living shows it's not necessary.

Windy: Exactly, but it is desirable. I think you have to watch your drift into, 'It doesn't matter,' as a way of coping because it does matter.

Anna: Yeah.

Windy: And then, if you are on your own, which who knows, it's unlikely but possible, who knows, but you're alone with you and the resourceful, caring aspects of you would actually come in handy there.

Anna: I'm also still interested in this sorrow thing.

Windy: Yeah. Sorrow is really saying, 'It is sad and sorrowful when I'm not getting what I want.' I think, in a way, hurt people feel more acutely with people who are close to them. It is an emotion that is related to closeness. So, you're with a man and he's a fallible man – he's got his strengths and presumably his weaknesses, and one of his weaknesses, we'll call it that, is that he's a bit impatient around leaving the house where you're concerned.

Anna: Yeah.

Windy: But you still would like him to be patient. You still would like him to be understanding. You're not getting it. You're not getting an apology. But what you can do is say, 'It is going to be, but do I need it or not?'

Anna: … And how do I do that without just ending up withdrawn: 'No, I don't need it'?

Windy: Well, by being watchful of that going into that withdrawn, 'I don't care,' and recognising that that's a self-protective mechanism.

Anna: Completely.

Windy: But that you can actually recognise, 'But I can protect myself while really recognising that I do care.'

Anna: Yeah.

Windy: 'Because, if I really didn't care, I wouldn't be hurt,' if you truly didn't care.

Anna: So, what is the benefit of thinking … 'I do care, I wish it were different. I don't actually need this because I can still keep going'?

Windy: It leads you to feel sorrowful but not hurt. In other words, I firmly believe that when adversity happens, we have a choice of feeling a healthy bad feeling or an unhealthy bad feeling.

Anna: OK.

Windy: And the healthiness of the bad feeling is not necessarily in the feeling itself but actually what it leads into.

Anna: So how would you describe what sorrowful feels like? What is sorrow?

Windy: It's the idea that, 'Look, I really want my husband to understand me more and even apologise for the way he's treating me. I'm not getting that. I don't need it but I really want it.' It overlaps with sadness in a way.

Anna: Yeah, OK.

Windy: And then you can say to him, 'Look, it would be nice if you were a bit more patient with me. You don't have to be but it would be nice if you were.' I recommend that because saying that keeps you connected. The thing about hurt is that you're looking to disconnect from somebody, and I think that activates the idea, in your mind, that disconnect eventually means being alone. So, if you could stay connected with him and say, 'Look, you don't have to do this and you may not do it, but it would be nice if you were able to be a little bit more patient because you know I've got a bit of an issue about leaving the house.'

Anna: Yeah. But I also wonder whether it points towards anything, for me, around sorrow from long, long ago, which means that I also block from letting it.

Windy: Yeah. I think you've learnt that sadness and sorrow were unhealthy emotions. I don't know what you were experiencing then, but that they are painful but they're not unhealthy.

Anna: Yeah. I think that, because I was so young when I did feel it, there really was obviously grief, sorrow.

Windy: That's right and, as you said, you had no words to deal with it.

Anna: And nobody.

Windy: You've done a tremendous amount of putting yourself back together. I really am impressed by the work you've done.

Anna: Therapy has been essential in this journey. This isn't something I've done on my own. But yes.

Windy: But there's also self-therapy.

Anna: Yes.

Windy: It's about taking this forward and recognising. So, as we approach the end of our session, Anna, maybe you could summarise what we've done and then we can see what you're going to be taking away.

Anna: I'm fairly bad at the summaries now because I have so many different things. I think the idea of keeping connected, that feels really important, the idea that hurt can lead to disconnect, because I think I have a tendency to withdraw and disconnect. And that is something that, going forward, generally, I would like to concentrate more on connection, as it were. The other idea of healthy and unhealthy emotions and healthy and unhealthy hurt – I'm not sure you said that but something like that. And also recognising that, when I feel hurt, what I feel is, in fact, some variation on sad; that that actually is a different way of being with myself. It's not like zooming off into nowhere-ville or braced, again which, in the end, takes me to disconnection, in a sense. Do I need it or not? And that's an interesting thing to think: 'Right now he's being a pain in the neck.' It's not the same as, 'Does that matter?' but, 'Do I need it?' which is a subtle variation on the theme, because then it's back to connection.

So, I guess, trying to summarise it as quickly as possible, the connection: something about connection and sorrow and back to the thing about, if I could actually imagine that I wasn't really going to be alone, the catastrophic aloneness thing, to recognise that that is a very old construct that is old, deep in me. How's that? That's fairly long-winded, isn't it?

Windy: No, that's fine. I think I would add the idea that the hurt states will be the ones to come up first, but, just because they come up doesn't mean you have to stay with them. And, although you might feel like withdrawing because that's what hurts does to you – it leads you to withdraw and sulk and all the rest of it – it doesn't mean you have to go that route. You could still choose to go against the grain, as I call it, and stay connected and assert yourself and things like that.

Anna: I'd also say another thing that's really important in this is actually talking to you about it, because I've never talked about this in this way with anybody because I've never identified it like this. And, so, immediately on the alone theme, I'm not alone because you're talking to me about this.

Windy: That's right.

Anna: And that actually also makes a huge difference. So, in terms of potentially internalising, as much as I can remember of this, so I look forward to having the transcript, that actually would be helpful for me because it would be like, 'That nice man was alongside me in terms of my internal world.' I mean, I will use you. I will use your words.

Windy: Absolutely. I look forward to that. OK, then, it's been a delight.

Anna: OK, great.

Windy: All the best.

[*I offered Anna my REBT-informed perspective because it seemed as though she did not have a helpful perspective of her own to address her hurt feelings. I think she found my perspective of interest and was able to take a few points from what I was saying that may be useful to her going forwards.*]

Anna's Reflections on the Session: 06/12/23

Why Did I Choose to Do This?

I saw an online ad for people willing to take part in a therapy session with Windy Dryden. I have a lot of experience of long-term therapy but no personal experience of very short-term work. I had been interested for a while in how single-session therapy would work as it seemed so different from what I had experienced. On a societal level, I also like the idea of a (possibly) more accessible, lower commitment (time and money) therapeutic intervention for people who identify one particular issue to focus on.

I was very aware of hurt which I was feeling repeatedly with my husband within the context of certain ways we interrelated. When I saw this opportunity to focus on hurt advertised, I thought, why not try it?

What Did I Expect?

I went into the session more with curiosity and openness than with the expectation I would "solve" this interpersonal issue. I was interested to hear what insight Windy might offer. Since I have quite a background already in psychotherapy, not having a solution was fine with me. I went into the session very willing to engage.

What I Experienced during the Session

I found Windy attentive and skilled. I did not feel a deep emotional connection, but nor did I feel a cold or clinical distance. I felt we were working alongside each other in a non-hierarchical way. I have had a lot of experience of therapy, and so I was able to 'place' myself in terms of not being overly vulnerable or particularly emotionally expressive, as it did not feel appropriate to do so within this context. Nor did the format move me to feel a deeper or unbounded level of emotional experience – it was more I was reporting thoughts and incidents within my life. There was a sort of brisk, 'let's get on with this' feeling.

What I Took Away from the Experience

I remember two basic takeaways from the session. The first was that my hurt might have roots in sadness. Feeling the sadness could help me not angrily withdraw in these painful interactions with my husband. The second was about a lifelong (since adolescence) fear I have of being catastrophically alone, related to my history of trauma and abandonment. Which also connects to the sense of hurt within the interactions with my husband.

Windy made comments about my not being catastrophically alone because I had myself. I really connected with this. When I was younger, I probably would not have connected with this so much as I did not feel I had a good sense of myself, only a negative, disjointed and shameful one. Plus, I wanted more than just to have myself anyway. But as a mature adult with much experience of personal therapy, I now feel I do have myself and so these words helped me update myself to today.

Postscript

I received a transcript of the session. It was interesting to see that some of what was said I did not remember (of course). I wondered if my takeaways were actually accurate for the session. I wanted to take on board the insights Windy offered and wondered if I had done so or had created some different version. As it was a single session, a follow-up discussion was not available.

But my two remembered insights feel valuable to me, whether or not they accurately represent what Windy meant. I think they are accurate enough!

Therefore, I found the single-session experience valuable.

12

Helping People with Problems with Unhealthy Jealousy

Helping the Client to Understand and Deal with Unhealthy Jealousy

Here are some ideas that I have found useful to introduce into my conversation with clients that can help them understand and deal with unhealthy jealousy.

- When a person experiences unhealthy jealousy, they hold a rigid and extreme attitude towards one or both of the following adversities: (i) They think that another person poses a risk to a valued relationship and (ii) they experience uncertainty related to the first threat (e.g. 'I want to know that my partner is not interested in any of the men she works with and therefore I have to know this. I can't bear not knowing'). When a person experiences unhealthy jealousy, they tend to take action to prevent what they fear and think that if they don't, then what they fear will happen, and also that uncertainty means that something bad is going on.
- The healthy alternative to unhealthy jealousy is healthy jealousy (sometimes called relationship concern).
- When the person experiences healthy jealousy (or relationship concern) about the same adversities, they hold a flexible and non-extreme attitude towards these adversities (e.g. 'I want to know that my partner is not interested in any of the men she works with, but I don't have to know this. It's a struggle not knowing, but I can bear it and it's worth bearing'). When a person experiences healthy jealousy, they don't take action to

prevent what they are concerned about and they think that probably nothing bad will happen if they don't. They also think that uncertainty does not mean that something bad is going on. In this and other matters they decide to go along with probability.

- When a self-devaluation attitude is a prominent feature of unhealthy jealousy, I discuss the importance of developing an attitude of unconditional self-acceptance as a solution.

- Yet again, if the person is interested, I will help them change their rigid/extreme attitudes to their flexible/non-extreme counterparts and help them think and act in ways that will support the development of these attitudes.

Transcript of My Work with a Person with a Problem with Unhealthy Jealousy

Therapist – Volunteer:	Windy – Lara
Venue:	Private session that took place on 07/08/23 arranged via Onlinevents
Time:	44 minutes 36 secs

Windy: So what's your understanding of the purpose of our conversation today?

Lara: That we'll have a one-time session. I will tell you what my main issue is, having already filled in the questionnaire and that we will be able to reach some sort of … steps forward, I guess.

Windy: And is it OK with you if I refer to the questionnaire as we go?

Lara: Yes, of course.

Windy: Sometimes in these sessions either people go off track or they elaborate far too much, so what I tend to do is to interrupt them to bring back to the focus. Is that OK with you if I interrupt you?

Lara: Yeah, that's fine. Thanks for telling me that.

Windy: And how can I best do that?

Lara: Well, however you like. Say stop or, 'Actually, can we just focus back on questions?'

Windy: So, something to do with my hands will help you to do that.

Lara: Yeah, I'm quite visual, so, yeah, let's do that. OK, thanks.

Windy: OK. So, you have a problem with jealousy. By the way, do you regard your jealousy as healthy or unhealthy?

Lara: Well, it depends how scratchy I'm feeling that day. I mean, it's not a constant. It's more situational. So, it depends what comes up.

Windy: When it comes up do you regard it as being healthy or unhealthy?

Lara: Oh no, unhealthy.

Windy: Why?

Lara: Well, it's a disproportionate reaction to a situation often and it ... comes from my own stuff, it comes from my own issues. It isn't like he is actually doing something terrible, but in my head I'm imagining that he is and that creates all kinds of panic in me, which comes out as jealousy. Yeah, so unhealthy.

Windy: So, what have you done that's been helpful to deal with this problem?

[*Again, this is a typical intervention in ONEplus Therapy. I hope to build on what Lara has found helpful in addressing her jealousy problem.*]

Lara: OK. Well, I am having ongoing therapy. So, we are working on attachment and feelings of safety. So, for me it is an attachment issue. In my questionnaire I've filled in about my parents are divorced, I have a lot of issues around being left. I guess my ultimate belief is that I will end up being left like my mum was left by my dad, men not to be trusted, so on, so on.... Sorry, I'm menopausal as well so my brain sometimes is like a tumbleweed moment where I've got a thought process going on and then all of a sudden, I haven't.

Windy: Don't worry.

Lara: I've completely lost track of where I was going with that.

Windy: I asked you what you found that was helpful.

Lara: Yeah. So what else have I found that is helpful? Trying to regulate myself, actually. So, trying to find moments where I can feel something coming up for me, I can feel it in my body, I can feel a sense of panic, I can feel it in my chest, I can feel a tightening, I can feel a sense of resistance in what's happening. And panic. Absolutely panic: 'Agh, he's going to leave me! He's going to run off with this person that he's just met,' who he's really got no interest in. So, yeah, I've done a body workshop recently, trying to understand when my body might suddenly become in a state of flight.

Windy: And, when you understand that, how does that help you?

Lara: It does help me because I can rationalise it. There's a sort of tipping point, isn't there? So, I suppose it's about seeing it before it reaches the tipping point and knowing what my other triggers are, and I think that's where therapy's been super helpful for me ... in a logical, cerebral sort of way. But it's just when it comes up immediately, if something comes up – so I'll give you a random example if you like?

Windy: Yeah.

Lara: Tell me if I'm going off at a tangent. So, he does a job which involves working with other people, a physical job, and he came home from work, and he made some joke about being paid for sexual services when he was at work. And, adult to adult, you might see that as just a funny moment. For me, I went to hypervigilant: 'Right, where are the signs of that? He's just saying that as a joke, but maybe he's just trying to cover the fact that is actually what happened,' this sort of rationale in my mind. 'Maybe he's having an affair and he's just trying to cover that by saying something ridiculous like that. Let me check his body. Are there any marks on his body? Does he smell different?' all these sorts of things, totally crazy.

Windy: So, on that episode, if we were to give you an ingredient that would've got rid of the jealousy, what would it have been?

Lara: ... A sense of reassurance.

Windy: Reassurance of what?

Lara: That that wasn't true.

Windy: Right.

Lara: A sense of safety, a sense of ... someone noticing that I felt like that.

Windy: It sounds like, if somebody's not around, it's the kind of assurance that this wasn't true.

Lara: I think it's fact-finding. I think I almost need to be able to look at what is truth and what is fantasy. I don't know if fantasy is the right word, but imagination. And at that moment in time, I am not looking at facts, I am not looking at the history behind this person in my relationship and all the good things that he does. I am totally in an imaginary place at that point: 'This could happen and that could happen and that could happen,' which is totally irrational and totally unreasonable because he's not that person. But I find it really hard to get back to what is rational, what is logical, what is real at that moment in time. I'm lost.

Windy: What have you tried to bring yourself back from that lost place?

Lara: At those moments in time? Well, actually, I've started expressing it. So I've started making it ... not explicit, overt – I've said at that time, 'Actually, when you say things like that, it's really triggering for me. I feel really vulnerable. I feel like … you're telling me this because you're covering something else and it makes me feel really insecure and it makes me feel really jealous and it makes me feel really panicked.'

Windy: And how does he respond?

Lara: 'Oh, I wish you'd told me that before. OK, I won't do that anymore. I won't make those jokes.' And, so being able to just talk about it and just express it rather than hold it inside … gets the monster out from under the bed, I guess.

Windy: And what happens to your jealousy at that point?

Lara: Then it just dissipates.

Windy: Right. So you've found that expressing yourself and how you're feeling is an important ingredient to deal with the jealousy.

Lara: Yeah, because it's almost like a thought spiral: if you're alone in your thoughts and that's where you're going with that, the only way that it can go is down.

Windy: What if he's not around?

Lara: To express it?

Windy: Yeah.

Lara: Then, yes, that's the difficult time, I think, because then I'm in my own head. If he's not around and that's already happened, that comment's been made, then I'm in that place again: that place of imaginary, 'Well, where is he right now? What is he doing? Who could he be with? Is it possible that something like that could be going on? Why would that be going on? But, yes, it could be going, couldn't it?' That would create a continuous spiral. So it is hard to stop myself.

Windy: In terms of the cold light of day, what kind of person is he?

Lara: Reliable, trustworthy, kind. He's a good man.

Windy: So, when you wrote here: 'Partner cheated on ex twice'?

Lara: Yes, but he did do that.

Windy: Yeah.

Lara: But, you know, people do it. I mean, it's complicated. He cheated because she cheated.

Windy: Like a tit for tat thing?

Lara: Tit for tat and then their relationship broke down and he reached out to somebody else. So, yeah, at the back of my mind it's really hard for me not to go to that place. I'd said to him, I've expressed that fear, 'Rather than you telling me that you are unhappy in our relationship' – we've only been together for three-and-a-half years, he seems alright, but, 'you would just tell me. You would just tell me that you're not happy rather than you going out and seeking that elsewhere.'

Windy: What did he say when you said that?

Lara: 'I wouldn't want to do that anyway. I'm happy with you. I wasn't happy in my relationship with her and that's why I did it.'

Windy: You say about yourself that you've always cheated.

Lara: Yeah, at some point.

Windy: Have you cheated on him?

Lara: Emotionally maybe at the beginning. Yeah.

Windy: Emotionally? What does that mean?

Lara: Imagining a romantic involvement with somebody else, somebody that I still maybe hankered for and text messages back and forth. So, in my mind, that's an emotional cheating.

Windy: And you did that at the beginning?

Lara: Yeah.

Windy: And now?

Lara: No. We're still in touch but that's it.

Windy: OK. You're smiling.

Lara: Well, because I can see how that looks.

Windy: How does it look?

Lara: Well, it looks like it could be misconstrued as that. But it isn't. But it's taken me a long time in a relationship to feel... that it isn't going to go wrong, and the thing is, when I panic, I suppose historically what's happened is I've panicked in relationships: 'Oh my God, I'm getting too close to somebody.... Get out or do something to mess it up or seek it somewhere else before I can get too attached to a person.' But ... with Sidney ... we have been able to get close. There have been times where I have pulled away and I have tried to create distance ... but this matters; this relationship has so much more value.

Windy: Right.

Lara: So, I don't want to do that.

Windy: Are you more vulnerable to jealousy because it matters?

Lara: Yes, exactly. Yeah.

Windy: Because it's really important.

Lara: Yeah, so important. This is finally somebody that ... [*pause*] really makes me happy. So yeah, there's a lot at stake.

Windy: So, what, for you, is the healthy alternative to jealousy?

Lara: To be accepting of light-hearted jokes, to be accepting of seeing someone who's my partner being given attention and time with other women and be OK with that and feel, 'Great, OK, yeah, they're flirting with him but that's fine. That will feel like a nice boost for him but that doesn't affect me.' I'd love to be able to get to that place.

Windy: You mean you want to be pleased for him if he's flirting with another woman?

Lara: Well, to be cool with it, yeah. To feel like, actually, he'd get a lot out of that.

Windy: Yeah, but you don't like it.

Lara: I don't like it, no.

Windy: So you're trying to be cool with something you don't like.

Lara: Yeah, I think because I don't want to restrain … his way of being too much, I guess, and I know that he'd get a massive reward from that.

Windy: Yeah, but you still don't like it.

Lara: No, I really hate it.

Windy: Exactly. The thing is, in working towards some emotional goal, I think we have to be clear first of all about what the heart of your jealousy is, which we'll get to in a minute, but also what is realistic in terms of your own preferences. And your own preference is that you would much prefer that he didn't flirt with another woman in front of you.

Lara: Yeah, and he does, and he is flirty.

Windy: What's wrong with not liking it?

Lara: Yeah. Can I give you another example of something that he did as well?

Windy: Sure.

Lara: So, it was New Year's Eve and we'd gone out. I hadn't been drinking because I was driving. He'd been drinking a lot. We went to my friend's house. This was 1 o'clock in the morning, we'd been to another party, we were coming back. I've got this friend called Abbie, and he's talked about her before being this little blonde. I clocked it when he said it. I thought, 'OK, so he fancies Abbie.' And he made it explicit. He said it in front of me and in front of other people something about, 'Yes, you're really hot, aren't you?' And I was a bit like, 'OK, clocked that one. I'm not going to say anything now. We're in a group of people,' but I saw her husband look at me and look at Sidney and be a bit like ... I was like thinking, 'What the fuck?' Sorry about the swearing, but I mean ... he was very drunk, and that is part of my rationale of not wanting to punch him in the face at that moment in time. But I was so furious.

Windy: Right, so you're not going to like that.

Lara: I didn't like that at all.

Windy: So, if you allow yourself not to like that and much prefer it didn't happen, what difference would that make to you?

Lara: If I didn't allow it to happen?

Windy: No, if you allowed yourself not to like it when it happened rather than be pleased for him.

Lara: Yeah, I'd feel a lot better. Also, where's the respect, is what I think. Where's the respect for me in that?

Windy: Right. But let's really get to the heart of your jealousy. It sounds to me like one of the things that is in there, which I'm not sure that you're very good at dealing with, is uncertainty.

Lara: ... Yeah.

Windy: Not knowing.

Lara: Yeah, that's true.

Windy: So maybe one of the things that we can do today is for me to help you to develop a healthier way of dealing with uncertainty.

[*On the basis of what Lara and I have discussed, I suggest that the heart of her difficulty with jealousy is dealing with uncertainty and being left – see below.*]

Lara: I do like things to be the same. I'm not good with uncertainty. That is absolutely true. There's a lot of risk involved.

Windy: The other thing is that the end result is that you're left.

Lara: Yeah.

Windy: Have you been left before?

Lara: Yeah, when my dad left.

Windy: How old were you then?

Lara: 13.

Windy: Are you the same person now as you were when you were 13?

Lara: Well, no, I'm not, but there's a part of that within me still, obviously. There's the essence of me, teenage me.

Windy: Of course, yeah. How do you think you'd cope if you were left by Sidney?

Lara: Well, I would just shut down emotionally. That's how I would cope, yeah.

Windy: How long for?

Lara: It's hard to say. I don't know. Until I felt that I could move forward and that.

Windy: That's right. There's a sense of, if he were to leave you, you'd shut down. What would you be doing in that shutdown period?

Lara: That would be an emotional shutdown, so that would feel nothing, just move on, bury that deeply, push that down – really healthy stuff – and just get on with it until actually 'fake it 'til you make it' was working and I could feel like life was OK again.

Windy: If you were dealing with it rather than burying it, what would dealing with being left be like for you?

Lara: Very painful. So painful. How would I deal with it? I guess I would write about it. That would be the first place that I would go to. I am good at thinking about things, not very good at feeling things necessarily because I haven't really accessed that part of me for a long time. I can now, but I would probably go there: I would write it down. If I'm able to write it down, I'm able to express. I'd be able to think my feelings, I guess.

Windy: Would you be seeking support from other people?

Lara: I probably would, yes. I'd reach out to girlfriends, yeah.

Windy: So, if we were to take the worst case scenario, which is that Sidney were to leave you and that that would be an emotional shock, yet you would deal with it by not burying your feelings, you would deal with it by writing, working it through like that, helping you to connect with your feelings, helping you to get support from your friends. What would that lead to, that process?

Lara: I suppose a sense of healing eventually.

Windy: So, I think what you do is, as soon as you think about being left, you go and stop thinking, stop processing.

Lara: Yeah.

Windy: And, when you stop thinking and processing, this horror becomes almost real rather than, when we look at it and we can actually see that it would be painful because this relationship really matters to you, that you'd be able to work it through both internally and interpersonally and reach a place of healing, rather than see that as something awful which you must avoid at all costs, how would you then see being left?

Lara: ... Yeah. Yes, it would feel differently, I guess, to be left.

Windy: You still wouldn't like it; you still would hate it in fact. It's almost like you're saying it's the end of the world horror, that's it, and you stop thinking. So, I think that's one thing that you can do: to actually help yourself to see that, even if this happened, and we don't know if it's going to happen, but if it does you will be OK eventually.

[In helping Lara deal with being left, I am bringing together strategies that she has mentioned herself. On this issue, I have not added any from my REBT-informed perspective.]

Lara: Yeah.

Windy: The other thing is dealing with uncertainty. Now, give me an example where uncertainty is a factor in all this with Sidney?

Lara: Well, it isn't just relationships. It's all aspects of my life. If I am unable to pre-empt, predict, look at a situation and know exactly what's gonna happen, then generally I don't feel very safe or I just don't it; I won't go there.

Windy: Let's have a look at your relationship with Sidney first 'cos you've volunteered for jealousy, and then let's see if we can help you to generalise that to other areas of your life later. How's that?

[Note that in response to my invitation to Lara to give me an example of dealing with uncertainty with her partner, Sidney, she generalises the issue. I suggest retaining the specific focus and

generalising later. She agrees. This is a typical strategy in ONEplus Therapy.]

Lara: OK, sure. So, with uncertainty, I suppose, if we were to go somewhere and do something ... if we'd made a plan to do something then I'm like, 'Great, OK, this is what we're doing.' I don't know, say we went to a festival – I don't like festivals, but we went to this festival and he got in a strop about something and wanted to go off and just leave me with all the children in the middle of this festival. And I was really upset, really horrified. All of a sudden there was uncertainty. I thought the plan was we were going to all be together and all the rest of it, and he was just going off. And in my head, I was like, 'Where's he going? Who's he going to be with 'cos he's certainly not going to be with me? And I'm being left, I'm being abandoned in the middle of a bloody field. What is happening right now?' That was very upsetting. That was very triggering for me. We had a massive row about that: 'How dare you leave me! How dare you!'

Windy: So, it sounds like in that situation is it a case of wanting to know what he was doing or wanting to know what he wasn't doing or what?

Lara: What's going to happen next, I suppose. Where am I in that? Where am I in relation to where he is and what are we doing, I suppose. I suppose for me the hard bit is when he's out of sight, out of mind and I don't know what's happening. There might be then uncertainty for me because I don't know what he's going to come back and say or come back and do.

Windy: So, you would like to know various things in this scenario: you'd like to know where he is, what he's doing, who he's with and where you stand and all the rest of it.

Lara: Yeah.

Windy: That's fine. On its own, that's not going to lead to jealousy. Would you be interested in my take on this?

[*Here, I am more definite in asking Lara for permission to offer my 'take' on how she unwittingly creates unhealthy jealousy in this situation. This perspective is informed by REBT – see Chapter 4.*]

Lara: Yes, of course.

Windy: I have to ask. It's polite to ask. So, in my mind, in my view, you start off with a perfectly reasonable desire: certainty/knowing what's happening matters to you. And that's fine. The question is, when you are in an anxious, jealous state, 'cos it sounds like you're in an anxious, jealous state in that situation, you actually hold one of four attitudes – two we can dismiss but I'll go over them anyway. One is, 'Great, I love uncertainty. I love being in this' – we'll forget about that. The second one, which probably we can forget about, is, 'It doesn't matter to me if I'm certain or not' – it does matter to you, so we can throw that out. So now you've got a choice of developing a flexible or a rigid attitude towards uncertainty. They both start off in the same way: 'I would like to know what he's doing, where he is and what's happening to us, and therefore I've got to know that. I have to know that. Not knowing that is unbearable. I can't stand it;' or, 'Yes, I would like to know what's happening, where he is, what he's doing, what it means to me, but I don't need to know that. It's desirable but I don't need to know it. And it's uncomfortable, me putting up with it, but I can bear it.' Now, which attitude do you think you bring to these episodes?

Lara: Not that one. The more rigid version, I guess.

Windy: Now, what would it be like for you if you did bring the flexible version and you really believed the flexible version?

Lara: That would be great because … yeah, it would be so much better for our relationship, I'd feel safer, I'd feel more relaxed.

Windy: One of the things you've done, and this happens to a lot of people, when you're in a rigid frame of mind towards uncertainty and you say, 'I must know and I don't,' you create a sense of unsafety for not knowing. And, after a while, your brain says, 'Uncertainty = unsafe.'

Lara: Yes, that is what I feel in my body.

Windy: Yeah, exactly. But, in reality, the most probable quadrant, if you like, is uncertainty but still safe, probably. This is what I'm saying, what do we know about the guy? Yes, he has cheated on his partner but reactively. He's not a Don Juan.

Lara: No.

Windy: He likes a bit of flirting occasionally. But, because you've actually trained your brain through this rigidity to see uncertainty as being unsafe, the only way you can calm down is to get certainty. But that's not the issue. It's actually to recognise that you cannot know and still be safe, because probably that's the case. We can't give you an absolute guarantee 'cos that's what you want. So, I think that one of the things you can do is that, when you start to get anxious in your body, you can then ask yourself, 'Am I demanding to know something? What am I demanding to know and do I need to know it?' Then, really important now, you need to make your behaviour consistent with tolerating uncertainty. What you do, if I can read from your form, what you were saying was you engage in all kinds of questioning and asking him things. Now, if you really want to deal with your jealousy issue, you're going to have to stop that.

Lara: Yeah, I know.

Windy: That's going to go against the grain, but that's important to do because, if you go with the grain, you maintain your jealousy problem.

Lara: Yeah.

Windy: So can you imagine a situation, for example, where replaying that scenario again – you didn't know where he was, and there you are and you're thinking, 'Look, I really would like to know where he is, but I don't know. I don't need to know. He'll come back when he's ready to come back. So, I don't need to ask any more questions in my mind, 'cos that's the other thing you're doing: 'Who's he with? What's he doing?' That's part of the, 'I don't need to know the answers to any of those questions. It would be nice, but I'll find out in the due course of time.'

Now, let me ask you a question about this. Do you regard yourself as a patient person or an impatient person?

Lara: Impatient.

Windy: And that's the other issue that you're bringing to the table. Not only are you saying, 'I have to know what he's doing so that I'm safe,' but, 'I have to know now.'

Lara: Yeah, it does feel urgent.

Windy: 'I've got to know right now.'

Lara: Yes.

Windy: You're not saying, 'I have to know, well, in 24 hours or 48 hours,' or anything like that, 'I have to know now.'

Lara: Yeah.

Windy: So, if you bring that to the table and say, 'Yeah, of course I'd like to know now, but I don't need to know now. My behaviour I'm going to bring to the table, so I'm not going to ask any questions, even though I may want to, I'm not going to ask for reassurance. I'm going along with the probability,' and the probability is what?

Lara: That he's not going to be doing anything bad.

Windy: That's right. That's it, and that's all we have in life is probability, and you're trying to make a new world, Lara's world, where it's possible to know things instantly, you want to know them, in the area of threat. Again, you can actually transfer that into other areas of your life, saying, 'I don't need to know this, I don't need to know that.'

Lara: Yeah, that's true, because I am hypervigilant in other areas of my life too, and I would always be wanting to know questions after questions after questions, and being able to predict exactly what the outcome's going to be in different situations. And it is quite tiring.

Windy: Yeah, because, 'If I can predict them', then what?

Lara: There's safety in that.

Windy: Yeah. But, you see, that's precisely the opposite. There's safety in giving up the need for certainty.

Lara: Yeah. I get it. I understand because I'm thinking that something's unsafe, therefore my body's responding to that in a way that makes it unsafe, and that's going back to my brain: 'I'm unsafe, I'm unsafe,' and it just creates this continuous feeling of feeling unsafe that I'm creating for myself.

Windy: But, if you can go back at that time to say, 'Look, I'm probably demanding certainty now. Let's go back. What am I demanding certainty about? Let's see if I can still want it but not need it and act according to that,' if you did that over time, I think what you would is to recognise that safety is not getting the certainty that you need, it's being able to not need it and to tolerate it. That's safety.

Lara: Yeah, OK.... That would feel great.

Windy: Well, it is a skill. That's the good news. The bad news is, unfortunately we haven't got a part of our brain we can rip out and take out the rigid attitude bit and put in the flexible attitude. That would be nice, but not in our lifetime, I think. But it is a skill and it is a skill that, if you're really wanting to get to grips with this jealousy issue, another issue related to uncertainty, you could do it.

Lara: Yeah. So, it's stopping, recognising where I'm at in that moment ... and identifying that perhaps I am being too rigid and I need just to take some time.

Windy: Reminding yourself that, yeah, it would be nice to know but you don't need to know and, therefore, you need to act according to not needing to know, and, therefore, you stop all the questions.

Lara: Yeah.

Windy: Even though there's a part of you saying, 'Ask! Ask! Ask!' because there's going to be. And, even if you ask a question, you could then say to him, let's say, 'Don't answer it.' Even if it's out of your mouth, you could say, 'Don't answer it.'

Lara: OK, yeah. So, if it's all too much, I can let a little bit out, but, yes, he doesn't need to, because, actually, yes, he's just reaffirming that sense of threat for me, isn't he, if he starts to go down that path of answering the questions. OK, yeah.

Windy: Yeah, that's right. I'm not against reassurance but I am against reassurance when you're not reassurable, and, when you're in this, 'I have to know for sure that he's not doing,' and he gives you an answer, you might say, 'Yeah, but that doesn't sound quite right,' and then you'll elaborate on that.

Lara: That makes a lot of sense.

Windy: Yeah.

Lara: ... OK, yeah.... [*Pause*] Yeah, it will be interesting to try it and see what happens.

Windy: Well, let's rehearse it. Imagine a situation that's coming up. Have you got a situation that's coming up with him, like you're going out somewhere?

[*Lara has found my REBT-informed 'take' on her unhealthy jealousy helpful. The next step is for her to rehearse it to see if she can apply it.*]

Lara: Yeah, he'll be going to a wedding without me. So, what about that?

Windy: That's great. When?

Lara: In a couple of weekends, and he's staying overnight, and his brother's going, I'm not going. They're friends of his from a long time ago. So, there'll be loads of people there that I don't know. It will be quite a party atmosphere. My brain's already going to, 'Oh, what if some girl tries to pick him up?'

Windy: So, the 'what if' is back to the uncertainty. Now, let's hear you get into the flexible attitude towards uncertainty and being able to tolerate it bit first. OK, over to you.

Lara: OK. I mean, I'm not really sure how to start this, to be honest. Is this a scenario where I'm talking to – are you him?

Windy: No, you're talking to yourself first of all.

Lara: OK, yeah. So, he's going to go to this wedding and I don't know who's going to be there. I don't exactly know what the sleeping arrangements are, I don't know what sort of state he's going to get into whilst he's going to be at this wedding, I don't know whether there's going to be decent phone reception there … and I have to be OK with not knowing the answers to those things.

Windy: Not OK with it but, if you like, uncomfortable with it.

Lara: OK. So, I have to be able to feel OK with sitting in the discomfort.

Windy: Yeah, 'Because I don't need to know the answers to any of those questions.'

Lara: Yes, I don't need to know the answers…. OK, yeah. I don't need to know the answers as to whether there's going to be any hot women there who want to flirt with him and … [*pause*] I don't need to know the answers to whether or not he's going to get really, really drunk and not know what he's doing.

Windy: Right, OK. That's right, you don't.

Lara: Wow, it feels really difficult even to say that because that isn't honestly how I feel at this point.

Windy: No, but what you feel is guided by your attitude on this occasion.

Lara: Yeah. So top down: I think it, and then my body feels it.

Windy: Yeah, even though you may not be aware of it, you're still appraising it because that's your habitual attitude.

Lara: Yes.

Windy: 'Lots of uncertainty, and I've got to know and if I don't know, danger is going to lead me.'

Lara: Yeah.... OK, yeah. I mean, like you say, I think it feels like the sort of thing that you need to practise a lot so that you do start to think that way.

Windy: Yeah, and going along with the probability: 'What I know about him is that, when he's drunk, he may get flirty,' but is that it?

Lara: Yeah, but I don't know because I won't be there.

Windy: I know, but what's he like as a person? I'm not saying on this occasion, but are we talking about somebody who, if he gets drunk, will go off and see if he can sleep around with the hottest women in the place or are we talking about somebody who, when he gets drunk, he might be a bit flirty but that's all before he falls asleep?

Lara: Yeah, but that's the thing, I don't know.

Windy: No, but you've been with him for how long?

Lara: Three-and-a-half years.

Windy: So, you know him much better than I do.

Lara: Yeah.

Windy: So, what I'm saying is, what's the probability?

Lara: Yes, and, when I'm rational about it, yes, the probability would be incredibly low.

Windy: Exactly. So that guides you, OK? So that's the other bit: 'I don't need to know and the probability is he's not going to be doing anything that I would really object to. I don't need to know that, but that's the probability.'

Lara: Yeah.

Windy: And I'm choosing to be guided by the probability.

Lara: Yeah, OK.

Windy: And, if you were guided by the probability, what would you do?

Lara: Make an active choice to not let it upset me so much.

Windy: Yeah, and not ask all these questions of yourself and of him.

Lara: Yeah. Yes, that's true.... [*Pause*] And I feel calm in my body when I think about it like that.

Windy: Incidentally, you can practise that, not obsessively, but just before he goes and when he's there. The other thing that I would say is, 'If the worst comes to the worst and he is shagging around and he is going to leave me, then I'm going to be,' in terms of what we were saying earlier, do you remember that?

Lara: … Yeah.

Windy: What did we say earlier about that?

Lara: I can't remember now. Well, it's not the end of the world, is it? I'm not going to die, for example.

Windy: 'I'm not going to die. I'm going to process it. I'm not going to bury my feelings. I'm going to write about my feelings, I'm going to process it in that way. I'm going to rely on friends for support and get through it that way.'

Lara: Yeah.

Windy: So now you've got what I call both ends covered.

[I had to guide Lara quite a bit through the rehearsal of her new attitude-based solution and I wished I had suggested that she rehearsed it again with me taking more of a back seat.]

Lara: Yeah.

Windy: The immediate uncertainty, which you're going to practise being flexible about, and what I call the distal fear of being left, which, when you start thinking it, you stop thinking about it because, in your mind, it's so bad. But, when we actually look at it, yes, it would be bad, you wouldn't want it, but you'd be able to process it and work it through.

Lara: Yeah. OK, thank you. Yeah…. Yeah, 'cos it is catastrophising as well, isn't it, to a degree and it's not real; it is in my imagination.

Windy: Yeah.

Lara: And yes.

Windy: But I think it stems from the idea that, 'Terrible things will happen if I don't know that things are OK, and this is one of the terrible things that will happen.' Now, if you really get to grips with dealing with uncertainty in this area and other areas of your life, then it could make a really big difference to you.

Lara: It would and it would take up a lot less energy as well, because it takes up a lot of thinking and a lot of energy, and also, I think, creates a disharmony in my relationship with him as well because, whilst he doesn't say anything, he's kind of aware of when that's going on for me. He can see it in my body and in my face and my behaviour. I think that can't be nice to be on the receiving end of that, especially when he hasn't actually done anything, to my knowledge, in this relationship.

Windy: Right.

Lara: And I do want this relationship to work.

Windy: Yeah, so I think, in order to make it work, do the bit that's in your control, which is working on changing your attitude. The point is, whether you have a jealousy problem or not, you still may not like him coming around and saying, 'Oh, he's been offered money for sexual services.' That may not be your cup of tea whether you have a jealousy issue or not.

Lara: Just horrible. Where my brain would go in that.

Windy: Yeah, exactly. So, you tell him things you don't like, 'cos the other thing that needs to be factored in here is that, if he is around, you can tell him how you feel.

Lara: Yeah, and that's definitely helping to express that. It just makes me feel so embarrassed, though, because I feel like it's just such crazy thinking.

Windy: Well, but you could actually say to him, 'Look, having worked it through, I still don't like not knowing things, but I don't need to know. And, so just be aware that, if you want to tell me, that's fine, I'd like to hear it, but I'm not going to drive you mad anymore with the questioning.'

Lara: Yeah. Well, yeah, little steps, I suppose.

Windy: Oh yeah.

Lara: Can I even just practise this? If I have this imaginary scenario in my head, I can just practise? I don't necessarily need to express that to him. I can just practise it in my own mind, practise saying these things that you said to me, and that will help diminish it. Then, actually, I don't even need to have that conversation with him necessarily.

Windy: That's right.

Lara: ... [*Pause*] It feels like that would be challenging, but... I really think I would like to try it. As soon as you said uncertainty, that, 'You don't like uncertainty,' that made me smile because I just thought that is totally it. Underneath all of those layers that's what's behind it.

Windy: Yeah.

Lara: … [*Pause*] Yeah, I feel like I need a little bit of time just to think about that, really.

Windy: OK. Well, you'll have that, and I'll send you the recording; you can listen to that.

Lara: Thank you.

Windy: And then you can go over the more practical things that we talked about there, make notes on it. Then later on I'll send you a copy of the transcript.

Lara: Cool. Thank you very much. That was very insightful.

Windy: Thank you. Are there any other questions or anything you want to say before we finish?

Lara: No, I don't think so. I feel a bit overwhelmed now. So, it would just be useful to just go away and sit with that quietly. Thank you.

[*We have covered a lot of ground in a short period of time and Lara's response indicates this. However, she will have two resources to consult later on: the recording of the session and the transcript that I routinely send to people who volunteer for my projects.*]

Windy: OK then. All the best then. Bye-bye.

Lara: Bye.

Lara's Reflections on the Session: 30/11/23

In my experience with Windy, I felt hugely understood. He identified my need for certainty very quickly and helped me to challenge that. He listened to my thinking around it and was able to offer me some alternative choices. I was so stuck in my way of thinking that I could not step back and see any other way. By showing me different options for new ways to approach my jealousy issues, he highlighted my rigidity in thinking about a situation and directed me to a solution using one of four scenarios/choices. Being able to see which ones I would/wouldn't be able to do made me feel like I was actively being accountable for my own actions towards becoming a less jealous person.

I went away feeling doubtful, thinking that it all felt very rushed and that perhaps it wasn't for me. I needed time to form a trusting bond with a therapist. And can be resistant to change! I was dismissive of the suggestions made and its effectiveness. I also questioned whether it was possible that someone I had just met would be able to facilitate any great change in my behaviour/thinking without knowing me very well.

Initially, it made no difference to my thinking. It felt like I wouldn't be able to apply this new way of thinking to any of the situations that have a tendency to crop up. But going over our transcript more recently, I can see that I have calmed down a bit in the time between our session and now (approaching four months). I can recall a couple of situations where I was able to be calm, and whilst I didn't entirely stop myself from going to a place of suspicion, I was, however, able to step back from my thoughts and hold still in my discomfort. It's difficult to break a long-held pattern of behaviour, but I feel like I am bringing awareness to my thoughts and can be more reflective rather than reactive. This has created a feeling of safety in my body and my mind. I feel less triggered by any obvious flirting and am not asking lots of questions around any activities he may have been doing when I'm not with him. Consequently, we have been able to connect with each other, as I am not coming off as suspicious and grouchy. And conversely, there have been fewer flirting incidents, so I wonder if he was doing it to create a game of some sort, but that's another story?! That is not to say I don't have moments of suspicion and jealousy, but I am trying.

13

Helping People with Problems with Unhealthy Envy

Helping the Client to Understand and Deal with Unhealthy Envy

Here are some ideas that I have found useful to introduce into my conversation with clients that can help them understand and deal with unhealthy envy.

* When a person experiences unhealthy envy, they hold a rigid and extreme attitude towards another person having something or somebody in their life that the person prizes but lacks (e.g. 'My friend has just got a new job, and I wish I had what she has and therefore I must have what she has, and I can't bear the resulting deprivation'). When a person experiences unhealthy envy, behaviourally they take desperate steps to get what they don't have and may try to spoil in action and/or in words what the other person has and enjoys or they may devalue the other person to others. Their unhealthy envy-influenced thinking is ruminative in nature and is focused on how to get what the other person has or on how to spoil things for the other person.
* The healthy alternative to unhealthy envy is healthy envy.
* When the person experiences healthy envy about the same adversity, they hold a flexible and non-extreme attitude towards this adversity (e.g. 'My friend has just got a new job, and I wish I had what she has, but I don't have to have it. I don't like the resulting deprivation, but I can bear it and it is worth bearing'). When a person

experiences healthy envy, they still might strive to get what the other person has, but only if they truly want it and not because the other person has it. Also, their efforts in this regard will not be desperate. They will neither try to spoil things for the other person in action or thought nor will they devalue the other person in their mind or to others.

- When a self-devaluation attitude is a prominent feature of unhealthy envy, I discuss the importance of developing an attitude of unconditional self-acceptance as a solution.

- Yet again, if the person is interested, I will help them change their rigid/extreme attitudes to their flexible/non-extreme counterparts and help them think and act in ways that will support the development of these attitudes.

Transcript of My Work with a Person with a Problem with Unhealthy Envy

Therapist – Volunteer:	Windy – Anne
Venue:	Private session that took place on 03/08/23 arranged via Onlinevents
Time:	48 minutes 53 secs

Windy: OK, Anne, what is your understanding of why we're talking today?

Anne: Well, what it is, is this is quite a longstanding issue for me and it's specific to a couple of my peers who are in my professional network. I would say I get quite triggered by them. … I think it's to do with that I look at what they've achieved and what they're achieving and… I suppose it's that I'm comparing myself to them and thinking, well, I've worked just as hard and, in some cases, have helped to support their development, but I still seem to be sitting in a position where I don't feel as if I've had the same level of success, don't seem to have progressed as much – but I suppose it's about me – as I would've hoped. And it manifests itself in, I think it's probably a resentment, that's a kind of envy of them, and the way that makes me feel is not very pleasant and not very nice.

Windy: Is it OK if I refer to your pre-assessment questionnaire as we go?

Anne: Yes, absolutely.

Windy: So, what if you were more of an operator? What would you have achieved if you were more of an operator? Because that's one of the things that you see: 'I don't want to be an operator. They're an operator,' and I'm just wondering what would've happened if you were more of an operator?

Anne: I've spent a lot of time thinking about this, and that totally nutshells it for me, and it's that term. If I had been an operator, I think I'd have done better. I think I would've progressed further.

Windy: Yeah. But you've chosen not to be an operator?

Anne: Chosen, or perhaps it's just the way I am.

Windy: What is it about being an operator that offends you?

Anne: … I think it's about particularly because I did work at a university and I was an academic, and I think it's like seeing people standing on shoulders of others ... and perhaps sometimes I kind of feel that perhaps those people sometimes do better disproportionately from how they're interacting, and I would say pick off certain people that can help progress them.

Windy: Would it be right to say that they are using them?

Anne: I suppose in that older kind of terminology, yeah, you say people are users.

Windy: Sorry, I am old, I use old terminology.

Anne: So am I.

Windy: What's the modern terminology that we should be using?

Anne: Operators. In some respects, there's that element of people who are really strong networkers as well. And, of course, we're all told that we should network. We're all told that we should make professional connections with people. And that's in all sorts of professions. Some of that just feels to me a bit false. It feels to me sometimes that, when people are doing that, it's like what can they get by doing it?

Windy: What do you think would've happened if you were an operator in this sense and they weren't: they were more like you, and you were more like them? What do you think would've happened?

Anne: They'd probably be sat here talking to you and feeling slightly bereft, perhaps. I know I'm doing, and I think that's what's unpleasant to me. ... These are people I'm close to. I don't really want to feel like I do.

Windy: So, let's suppose then, and this is another scenario, that none of you are operators, what would happen then?

Anne: None of us are operators. Well, I think I'd have done better than them. That's the truth.

Windy: Given a level playing field, then, then you would've done better.

Anne: Possibly.

Windy: If you were an operator and they weren't, you would've done a lot better, and they're operators and you're not, they're doing better. So, when you envy them, what do you envy?

[*While there is no place in ONEplus Therapy for 'person assessment', there is a place for a contextual assessment of the person's nominated problem and that is what I have been doing up to this point – modifying the relevant variables in the service of gaining a contextual understanding of the issue.*]

Anne: … [*Long pause*] I think what I'm envying is the … [*pause*] progress that I can see that they're making, whether that be through working with other people, and in the academic world, it's about the publications that you write, isn't it? It's also about having a job and getting promotions and things like that as well.

Windy: What area of discourse were you involved in?

Anne: I'm a sports historian, which is niche, very niche – sports history.

Windy: And they're sports historians too?

Anne: The older peer is ... and the younger one is a historian/sociologist but is working in the same topical area as I do. In fact, I've been that person's supervisor, and I'm working on a project with that person now. And that's why it's problematic because both of those people are close.

Windy: They're in your face, so to speak.

Anne: Yeah, and it's hard for me. But then again, there is this contradiction in it because they obviously do have abilities and talents.

Windy: It's interesting that, when you get envious, what's your mindset? In the moment when you're envious in this way, I guess you regard your envy as unhealthy or healthy?

[As I have shown when discussing the REBT-informed conceptualisations of the common emotional problems that appear in this book, a distinction is made between healthy and unhealthy negative emotions. Here I am asking Anne whether she regards her envy as healthy or unhealthy.]

Anne: Oh, it's unhealthy, isn't it?

Windy: Well, some envy is healthy because with envy, you could say, 'Oh, this person's got this. How do I get it? What can I learn from them?' You can have that kind of more admiring type of envy.

Anne: I think this is why I thought it would be a useful exercise just to talk to somebody who's fully detached from it because, in my view, it's not healthy.

Windy: No. So, when you are in that unhealthy frame of mind, I just want to get a quality of what you focus on.

Anne: … I don't almost feel like I'm focusing on it. If I'm in that situation, it's like I'm triggered. It's not a focus. It's almost like reactive.

Windy: Yeah, OK, but what are you thinking, whether you're focusing on it or you're triggered?

Anne: Well, I would be thinking along the lines of … in the case of the younger one, 'Stop going on about all of the things that you're doing as if they're some kind of big deal.' That's what's going in my head. And probably not helped by the situation that we're in a group of people, and everybody's going, 'Oh, isn't that amazing? Isn't that brilliant?' and it's like, 'Well, actually, it's quite normal what that person is doing. It's not a big deal.' So that kind.

Windy: So, what do you envy then? Let's take her first of all.

Anne: Right, OK. Actually, I suppose, thinking about that question … I'm not necessarily so much envying what she's doing. I think I get envious in that situation because everybody's saying how amazing what that person is doing is, and it's not. It's just potentially some of that stuff is just quite normal things to be doing and why are you getting this almost over-celebratory reaction. And also, quite a lot of the stuff that she does is not stuff that she's just done by herself; it's stuff that other people are assuring up because she's a younger researcher. I mean, she's a PhD student. So, I suppose what goes with that is that element of you've got to encourage PhD students, but at the same time, you've got to be realistic in what you're telling them is fabulous and what you're telling them is regular. So, I don't know, maybe I feel like she's a bit attention-seeking, and I just don't like that.

Windy: Let's see if we're talking about the same emotion because envy, for me – and I'm interested to see how you define it – has got that quality that somebody has got something that you haven't got and you want.

Anne: Yeah.

Windy: So, I'm just listening to you through that lens and thinking, 'Well, what does Anne want that she hasn't got that this person's got?'

Anne: … [*Pause*] Yeah. Possibly, perhaps it's the kind of praise and recognition that this person is getting when I think of a lot of things I've done in the past.

Windy: One of my virtually earliest memories, and I think I do remember it because I kept on being reminded of it, when I was very young I went to the circus and the clowns were going and everyone was laughing and joking at clowns, and I got up and I said, 'And I've got a cough, Mister,' in other words, 'Give me some recognition. I want some attention. I've got a cough, Mister.'

> [*Maybe it would have been better to ask Anne for her permission for me to make this related self-disclosure.*]

Anne: Yeah.

Windy: So, it sounds like you want some of that praise.

Anne: Well, I think there is an element of that, and it's not because I haven't had praise from people, but it's just that it's something about what is being praised, I think, as well.

Windy: She doesn't really deserve that much praise, does she?

Anne: Well, no, for that person, that's kind of what gets under my skin. And, in fact, in those meetings I'd actually like to say to people, 'Can you just stop going on about that?'

Windy: 'It's just a cough, Mister. There's nothing special about it.'

Anne: A bit. There is a bit of that in it. So, I'll give you an example. So, again, because I'm in a little research network, and, again, in some respects ... it's enmeshed because this researcher started off under my supervision and a colleague's supervision as a Master's student researching in what was essentially my main area of expertise. And I think at that point ... and I would never have withheld my ongoing and full support in that situation, and obviously, you give that as part of your academic role and your job, but I think from that point onwards ... [*pause*] ... because of that, we've stayed connected because we do have a mutual research interest. Obviously, I benefit from that as well, and that's what I think makes it difficult because I can't completely detach from it because we're invested in the same kind of research... But it's almost like I feel like she's running away with it, in some respects as well. It's not just that thing about her being elevated. It's about ... seeing, perhaps, progress that she's making, and I'm kind of thinking, 'How has somebody who's not been in the game that long, how are they doing so much, and how are they managing to get so much traction in such a short space of time?'

Windy: And you suspect it's because she's an operator?

Anne: ... She's an arch networker, for sure, which I know I'm not ... and I'm not comfortable making those.

Windy: So, in a way, if we were to look at it, because envy is this thing about, 'Somebody else has got something that I don't,' and I want to zero in on that – is it the praise? What has she got that you haven't got that you want at the moment, that you envy, if we were going to really focus on that?

Anne: ... [*Pause*] I suppose it is ... [*pause*] and I'm not sure whether I want it now or whether there's something a bit retrospective about it as well, in that I'm thinking, 'I wish I'd have had all those opportunities and contacts when I was studying the same research,' and I miss those.

Windy: 'She's got now what I wished I had then.'

Anne: A bit, yeah. I think it is that.

Windy: Yeah, which you may have been able to get if you'd been an operator then.

Anne: I may have done. I think as well, one of the things that's going with this territory at the moment is the research now is very on trend. It's research on the outdoors, so all the stuff is about health and wellbeing and all of that.

Windy: So, it may well be that it's a combination of things that she's doing something very sexy, on-trend, she's an operator. And you were doing research that wasn't that sexy, and you weren't prepared to be an operator. But I don't think you see the full picture, do you? You don't say to yourself, 'Look, OK, she's doing well, she's got what I want, but, in a way, back then, I wasn't really working in a very trendy area, so that was a bit of a drawback. I wasn't prepared to be an operator; that was a drawback. So, she's benefiting from things that I didn't have the opportunity to have, and I wasn't prepared to do.'

Anne: Yeah.

Windy: I mean, if you looked at the whole picture, what would that do to your envy?

Anne: ... [*Pause*] What it would do, it rationalises it for me. But I suppose, as well, just thinking a bit more about not being prepared to do something, but I think there's a bit more to it than that. I come from a working-class background, and my brother and I were the first people in our families to go to university, and I think I was very deferential to an extent, even in my professional life, being very deferential to people who are considered to be higher status in the university system.

Windy: Respectful, you mean?

Anne: I wasn't the sort of person who would knock on my supervisor's door and say, 'Can I do this?' or, 'I can do this, I can do that.'

Windy: Do you wish you were or you're glad you're not?

Anne: Well, I think I tell myself that I'm glad I'm not; I don't want to be like that. But I think probably, on reflection, at the age that I am now, I kind of think, well, actually, I wish I had had that confidence and been more … not worried about putting myself out there.

Windy: There are a couple of factors here which I think we have to be clear about. One is the putting yourself out there, which you wish you had been more like that, and I think you look at this young woman and you see her as being full of the confidence and you go, 'I wish I was like that.'

Anne: Yeah.

Windy: But the other element is the using bit. I just wonder, if you were confident back then, would you have also been an operator or would you have drawn the line and said, 'Actually, I'll knock on people's doors, I'll put myself forward, but I'm not going to use them'?

Anne: Yeah. I think there might have been a bit. … [*Pause*] I don't know, I like to think of myself as a fair person in terms of playing fair with the people that I work with…. And, in fact, in some respects I would say that it's probably almost like I'm probably a bit too like that.

Windy: Yeah, and do you wish that you weren't or that you're glad that you are?

Anne: No, I'm glad that I am, but I just wish other people would like....

Windy: What?

Anne: I wish everybody played fair with everybody.

Windy: Yeah, and I wish everybody had a full head of hair. Where does that get us?

Anne: Yeah. But I do kind of ground that ... in the sense of the way I work with people and things like that.

Windy: Part of it, the picture is – we're putting it together with her – it's like you look at it and you say, 'This person is being praised for something normal. But I guess that's part of the changing structure of academia or maybe there's something about her that elicits that. And, as I look at her and what she's achieved, she has part of what I wish I had. I wish I was more confident and outgoing, be prepared to knock on people's doors. But I'm glad that I'm not somebody who used that to my advantage, because one of my core values is playing fair. I wish that the world shared that core value, but, sadly, it doesn't.' Obviously, it doesn't because, if it did, she wouldn't have had all the benefits because she would be playing fair. 'So, I wish it was like that, but it's not and, therefore, let's stand back and have a look at what I have achieved, given the fact that I came from a situation of deference and didn't do these things, and look at what I've achieved as a result of not doing these things.'

Anne: Yeah.

Windy: Part of unhealthy envy is you don't stand back and have a look at what you have done. You're just so focused on what the other person's doing.

Anne: Yeah.

Windy: And I think that one of the ways that you can deal with this particular woman is to remind yourself of the whole picture. I know it's lengthy, but I think you can condense it in your own way. But the ingredients seem to be, yes, she's getting the benefits that you're not getting, the praise that you're not getting, but she's partly getting it because, although she presumably has some talent, she's confident, she's prepared to be an operator and she's working in a very sexy area and putting all of those together. 'I wish I was like that. I'm glad I'm not an operator because I believe in the values of playing fair. What I've achieved is, actually, a result of my talent rather than my confidence and my social operativeness. So let me have a look at what I've done.' So, if you embed the initial reaction in that frame, what effect does doing that have?

Anne: … Yeah, I think what you were saying about reframing and thinking about what have I managed to achieve, is an important one. Interestingly, actually, I was having a conversation with my son last night because I'm going to Japan in September to do with research. I was just talking about it, and he said, 'Mum, you know that's a good deal, that is, going to Japan,' whereas I don't tend to see things as a big deal, and perhaps that's a bit as well. I don't see things like that as a big deal. I think, 'Well, yeah,

I've been invited to go, but then equally somebody else could be invited to go.'

Windy: Yeah. 'The only time that I'm going to recognise that it's a big deal is if I'm the only person in the universe that could possibly be invited.'

Anne: ... Yeah, probably. Actually, that's probably about it. And I can extrapolate that out to lots and lots of scenarios: when I see things on TV where people are having a big hoorah about things.

Windy: In other words, 'For me to recognise and own something that I've done that's achievable, nobody else could possibly have done it.'

Anne: Well, not nobody, but it would be something that was perhaps more rare.

Windy: OK.

Anne: ... Because, in the grand scheme of things there are people out there all of the time doing really amazing things that are worthy of being praised.

Windy: Right. But, if you can stand back and say, 'Yes, despite the fact there are other people that can do it, I'm still pleased that I've been invited.'

Anne: Yeah, I suppose so. So that thing about what I have achieved, perhaps not underselling myself to myself.

Windy: That's right, yeah. It's almost like saying, 'Looking at this person's CV, I wouldn't offer her a job.'

Anne: Yeah.

Windy: Why don't you revisit your CV but this time from a different perspective? Look at it from the point of view as a working-class woman, first to go to university who didn't have the confidence to knock on doors, that wasn't prepared to use people, have a look at it from that point of view. It would be interesting to see what you think.

Anne: Yeah.

Windy: Shall we move on to the other one?

Anne: Yeah, if there's time.

Windy: Of course, there's time. Are there any common elements of looking at this particular scenario that we can transfer to the other scenario?

        [*I have done too much of the work for Anne on the previous issue. It would have been better, for example, if I had asked Anne what she is going to take away from our discussion rather than me summarising it. However, I do ask her for the elements that are common to the situation that we have discussed and the one that we are going to discuss.*]

Anne: Yeah. It's quite interesting because they're quite significant ages apart.... And the second person, again there's no doubt about it, this person does work hard, they deserve to be where they are, but I don't know if this would be more classic envy, because actually I do look at that person and think … [*pause*], 'How are you in that position but I'm not?' … And I suppose there's lots of circumstances. I suppose, thinking about CVs, if you looked at both of our CVs … this is a person who ticks, ticks, ticks, ticks every single box to jump, jump, jump, jump. But, then again, I look at that person and I just ... [*pause*] can't really detach very easily from their achievement in comparison to my own.

Windy: How would you describe their achievement in comparison to your own?

Anne: ... It is deserved.... It is deserved.... [*Pause*] But, again, it is also built on this real strategising and networking with various people. All the people you see that person working with are all people who actually are pretty good academics, and it's almost like there's this real strategising about where to go next and who to work with next. And, anything that doesn't serve their purpose it's like, 'I'm not getting involved.' Even if it was a good thing to do, intrinsically good, they wouldn't do it.

Windy: So, she's self-serving.

Anne: I think so.

Windy: Are you self-serving?

Anne: Probably.

Windy: You are?

Anne: Probably.

Windy: In that strategizing...?

Anne: Not in that sense.

Windy: Would you like to be as self-serving as she?

Anne: No.

Windy: So, what sorts of disbenefits have you experienced for not being as self-serving as she has decided to be?

Anne: Well … I suppose some of the things that I've tried to – I don't know, sometimes when I think about it, I think it's about me; it's not about that other person. It's about that I haven't been as efficient or I just haven't been as skilled in trying to make certain relationships work, for example, professionally, and that's the point.

Windy: And how do you view yourself for not having those skills or not being as skilled, I should say?

Anne: Well, I think it makes me look a bit stupid, actually.

Windy: Now, let's take that out of it. If we took that out of it and you said, 'Actually, I'm not stupid. I'm an ordinary human being. My worth wouldn't have gone up if I did have those skills, but I wish I had them.'

Anne: Yeah.

Windy: I wish I had them, but I'm not stupid for not having them. I'm the same worthwhile person whether I've got them or not.' Now, that attitude, would that make a difference to you when you looked at what she was doing?

Anne: … [*Long pause*] I'm not sure it would, really.

               [*Here, I am assessing the potential role of self-devaluation in Anne's unhealthy envy. She makes it clear that this is not a factor. However, later it does seem that lack of self-validation is a factor. It is cleat then that for Anne self-devaluation and lack of self-validation are different concepts.*]

Windy: OK. So, if we gave you one ingredient that would solve the envy problem with her, what would it be?

Anne: Now, this is going to sound really horrible, what I'm going to say next. I wish something would go wrong for her just once. I just really wish that a project or something that she was working on would run into some kind of problem rather than everything seeming to just ch-ch-ch-ch-ch, fall into place.

Windy: So, it sounds like, whether or not the strategising, what you envy is the fact that things have continued to go right for her.

Anne: Yeah.

Windy: And you wish that you had had that in your career?

Anne: Yeah, sometimes I do. Yeah, I do sometimes wish that things had been a bit smoother. Yeah, I do.

Windy: If it had gone smoothly for you, what would that have changed in how you view yourself or her or the world? What would that have changed for you?

Anne: I probably would've felt a bit more validated for the amount of effort.

Windy: Validated by whom?

Anne: Well, by the system, I suppose, because it's the system that you're sat in, isn't it, that validates you, that makes you feel valued or makes you feel as if what you're doing is worthwhile. It is about how you feel yourself, but the system does, and I suppose that's ultimately what work does to people and particularly something like academic work is particularly vicious from that point of view. It's competitive. Whether people like it or not, it's competitive. And so you're in this system that judges you by certain marks of success, which is kind of right, isn't it, wherever you work?

Windy: But where's the role for self-validation?

Anne: … [*Pause*] Well, I suppose there is a role for self-validation, just in terms of perhaps projects that you do that you've achieved, help that you might give to other people that makes you feel satisfied in what you're doing.

Windy: And what happens if you could validate yourself in the direct face of lack of validation by your institution or your organisation? What difference would that make?

Anne: … I suppose it does make a difference, but just maybe the top and bottom of it is, is it's not the same as … being promoted in your job or even having a job.… [*Pause*] So there's that as well.

Windy: Yeah, sure, but again what's better for your mental health: striving for other validation or working towards self-validation?

Anne: … [*Long pause*] Probably self is more important, but you can't discount.…

Windy: No, I'm not asking you to discount. I'm asking you to recognise that, yes, it would be better if the organisation had validated you and it probably would've done if you were more like her. But you're not, and I think that that's the rub. But, given the fact you're not for all kinds of reasons, that's a disappointment and you could say, 'I wish I was more like her, but, ultimately, I'm in charge of my validation. And for my mental health and for dealing with envy, it's about self-validation rather than wanting to bring her down.' The envy that you're talking about is what we call an ugly emotion.

Anne: It is very, I know.

Windy: So, it's about, 'If I can't bring myself up, I want to bring them down.' The other thing is it's important for you to accept yourself for feeling envious, because you can really condemn yourself for feeling that way, but it's part of the human condition. I'm just thinking, if you could really recognise that, 'Yes, I wish I did have the organisational validation that she's got and this other one is on the way to getting,' it sounds like.

Anne: That's it.

Windy: She's going to bypass you.

Anne: Yeah, exactly it. In a sense, they've both done that.

Windy: Yeah, but they've both done that because they have got things that you haven't got, are prepared to do things that you've not been prepared to do and are self-promotional in the sense that is far beyond that you have even thought of doing, in a way. In this unfair world, they're getting the benefits that you could've got if you were like that, but you're not.

Anne: No.

Windy: But you can actually still validate yourself, particularly in the context of what you have achieved, given the fact what you brought to the game as Anne, not as Bloggs and Bloggs. And then you could say, 'Yeah, I wish I was more like that, but—

Anne: But I'm not.

Windy: 'But I'm not. In some senses, I don't want to be. And, in any case, that ain't changing my worth because I'm in charge of that. I'm in charge of whether I validate myself or not.'

Anne: Yeah.

Windy: Can I share a personal example scenario with you?

Anne: Yeah.

Windy: I've published 265 books. How many awards from British therapy and counselling associations have I received?

Anne: I hope you're not going to say none. I hope you say some, but probably not as many as the books that you've been published.

Windy: That's correct but how many do you think I have received?

Anne: Ten?

Windy: None.

Anne: ... Yeah.

Windy: And why is that? And I'll tell you why. Because I don't network. I just concentrate on what I do. I enjoy what I do. Yes, when I see people getting OBEs here and awards here, I say, 'Yeah, that would be nice, but that isn't me, because I have chosen to do what I want to do.' And, in some senses, if you look at it and stand back, you could say, 'Yes, I wish I was more like that. No, I'm glad I'm not like that.' One is very self-promotional – she's got talent but she's very self-promotional in the sense of not regarding other people. She seems to edit out other people: if it's not going to benefit her, she isn't going to do it. And you have to ask yourself, 'Am I like that? Do I want to be like that?' And you don't. And you don't want to be somebody who uses people. And that has a price.

Anne: Yeah.

Windy: In the same way as my 265 books, and I've decided not to do any bloody networking because I don't like that kind of thing and that comes at a price.

[*Again, I self-disclose without asking for permission here. Also, I could have checked whether this self-disclosure was helpful to Anne.*]

Anne: Yeah.... Stepping back, I get that and I think that thing about looking at the CV and everything and just perhaps mapping a bit what I've done and what I'm doing moving forward, probably will be helpful. But I think that the thing ... that I think will potentially continue to be a bit of an issue for me is having that direct contact with those people and that kind of sense.

Windy: That's why you need to prepare your mind just before you go into the situation, just like when you go into an interview you prepare for the interview. You need to prepare your mind for this by going over some of the things that we've been talking about, because, if you don't prepare your mind, your mind will revert to what it's been doing.

[I make the point that this new way of thinking needs to be practised and that Anne can do this practice before she meets with the two women under discussion.]

Anne: Yeah.

Windy: And you don't need to practise that. You're good at that. But you do need to practise, and it is a skill. It is a skill what I'm talking about here, but it's a skill that if you practise it and allow yourself: the first thing is you are going to be envious maybe, so you need to respond to that. And what does that prove? Either it proves that you're a horrible person with an ugly emotion or it proves you're an ordinary human being, and human beings suffer from envy. You go back into the Old Testament and you'll find loads of examples of envy in there.

Anne: Yeah.

Windy: Cain and Abel, maybe. Why don't you summarise what we've talked about today?

Anne: Now?

Windy: Yes, now.

Anne: That's a tough one. Yeah. So ... [*pause*] that's quite hard, actually, thinking about it, summarising it.... [*Pause*] So, I suppose ... [*pause*] I think I've got to think more about ... [*pause*] what my achievements are and ... [*pause*] the kind of circumstances that I've kind of progressed in and acknowledge that the conditions and the circumstances that belong to me are about me and my values as a person.... [*Pause*] And, perhaps, those other people, my peers, they're different people to me; the way that they do things is the way they do things. It's not my way. And, although that's led them to get a kind of success that I would quite like to have for myself, I'm not prepared or I'm not somebody who's going to move and do things in the same way as they do. And, I suppose, taking that forward a bit, by definition that means that the outcomes for me are going to be different.

Windy: And it still would be nice to have what they've achieved, but you need to put that into a context. That summary's beautiful. I think what I'm saying is that's what you need to touch base with before you go into meetings know that they're there. You need to prepare your mind for that to the point that you can do it quite quickly and maybe with shortcuts and certain phrases that might come to mind. But, if you did that, I think you'd solve the problem.

Anne: Yeah. I think, actually, that thing that you just said there, that's what I've got to actively remember, actually, to do, because sometimes you go into meetings and you're on the hop; you come from one task to the next.

Windy: Right, but you know where you can go to prepare? There's always the toilet. Go into the toilet and prepare your mind.

Anne: That's interesting, actually, because I'm in direct contact with the older peer and she contacts me and says, 'We've got a conference at the end of the month. When are you going? Will we be meeting up?' and it's like, 'Well, yeah,' because I do want to see her. So I'm going to the toilet first.

Windy: Go to the toilet first because you're not going to solve the problem by avoiding her and the other one.

Anne: No, I know.

Windy: You're going to be maintaining the problem.

Anne: Yeah.

Windy: So, it's about practising the mindset that you beautifully summarised before you go and meet her and while you're there if you need to, but recognise that, yeah, she may well end up with greater accolades than you. I just have to remind myself, when I see other people getting things that I would like, I say: yeah, but I've chosen the pathway. I could've chosen to sit on committees and join associations and that may have helped me, but it's not me. It would've bored me silly. I wouldn't have wanted to do that.

Anne: Yeah.

Windy: So, it doesn't matter if I do 300 books, I'm still going to be the same. I accept that. I just concentrate on it because I enjoy it.

Anne: Yeah.

Windy: And that will enable you to focus on what's
              important to you rather than focusing on what they
              have that they've got through means that you
              wouldn't have actually wanted to do the things that
              they've got. It's lovely to talk to you. I'll write to
              you in three months' time, and you can give us an
              update on how things are going, for the book.

Anne: OK.

Windy: Nice to meet you.

Anne: Thank you so much for the opportunity. It's been
              good to talk it through, to be honest.

Windy: Good, excellent. All the best.

Anne's Reflections on the Session: 30/11/23

Until the ONEplus Therapy session, I could only talk to myself
about the envy I felt when interacting with two close academic
peers – I couldn't share how I felt with anyone in my network
because we mingled with the same people at conferences and
through social media channels; I was certain my partner would
dismiss or deride the way I felt. Just having a chance to speak my
feelings of envy to a therapist was an opportunity to potentially
manage the spiteful thoughts that had spoilt my interactions with
people who I otherwise felt were closer to being friends than
professional peers.

   Because I had already provided an outline of my situation, I
went into the session confident that Windy had already grasped
what was happening with me – we were not starting from scratch,
so there was an instant conversational connection. The ONEplus
Therapy time was fully focused on getting to the heart of the

issue, helping me make sense of it, and identifying strategies to alleviate it. Having another perspective was (and has continued to be) helpful: through Windy's questioning, I was enabled to reflect on how the situations I've experienced during my professional life, coupled with my ways of doing things, are completely different to those of the two people I envy. From talking it through in session, I'm beginning to ease up on myself and recognise that my professional outcomes are inevitably different to those of the people I envy. Windy helped me to recognise that understanding this will not necessarily stop the envy being triggered, but can moderate the emphasis in my thinking which, in turn, can temper the strength of the emotion. In this respect, I had to take ownership of where I am professionally, I was also invited to consider my achievements as worthy in themselves – without the need to compromise them through comparisons with particular others. The session also gave me permission to accept the way I feel because, to quote Windy, envy is a human emotion 'even if it [the vengeful kind] is a bit ugly'. I know now that it's important to maintain awareness of how my envy strikes in real-time and, by doing so, draw on the perspective achieved through ONEplus Therapy, i.e. switch the focus to my achievements first rather than those of my professional peers. By consciously applying this line of thinking, I can actively prepare for any occasions when I know I'll be coming into close contact with these peers and/or others who might praise them. In the short term, the impact of the session was striking – I met one of my envied peers at an academic conference the week after and generally felt less tense during conversations focused on how things were going with our jobs or past and present projects.

I'm not sure if writing a reflection about ONEplus Therapy is typical but revisiting the transcript twelve weeks later was almost like reliving the encounter again: the transcript reminded me to stay aware of how I might get caught out by feelings of envy. I can revisit the therapeutic conversation as and when I need to – when I read back over it, I feel reassured by the perspective it provides. Experiencing envy is unpleasant, but now

I understand it can be managed – I just need to remind myself to shift the focus to myself and what I've achieved rather than getting hung up on the achievements of others.

14

Helping People with a Mixture of Common Emotional Problems

My original intention in this book was to provide transcripts of nine single sessions with people each experiencing one of the major common emotional problems that I covered in this book. However, I decided to include my interview with Beau as it demonstrates that it is not always possible to work with a client who has only one common emotional issue and that sometimes one needs to be flexible and work with a mixture of such problems.

Transcript of My Work with a Person with a Mixture of Common Emotional Problems

Therapist – Volunteer:	Windy – Beau
Venue:	Private session that took place on 16/08/23 arranged via Onlinevents
Time:	45 minutes 59 secs

Windy: Hi Beau, how are you today?

Beau: I'm good, thank you, Windy. Nice to see you.

Windy: Nice to see you. And what's your understanding of the purpose of our conversation this afternoon?

Beau: So … you offer single-session therapy and we're here to work on my issues of hurt.

Windy: Two things before we get going: is it OK if I refer to your pre-session questionnaire if needs be?

Beau: Sure.

Windy: And, if I need to keep us focused by interrupting you, is that OK with you?

Beau: No problem.

Windy: How can I best do that for you?

Beau: I mean … I'm pretty flexible. I'm quite used to therapy and my supervisor's quite direct. So … I mean … whatever works for you.

Windy: So, if I say, 'May I interrupt you?' then that's OK?

Beau: Sure, yeah.

Windy: So, what would you like to achieve by the end of the session on this issue?

              [*Here I ask for Beau's session goal.*]

Beau: Yeah … I have been thinking about this and I guess, because a lot of the hurt involves family members that are very close to me – my mother and my two brothers – and I have had a lot of help with it already in terms of supervision, therapy, etc. If there was any new level of understanding or insight, that might be useful. I'm also currently weighing up a decision as to whether to carry on straight into my dissertation year, continue living in this hell, this turmoil and just power through, write the dissertation and then get on with it and leave the home, the house I'm living in at the moment that I share with my family. Or whether to try and maybe take a year out and focus on getting a better paid job so that I can leave sooner rather than later. So, it's a bit of a difficult decision I guess I'm at, at the moment.

Windy: Does dealing with your hurt feelings impact on making that decision?

Beau: Can you say more about the question?

Windy: I think we have to talk about whether you consider your hurt to be healthy or unhealthy for you and, if unhealthy, what's the alternative. I think if you experience the alternative rather than hurt, would that impact on the decision that you just outlined?

Beau: … Well, I guess my hurt … I think it's kind of healthy.

Windy: So why are you seeking help for it?

[*The purpose of this book is to show how ONEplus Therapy can be used to help people experience common emotional problems. Since Beau regards her feelings of hurt as healthy, it poses a dilemma for me in terms of the work I am doing with her in the context of my purpose in writing the book.*]

Beau: … [*Pause*] That's a good question … yeah. Even though I am in this training, maybe it's some kind of magical thinking that I'm hoping for. I don't know.

Windy: And what would that magical thinking be if you were to spell it out?

Beau: … [*Long pause*] Well, like I said, maybe there's a new level of insight but, given the in-depth work that I've been doing in terms of my training and therapy, etc., maybe there isn't.

Windy: Right. Look, let me outline my take on hurt. Before I do that, why don't you tell me what your definition of hurt is so that I can understand where you're coming from, then I'll outline my views on hurt so you can understand where I'm coming from, so we're going to be talking the same language?

Beau: I guess I'm thinking of pain, really, emotional pain rather than physical, although that does come into it too, the physical…. And it's really for me … I suppose, a deep sadness … and it does reside very, very deeply…. And I suppose I feel quite hurt in terms of this current situation…. I feel hurt that the people that I love and that did once really care very deeply for me – and I was a very loved baby – to see that change has been extremely difficult to deal with and very hurtful.

Windy: And what are the consequences of that hurt for you?

Beau: A deep longing for relationships with these people. That's not the logical part, though. That's more emotional. The logical part does not want to have a relationship with these people given what's happened, and I've detailed that in the form…. Yeah, sorry, could you repeat the question again?

Windy: What are the consequences of the hurt for you?

Beau: … Yeah…. [*Pause*] So … yeah … it just feels really unresolved … I suppose … and maybe it can't be resolved … certainly not while I'm living there.

Windy: Right, OK. There are two types of resolution, as you probably know: interpersonal resolution and intrapersonal resolution. Which of those two do you think can't be resolved?

[Here I am looking for a focus for the session.]

Beau: I would say the interpersonal at the moment can't be resolved.

Windy: And what about intrapersonal? How resolved do you feel about this issue?

Beau: I mean, sometimes I do feel quite resolved, in a sense, by it, because this is the situation.

Windy: I want to find out from you what are the elements of your intrapersonal resolution.

Beau: Yeah. Yeah … this is the situation as it is, and I have tried to have conversations with them but it's just not possible while we live together, and I've learnt that the hard way. And, so there is just a quietening of the way that I feel. Acknowledging it, I suppose.

Windy: Well, it sounds like you're acknowledging it and accepting it.

Beau: … Yeah.

Windy: Accepting in a sense that that's the way it is doesn't mean that you like it but you acknowledge and accept the fact that it is a very difficult situation but that's the way it is.

Beau: That is the way it is, yeah.

Windy: What about times when you don't feel intrapersonally resolved?

Beau: ... Yeah, I guess those are the times where they might try to provoke an argument with me, which happens fairly regularly. And, with the support of therapy, it's this whole thing of just de-escalating, walk away – which I do manage to do most of the time, but they're family, they know how to push buttons. And sometimes that works and sometimes I then get invited into the game.

Windy: And you choose to accept the invitation?

Beau: I do, yeah. Sometimes, I feel like the real deep Child part of me just takes over. Sometimes, I'm able to connect to that part and talk to that part.

Windy: And, when you talk to that part, what do you say?

Beau: ... [*Pause*] I guess I would say something like ... [*pause*], 'This isn't useful.... [*Pause*] This is an overreaction. Don't accept the game invitation,' something along those lines.

Windy: So, it sounds like sometimes you get caught unawares.

Beau: ... Yeah, that happens a lot. A lot of the time, I'll come home from work, and it'll just be like, 'Wow!' and then I have to react.

Windy: OK. It sounds like, when you're on your own, you can come to an intrapersonal resolution; you can accept the sad reality of what is. And you were loved as a young baby, but you've got a lot of, from what I read, abuse to deal with. And, for pragmatic reasons, it's difficult for you to get out of it, and one of the decisions you outlined earlier is, 'Do I stay in this situation, try to blast my way through it and get my dissertation done or do I put that off and go and earn some money and live outside?' And I get that.

One thing that I might be able to do is, first of all, to outline what I consider to be hurt, if you're interested, and then contrast the healthy hurt with unhealthy hurt, 'cos then you'll be able to know where I'm coming from. So, would you like me to do that?

[I return to the topic of hurt and offer to explain my take on the difference between what I am calling here 'healthy hurt' and 'unhealthy hurt' to see if this will help us get a focus for the session.]

Beau: Yeah!

Windy: In terms of language, hurt I contrast with sorrow which I see as the healthy alternative to it. It doesn't matter. We can use healthy hurt and unhealthy hurt. That's not the issue. The issue is what differentiates healthy and unhealthy hurt, so to speak, is the effect on you, the person. And, from what you've been saying, healthy hurt comes from an acceptance of what is but a longing, and it can be a strong longing, that things were different but also an acknowledgement that, sadly and regretfully, it doesn't have to be the way you want it to be because it isn't. And that leads you to, in other circumstances, keeping the communication lines open, not sulking, not feeling sorry for yourself, not feeling badly about yourself. That's healthy hurt. Both hurts are about the same thing. Hurt is often about close relationships although it can be about other relationships but most often. It's either about an acknowledgement that you're more invested in the relationship than they are in wanting to make it good, in a way, 'cos I think they're invested in some level about wanting it to be bad. I don't know. So, there is an investment from their part. But often the idea is that, 'I'm being treated in a way that I don't deserve.' There's a sense of undeservingness in there: 'I haven't deserved this.'

With healthy hurt it's, 'I don't deserve this but, sadly and regretfully, just because I don't deserve things, it doesn't mean that I have to get what I deserve 'cos the reality is the reality.' Unhealthy hurt is really saying, 'Because I don't deserve to be treated this way, it shouldn't happen.'

[*While I am clear in outlining the differences between healthy and unhealthy hurt, I do not ask Beau which form of hurt she experiences. I assume that it is the healthy form based on her previous remarks on the subject. This is an error and I wish I had checked things out more with her on this point.*]

Now, I think, from what you're saying, Beau, most of your hurt is healthy. I think that the bit I can maybe add value to this is to help you to prepare yourself so that you're not caught unawares, helping you to go in there and, even if you are pounced upon as soon as you get into the house, you've actually prepared yourself outside of the house for this. There is one place that you can go even if you are in the house that will give you privacy so that you can prepare to deal with all of the crap. Do you know where that is?

Beau: I'm thinking my bedroom but I don't think you are…!

Windy: No. I'm thinking of the toilet.

Beau: Right…. The toilet?

Windy: People aren't going to come into the toilet. They might barge into your room, unless you've got a lock on it.

Beau: I actually don't have a lock on it but it's part of the injunction that they can't come in my room.

Windy: Or you might say to them, 'Look, I'm bursting to go to the toilet,' and then come up to your room and then prepare for yourself to go down. And I'm wondering how much you prepare yourself in advance to deal with this crap.

Beau: Not at all, really.

Windy: So maybe I can add value by helping you to do that. The deep longing is present in both healthy and unhealthy hurt, but I think the acceptance you're combining, and I think you do that most of the time; you combine the acceptance with the deep longing.

Beau: Yeah.

Windy: You say, 'Just because I have this deep longing it doesn't mean that it has to be different. It just means I have this deep longing. I really wish my family were as they were when I was a baby, but they're not, but I still long for that.' That's not the problem. But it is what it is. Now, if we take this issue of preparation, how much time do you spend outside of the house?

Beau: Not a huge amount. I'm working part time and I'll go out and socialise occasionally. Because of the course I'm spending a lot of time writing.

Windy: For example, can you predict when you are going to come across one or more members of your family in the house?

Beau: ... Yes. It's never in my room or even upstairs. It's kind of always in the kitchen, really.

Windy: Right, OK.

Beau: And it occurs when my brother is drunk, usually.

Windy: Like a good cook does the preparation before they create a meal in the kitchen, let's see if I can help Beau to be a good mental cook or psychological cook, doing her preparation. So, let's hear it out loud and how you would prepare yourself for going downstairs into the kitchen with the possibility of facing this. Incidentally, even if you don't face it in reality, you've done the preparation. So how would you prepare?

               [*It would have been better if I had asked Beau if she wants to focus on preparing herself to meet her brother in the kitchen rather than proceed as if she does.*]

Beau: So, normally, there's an internal bracing. So, I guess I do prepare. I guess I think about ... there's a certain relaxed part of myself that I'm able to be in my space in my room, but, when I go outside of that, I'm not relaxed. I guess I am 'on guard' in terms of who I might face. Even if there's no one in the kitchen, someone could then walk in the kitchen. Is my brother doing it to be antagonistic or is he just coming in to get a glass of water? Does he want to have an argument? Is this intentional? So, I suppose there is a little bit of preparation in terms of what I might face, but not really in terms of how.

Windy: Do you like cricket?

Beau: No...!

Windy: Well, do you know about cricket?

Beau: A bit, maybe.

Windy: There's a batsman and a bowler.

Beau: Yep, with you so far!

Windy: And there are fielders, but the fielders, for the point of view of this analogy, are not important. What you're doing, in your preparation, is you're trying to figure out what kind of ball the bowler is going to bowl, and that's it. Preparation from the point of view of the batsman is, 'Look, if the bowler does this, I'm going to play this stroke. If the bowler does that, I'm going to play that stroke. If the bowler does the other, I'm going to play the other stroke.' So the emphasis is not on what they are going to do, but, 'Here's a range of things that they're going to do and this is what I'm going to do if they do it.' Now, what would happen, do you think, if you did that kind of preparation?

Beau: Yeah, that sounds useful.

[*Helping Beau to prepare psychologically for encountering her brother in the kitchen becomes the focus for the rest of the session*]

Windy: So, let's hear you do that preparation out loud, if I can help you to do that.

Beau: OK. So, if he comes in and doesn't seem antagonistic and maybe he is just coming in to get a glass of water, that means I'm OK; I don't need to necessarily do anything. If he comes in and I can sense his agitation, then he's obviously really wanting to have an argument. I'm going to hazard a guess that he's drunk. Really, from having conversations with people, what I should do is just walk out, but there's a part of me, maybe it's that really strong Child part that wants to go in there to finish what I went in there to do, be that to put my plate in the dishwasher or to make a cup of tea or whatever it is or make dinner or whatever it might be. So, I do recognise in myself that that Child part is really strong and it really does take over the Adult part of me.

Windy: And 'If I, at that point, I recognise he's drunk and I leave the kitchen without doing what I've come to do, then how do I view myself or the situation if I withdraw in that way without completing what I've come in to do?'

Beau: … I guess then it's kind of like a loss or something.

Windy: A loss of what?

Beau: … [*Pause*] A loss of … [*Long pause*] I don't know, the goal that I set out to do, the reason that I went into the kitchen, but also something's coming up for me about winning and losing.

Windy: Right. Yeah, what have you won and what have you lost? 'If I put the cup into the dishwasher, I've won,' what?

Beau: … [*Long pause*] Achievement? I don't know. I notice I'm saying 'I don't know' a lot, which I'm wondering about....

Windy: I'm hearing that somehow, 'I've not let him stop me from doing what I want.' There's an autonomy issue. 'I have to finish what I've started. I'm an autonomous individual and, if I want to put a cup in the dishwasher, I'm going to do it.'

Beau: Yeah!

Windy: Right. I get that. But, interestingly enough, that's not autonomy. Do you know why? 'Cos you're not choosing. Do you know why that's not autonomy?

Beau: It sounds like script. It sounds like the Child part has taken over.

Windy: And also, you're not choosing to retreat for good reasons. A good army commander is not saying, 'Right, we've got to go in there no matter what happens,' and then say, 'Wait a minute, if we go in there and this happens, let's beat a retreat because it's better for the army. We can come back and put the cup in the dishwasher later.'

Beau: Yeah, that's really useful.

Windy: So, maybe part of your preparation is, 'Look, if my brother is in there and he's drunk, I'm going to make a tactical retreat for my mental health.'

Beau: Yeah.

Windy: 'And that's my autonomy because I'm choosing to retreat temporarily.' Go back later when he's not there and put the cup in.

Beau: Yeah.... [*Pause*] And that's helpful because so many people just say, 'Just leave the kitchen. Just leave the kitchen.' And I hear that, but there's that part of me that's like, 'But no.'

Windy: Yeah, exactly, because what they're saying ignores the psychological issues that are there for you. Unless they're dealt with, you're not going to leave the kitchen. I'm saying let's have a look what's involved. Of course, you want to be autonomous and put the cup in, but there are times and places to put the cup in, and there are other considerations like your mental health or, 'What's best for me? What's best for Beau?' So, looking at it that way and having that as part of the preparation, what would that sound like?

Beau: ... Are you asking me now?

Windy: Yeah.

Beau: ... Well....

Windy: 'If I go into the kitchen to put my cup in the dishwasher and my brother's drunk,' what?

Beau: … I guess, to take care of me, thinking about autonomy and the appropriate Adult here and now reaction or response would be to take care of myself and de-escalate, as my therapist would say, and leave the kitchen.

Windy: Yeah, and recognising, 'There's still a part of me that still wants to put it there, there and then, but I don't have to access and make that part of me the dominant one. I'm not going to kill it off. I'm going to recognise it's there but I'm not going to access it. I have a choice about which state to access.'

[One of the common interventions that I make in ONEplus Therapy is to help people see that they do not have to 'kill off' or attempt to eradicate parts of themselves, but to acknowledge the existence of such parts and use that acknowledgment as a prelude to making a choice concerning which part of themselves with which to go forward.]

Beau: And the army analogy's really helpful, 'cos of course a commander wouldn't say you go in and all costs, no matter what.

Windy: Yeah. You know when that happens? You know a good example of, 'We'll go in there at all costs'? Do you know when that was?

Beau: No?

Windy: The Charge of the Light Brigade.

Beau: I don't know The Charge of the Light Brigade!

Windy: The Charge of the Light Brigade – I'm going to give you that as a homework assignment: read about The

Charge of the Light Brigade because it's what we're talking about here. So, have we covered all the possibilities with your brother?

Beau: ... I think so. I like the bowler and bat analogy.

Windy: Yeah. I think the other thing is for you to get in touch with your resourcefulness before you go in, because what you're doing by preparing, 'What's he going to do?' is you're not getting in touch with your resourcefulness, which is, 'And, if he does this, I'm going to do this because I'm resourceful enough to do that. If he does that, I'm going to do this because I'm resourceful enough to do that and, if he does the other, I'll do this because I'm resourceful enough to deal with the other.'

Beau: ... [*Pause*] And I think, even though it often ends in an argument, it's so interesting that I haven't been preparing for it, 'cos it's an inevitability.

Windy: Yeah. So, who else do I have to help you to prepare to deal with down in the kitchen?

Beau: It's just him, really. I live with my mum and my brother.... My mum is with the 'words', not so much the violence. So, it's interesting. I feel when she goes on and on and on at me, I do feel an internal tussle, I guess, between Adult and Child, but I am more able just to walk away. It really annoys me, and I do feel my buttons being pushed, but for some reason, it's easier for me to walk away with her than it is with him.

Windy: Right. So, are you saying that I don't need to help you to prepare to deal with your mother because you're doing a good enough job, in your view, on that, or what?

Beau: Well, it might be useful to talk about 'cos I think sometimes ... [*pause*] ... yeah, it's more ... I guess the word hurt is coming to me: I still feel hurt. There's just a silly example of I've been meaning to give the dog a bath for a while, and he's been ill, and I haven't been able to do it because he's been ill. And the other day was the perfect opportunity and it was quite late in the day, it was like near his dinnertime – he has dinner at five and I decided to do it at half past four – and there was this whole thing between the two of them about the time that I'm choosing to give the dog a bath and what a big issue it was. And then my mum starts bringing up the past of when the dog was dirty, and so-and-so and I didn't bath him then but I'm bathing him now. And she said, 'Do it another day,' or something, and my Child response said, 'It's now or never!' And, of course, that just gave them ammunition and she then said to him, 'Well, it's now or never!' ... It was just this big deal.

Windy: So, if you had prepared for that, what would that have sounded like in advance? That involves you predicting, 'What is my mother likely to say if I go down and want to bath the dog now?' You've got to predict based on your knowledge of her about what she's likely to say that you're going to feel hurt about.

Beau: ... Yeah. It's difficult to predict what she will say, but what's a certainty is I will feel a reaction and I will feel pulled, and I will feel quite Persecutory towards her. I don't act on it.

Windy: Persecutory in what sense?

Beau: So, I feel that what's being said – we're talking about her – by her is persecutory towards me and then the game invitation is to Persecute back then.

Windy: OK. So how can you deal with her Persecution? How can you prepare to deal with that?

Beau: … I mean, that is the million-dollar question, Windy?

Windy: What are your options?

Beau: What are my options?

Windy: Does that mean, if I come up with a good solution, you'll give me a million dollars?

Beau: If I had a million dollars, I'd be out the house, Windy!

Windy: That's true.

Beau: When I win the Lottery, we can revisit this conversation.

Windy: We can revisit this conversation, right. So, 'If she Persecutes me,' what are the options?

Beau: Well, my usual is to … just be silent, just let them talk. I guess it's just internally pushing down how I feel. That's how I've been.

Windy: OK. Any other options other than suppression?

Beau: … I could try acknowledging that what she's saying, maybe her intent is to invite me into this game and to Persecute her back. Acknowledging that and deciding to not react, acknowledging that I'm pissed off, that I'm hurt, that I'm angry right now in this moment.

Windy: What are you hurt about if she Persecutes you under those circumstances? What are you hurt about?

Beau: I guess there's always an issue to be found in something I've said or done, and it goes back to what I wrote in the form about the cultural injunctions and always – I don't like to say always, but being favoured by a man in my culture. It's just like I had to take my brother to court to stop the violence.

Windy: When you say favoured by a man, you mean that she favours your brother over you?

Beau: Yeah, and the culture. So, I had to take my brother to court to stop the violence. And then somehow that was still – in her eyes – my fault.

Windy: What do we know then? We know that in your culture there's a favouring of the man over the woman. That is irrespective of how well the woman behaves and how badly the man behaves.

Beau: Yeah.

Windy: And you wish it wasn't like that.

Beau: Yeah!

Windy: How strongly do you wish that it wasn't like that?

Beau: With every fibre of my being.

Windy: Right. So now I've got my work cut out for me, because I want you to come up with now what a flexible attitude and what a rigid attitude would be about your desire.

Beau: So a flexible attitude would be: this is the way it is. I'm not going to change the views of the entire country of Mauritius. It's not likely that that's going to happen. Or even my mum alone, even one person. History has taught me that that's not going to happen. So I guess to be flexible I need to accept that that is the way things are.

Windy: Yeah, and I would add, 'And, very sadly and regretfully, it doesn't have to be the way I want it to be. It really doesn't have to be the way I want it to be. And, given the reality, what's really important to me is that I treat myself as I want to be treated.'

Beau: … [*Long pause*] Yeah. I guess I've been trying so hard to treat others the way that I want to be treated, and I'm not always successful with that either, but I often forget to treat myself that way.

Windy: That's right. And I think maybe part of the preparation with your mum is to prepare yourself to say, 'Look, chances are I'm going to be Persecuted because I'm a woman, and that's unfair, but, sadly and regretfully, that's the way it is, and it doesn't have to be the way I want it to be. But I'm not going to Persecute myself. I'm going to treat myself as,' what?

Beau: … [*Long pause*] I guess as a human being that has needs but is not always going to get those needs met.

Windy: Certainly by them.

Beau: Certainly by them.

Windy: And those needs are gone have to be met outside the house.

Beau: Yeah.

Windy: So, what if you prepared yourself like that? Every time you know you're going to see your mother, you say, 'Look, chances are, if she persecutes me, I don't like that, it's very unpleasant, and it's culturally determined, and that's unfair, but that's the way it is and it doesn't have to be the way I want it to be. And I'm not going to treat myself like that. I'm going to treat myself as a human being who's in a bloody tough situation, but I'm not going to let myself be defined by the way I'm treated. I am not the way I am being treated.' What would happen if you prepared yourself like that?

Beau: I really like that. I think it's incredibly useful … and I think it will really help my mental health.

Windy: Yep, and that's what we're talking about. I've got a couple of things in here – it would be nice if I waved this[29] and, 'Right, the whole of Mauritius is now going to be changed, or at least Beau's mother.' Sadly, that isn't going to work, so we'll put that away. But what you can do is you can prepare yourself for that, and that's going to take discipline. That's going to take you reminding yourself that in your house you're going to have to do the unnatural

---

[29] I have a small number of objects that I use as therapeutic aids and here I am waving my magic wand.

thing that most other people are not going to do in this situation. Most other people go into the kitchen and put a cup into the dishwasher without facing crap, but they don't need to prepare for that. You have an opportunity to an unusual thing but for good healthy reasons. I'm wondering whether part of your strength, Beau, do you see yourself as somebody who has the discipline to do that regularly?

Beau: ... [*Pause*] I can see myself doing it the majority of the time. Like with this whole de-escalation thing and walking out, obviously now with you there are many added layers to that, but, even with the de-escalation alone, there were times where I would give in, and that's part of being human.

Windy: Sure.

Beau: We make mistakes and we're not perfect. One day is it inevitable that that Child is just going to take over? Maybe.

Windy: Well, yes. So maybe also you need to prepare. There's a process and, if we slow it down, because I think it's useful to slow it down, which says, 'There's a Child part of me that ends up by taking over.' Do you recognise that there's a difference between an urge and an action?

Beau: Yeah.

Windy: What's the difference?

Beau: ... I guess I would think of the urge as the Child part and it's reactive and it doesn't think. And I guess the action part could be construed as maybe more Adult, having thought through options.

Windy: Well, I was thinking of something different. Even if we take the Child part, you can recognise, 'Wait a minute, my Child is wanting to say something, is wanting Child to get involved. That's the urge of the Child. But the Child doesn't have to act on that urge because I can come in and parent the Child and say, 'OK, it's understandable that you want to say that, but let's get together because our mental health is involved.' Do you see what I'm saying with the urge and the action there?

Beau: Mmm [yes].

Windy: I think you've got to learn to recognise the signs that the Child is revving up and has an urge to say something. Then, at that point, come in and parent the Child in the way that is going to lead you to preserve your mental health.

Beau: … Yeah, and I think that's where the work is because sometimes the way that my brother will, not physically but hit me with something when I walk through the door….

Windy: Right. So, part of the preparation is, not only preparing for how you're going to respond if he acts in a certain way, but how are you going to respond if the Child in you comes up and wants to get involved in ways that you would later regret.

[*So, there are two aspects here: Beau preparing to deal with her brother and Beau preparing to deal with her Child part.*]

Beau: Yeah.

Windy: That's the work that you also need to do in the preparation.

Beau: Yeah.

Windy: Do you want to summarise what we've done today and what you're going to take away?

Beau: A lot.... So, talking about my options, really. So, when it comes to my brother, thinking about the bowler and the batter analogy; what are the various ways that he might respond, and really thinking about that. Really, it's one of two ways: he's either going to come in and not provoke or he's going to want an argument. And I guess it's thinking about what I'm going to do when that occurs.... [*Pause*] And, again, just going back to what I said about the usefulness of the army analogy and my homework – really useful. And with my mum I guess there was a part of me that thought ... not that I've got that bit nailed because I definitely haven't and that's why I'm here, but just that added layer of talking about that I'm not going to change an entire country and I'm not even going to be able to change my mother, and I know that.... It's just been really useful to think about and how much, especially with doing the course, I've realised that imbalance of male/female in the world but particularly in my culture. And I'm not going to change it and I have to just accept that it's a bit shit.

Windy: Yeah, and you really want your mother to not Persecute you but that doesn't mean that you have to get what you want because you get what you get.

The bowler is in charge of what the bowler throws down, you're in charge of the strokes that you play.

Beau: Yeah.

Windy: Finally, what about the bit about preparing to deal with your Child part?

Beau: Yeah, and I think that's going to be the toughest thing probably. Not to get into too much TA, but that's really where the deconfusion work is with the Child. It's so powerful.

Windy: I would say learning to recognise the beginnings of that state coming up and intervening early. Also, learning to do it, not only before you go into the situation but to hold that as much as you can and to intervene with yourself while you're in that situation because the Child is always going to want to come up. That's not the issue. It's recognising that and protecting the Child, in a way, while protecting yourself. It's protecting the Child and protecting you.

Beau: Yeah. That's really meaningful, what you've said there about protecting the Child, because I guess I definitely, as a child, didn't feel protected. So maybe I've got a chance to try to do it now.

Windy: Try to do it now, OK. We started off looking to add some value. I hope I've done that for you.

Beau: You really have.

Windy: Thank you very much for coming.

Beau: Thank you, Windy. Thank you so much! This has been, like I say, really meaningful.

Beau's Reflections on the Session: 28/11/23

Having seen Windy in action before, I had an idea of what to expect. As I had a lot going on at the time, it was challenging for me to home in on what exactly I wanted from the session. I thought Windy did an excellent job of rooting through the weeds and getting to the immediacy of what was needed at the time particularly as I wasn't entirely sure myself.

I felt we connected well, and there were some light moments of humour during the session, which I enjoyed. But we worked hard, and it was challenging work.

Much of what Windy said unlocked a lot for me internally; for example, the army references/not going in at all costs.... Winning and losing was also helpful – especially as there was a similarity with my regular therapist who said, 'it's like you are in a war', which cemented my understanding of why I often have to 'win'.

I regularly talk about TA's ego state model in my own therapy, in my therapeutic work with my clients, and my therapist and supervisors talk about 'parenting the Child' again Windy tapped into something when he talked about '*protecting* the Child' and I found his new insight helpful. It made me think of little girl Beau, who I couldn't 'protect' then – but I can now.

What was interesting was in the days since the SST, the game invitations were being 'sent' and I found myself accepting the invites and getting into arguments. I'd give myself a hard time for not being able to internalise Windy – and because I went in at all costs. My regular therapist helpfully reminded me that my fight or flight response is to fight – so under pressure that's exactly what I do. It's been very challenging to 'train' myself out of something that's instinctive. In the weeks after SST, I have been able to decline the invites and internalise Windy somewhat. It's a process.

I feel proud of my achievement. Proud that increasingly, I have been able to 'not' go in at all costs – and I am incredibly grateful to all the layered therapeutic interventions I have had, which in my opinion, have complemented one another beautifully.

15

Some Final Observations

In this final chapter, I will draw together some themes based on the submitted reflections of the volunteers that appear at the end of their respective chapters. Each of the volunteers (all therapists who signed up for a single session on their struggles with common emotional problems) agreed to provide their reflections on their particular session with me. In my email to them, I wrote as follows:

> *I hope you are well. You kindly agreed to provide a 500-word reflection on the single session we had for my book: ONEplus Therapy with Common Emotional Problems. Your reflection will go at the end of the chapter, which will contain the transcript of our session. I am happy for you to structure the reflection in any way you wish. However, I think readers would be interested in:*
>
> - *What your experience was in having the session with me*
> - *What you took from the session and*
> - *What difference it made to you.*
>
> *I look forward to receiving the statement by no later than Thursday 30th November 2023.*

I was thus asking for their views on the process of the session and its outcome. As is my practice, I sent a reminder email on 23 November and, where relevant, the day before the piece was due.

I have structured their responses by using the following categories:

- The value of the session
- The therapeutic relationship
- My contribution to the session

- Therapeutic factors
- Takeaways
- Outcome

The Value of the Session

Four volunteers commented on the value of the session for them.

- Jane ['Guilt'] said that the session gave her an opportunity to air her anxieties and guilt concerning her relationship with her brother. She further said that the session allowed her to sit with and confront her guilt.
- Anne ['Unhealthy envy'] said that her session with me gave her the opportunity to talk about her envious feelings with someone that she couldn't talk about elsewhere.
- Libby ['Unhealthy regret'] felt that the session was valuable in that it gave her a sense of control
- Beau ['Mixed emotions'] remarked that her session complemented other therapy that she had.

The Therapeutic Relationship

Five volunteers made reference to their therapeutic relationship with me.

- Jane ['Guilt'] and Anna ['Hurt'] made similar comments. Jane said that her relationship with me was neither warm nor cold and neither harsh nor soft in nature, assertiveness and boundary-setting. Anna said that she did not feel a deep emotional connection with me nor a cold, clinical distance. She said we were working alongside one another in a non-hierarchical way. She said that there was a brisk, let's get on with it feeling to the relationship.

- Beau ['Mixed emotions'] said that we connected well with light moments of humour. She noted further that we worked well together and that it was challenging work.
- Margaret ['Depression'] said that she did not feel unsafe and that she had the confidence in the relationship that she could be open with me.
- Robert ['Shame'] experienced me in the relationship with him as more forthright than he expected, which helped him engage in the process.

My Contribution to the Session

Nine of the ten volunteers commented on my contribution to the session.

- Four volunteers referred to my use of questions. Anne ['Unhealthy envy'] said that my questioning helped her to reflect on situations related to her feelings of envy and how her experiences were different to the women at work whom she envied. Margaret ['Depression'] also mentioned that my questions helped her to reflect and self-analyse. My direct yet compassionate questioning struck Jen ['Anxiety'] and Libby ['Unhealthy regret'] said that the structure of my questions helped her to understand how she was viewing the situation that she was discussing.
- Four volunteers mentioned feeling heard, supported or understood by me. Both Margaret ['Depression'] and Libby ['Unhealthy regret'] felt heard and supported, Robert ['Shame'] felt heard and understood and Lara ['Unhealthy jealousy'] felt hugely understood.
- Two volunteers referred to being challenged by me. Robert ['Shame'] mentioned that my challenges were really important for him and Margaret ['Depression') said that my challenges were gentle.
- Anna ['Hurt'] said I was attentive and skilled.

- Jen ['Anxiety'] enjoyed my style provocative humour.
- Jane ['Guilt'] said that my consistency helped her to regulate and settle into the session.
- Tab ['Unhealthy anger'] said that I created a space so that she could unravel the layers of her frustration and anger.
- Libby ['Unhealthy regret'] mentioned that I helped her to hold the sadness of loss and gratitude of what she has.

Therapeutic Factors

Volunteers mentioned a range of therapeutic factors in their reflections.

Having Another Perspective

The main therapeutic factor mentioned by volunteers (six of them) is what I refer to here as 'having another perspective'.

- Anne ['Unhealthy envy'] used the term 'having another perspective' in her reflection on our session, which she found useful.
- Libby ['Unhealthy regret'] mentioned that my questioning (see above) helped her to get some distance and gain a different perspective. Additionally, and more specifically, she found my distinction between healthy and unhealthy regret interesting and useful.
- Tab ['Unhealthy anger'] found my distinction between her primary problem and her secondary problem useful and helped her to deal with the rigidity associated with the latter.
- Lara ['Unhealthy jealousy] mentioned that it was helpful when I offered her some alternative choices in understanding and dealing with her jealousy issue.
- Jen ['Anxiety'] said that it was helpful when I pointed out that I did not think that she had a phobia; rather, she

needed to develop a healthier attitude to having her blood pressure taken.

- Beau ['Mixed emotions'] found it helpful when I offered her the insight that she needed to 'protect her Child' rather than 'parent the Child '.

Other Therapeutic Factors

Volunteers mentioned a range of other therapeutic factors:

- Strategies and techniques were mentioned by three volunteers. Anne ['Unhealthy envy'] mentioned that it was helpful to be offered strategies to help her prepare herself to deal with envy in relevant situations. Margaret ['Depression'] commented on the helpfulness of an imagery-based technique to distance herself from troubling thoughts. Finally, Robert ['Shame'] mentioned that he found it helpful when I showed him my use of my wooden 'I' (see Chapter 9), which stresses the complexity of the self and that one cannot legitimately rate the whole of 'self' based on some of its parts.
- The value of focus was mentioned by three volunteers: Anne ['Unhealthy envy'], Robert ['Shame'] and Beau ['Mixed emotions].
- Contracting and clarity were mentioned by Jane ['Guilt'].
- Anne ['Unhealthy envy'] mentioned the value of being helped to make sense of her experience.
- Two volunteers mentioned the pre-session questionnaire, recording and transcript as therapeutic factors. Anne ['Unhealthy envy'] said that the *pre-session questionnaire* helped her form an instant conversational connection with me and that the *transcript* provided a reminder of the solution. Robert ['Shame'] said that listening to the *recording* helped him to appreciate and understand the journey we had covered in such a short period of time.

- On the debit side, Lara ['Unhealthy jealousy'] felt rushed in the session.

Takeaways

An important feature of ONEplus Therapy concerns what people take away from the session that they can implement after the session has ended. Four volunteers made spontaneous mention of such takeaways.

- Anna ['Hurt'] mentioned that she took away two points: (i) Hurt has its roots in sadness. Feeling the sadness could help her not angrily withdraw in painful interactions with her husband, and (ii) she had a fear of being catastrophically alone, but that was not catastrophically alone because she had herself.
- Jane ['Guilt'] also mentioned that she took away two points: (i) She doesn't have to step back into the role of rescuer and (ii) she can forgive herself for colluding with her family's avoidant tendencies.
- Tab ['Unhealthy anger'] took away the point that when she notices herself getting worked up, she can ask herself what she is avoiding and if this coming from a rigid place she can allow in acceptance and compassion.
- Libby ['Unhealthy regret'] took away the point that even in one session she can pull some threads in her original story to imagine other possibilities.

Outcome

As I gave volunteers between three and four months to write their reflections after their session with me, sufficient time had elapsed for them to gauge what difference the session made to them if they chose to address this issue in their reflective piece. Seven volunteers wrote in their reflections what they gained from their session with me.

- Anne ['Unhealthy envy'] said that her session with me helped her to (i) ease up on herself, (ii) accept the way that she feels, (iii) feel less tense with the colleague that she envied, and (iv) prepare to deal with envy-related situations.
- Lara ['Unhealthy jealousy'] said that initially, the session made no difference to her thinking and that she did calm down a bit subsequently. She also reported feeling less triggered by her partner's flirting.
- Beau ['Mixed emotions'] also said that initially, she accepted invites (from her family) and got into arguments with them, but later, she did not do this and was able to internalise what we had discussed.
- Libby ['Unhealthy regret'] said the session helped her to feel less hard on herself and to have greater self-compassion for the way she was at the time.
- Tab ['Unhealthy anger'] said that the session helped her to generally feel calmer not just physically but like her mind has been on holiday and has returned refreshed.
- Robert ['Shame'] said that the session 'changed a small part of me for the better, and I would summarise this as challenging my relational model when it comes to feeling heard, supported and helped. I guess I always believed that it was trust that enabled personality transformation, but now I wonder whether my focus on trust might sometimes just be getting in the way'.
- Jen ['Anxiety] said that the session helped her to take her blood pressure regularly when, before the session, she was anxious and avoided doing so.

Conclusion

In conclusion, it is my view that a single session of therapy focused on common emotional problems can be useful and that volunteers found salient aspects of the practical applications of the single-session mindset to be therapeutic and helped most of them to derive benefit from the session.

References

Beck, A.T., Epstein, N., & Harrison, R. (1983). Cognitions, attitudes and personality dimensions in depression. *British Journal of Cognitive Psychotherapy, 1*(1), 1–16.

Bordin, E.S. (1979). The generalizability of the psychoanalytic concept of the working alliance. *Psychotherapy: Theory, Research and Practice*, 16, 252–260.

Cannistrà, F. (2022). The single-session therapy mindset: Fourteen principles gained through an analysis of the literature. *International Journal of Brief Therapy and Family Science, 12*(1), 1–26.

Colman, A. (2015). *Oxford Dictionary of Psychology.* 4th edn. Oxford University Press.

Dryden, W. (2011). *Counselling in a Nutshell.* 2nd ed. Sage.

Dryden, W. (2013). *The ABCs of REBT: Perspectives on Conceptualization.* Springer.

Dryden, W. (2016a). *When Time Is at a Premium: Cognitive-Behavioural Approaches to Single-Session Therapy and Very Brief Coaching.* Rationality Publications.

Dryden, W. (2016b). *Attitudes in Rational Emotive Behaviour Therapy: Components, Characteristics and Adversity-Related Consequences.* Rationality Publications.

Dryden, W. (2019). *Single-Session 'One-At-A-Time' (OAAT) Therapy: A Rational Emotive Behaviour Therapy Approach.* Routledge.

Dryden, W. (2021). *Seven Principles of Doing Live Therapy Demonstrations.* Rationality Publications.

Dryden, W. (2022a). *Single-Session Therapy: Responses to Frequently Asked Questions.* Routledge.

Dryden, W. (2022b). *The Rational Emotive Behaviour Therapy Primer: A Concise Introduction.* PCCS Books.

Dryden, W. (2023a). *ONEplus Therapy: Help at the Point of Need.* Onlinevents.

Dryden, W. (2023b). *Single-Session Therapy and Regret.* Onlinevents.

Dryden, W. (2024). *Single-Session Therapy: 100 Key Points and Techniques. 2nd edition.* Routledge.

Dryden, W. (2025). Bringing a single-session mindset to counselling in an online health service. In M.F. Hoyt & F. Cannistrà (eds), *Single Session Therapies: Why and How One-At-A-Time Mindsets are Effective.* Routledge.

Ellis, A. (1957). Rational psychotherapy and individual psychology. *Journal of Individual Psychology, 13*(1), 38–44.

Ellis, A. (1994). *Reason and Emotion in Psychotherapy.* Revised and Expanded Edition. Birch Lane Press.

Flaxman, P.E., Blackledge, J.T. & Bond, F. W. (2011). *Acceptance and Commitment Therapy: Distinctive Features.* Routledge.

Hoyt, M.F. (2011). Foreword. In A. Slive & M. Bobele (eds), *When One Hour Is All You Have: Effective Therapy for Walk-in Clients* (pp. xix–xv). Zeig, Tucker, & Theisen.

Jacobson, E. (1934). *You Must Relax.* Whittlesey House. A Division of the McGraw-Hill Book Company, Inc.

Lemma, A. (2000). *Humour on the Couch: Exploring Humour in Psychotherapy and in Everyday Life.* Whurr.

Simon, G.E., Imel, Z.E., Ludman, E.J. & Steinfeld, B.J. (2012). Is dropout after a first psychotherapy visit always a bad outcome? *Psychiatric Services, 63*(7), 705–707.

Young, J. (2018). SST: The misunderstood gift that keeps on giving. In M.F. Hoyt, M. Bobele, A. Slive, J. Young & M. Talmon (eds), *Single-Session Therapy by Walk-In or Appointment: Administrative, Clinical, and Supervisory Aspects of One-at-a-Time Services* (pp. 40–58). Routledge.

Index

Index

www.ingramcontent.com/pod-product-compliance
Lightning Source LLC
Chambersburg PA
CBHW071220290326
41931CB00037B/1484